ON TO **SMALLTALK**

Patrick Henry Winston

Massachusetts Institute of Technology

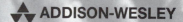

ADDISON-WESLEY

An imprint of Addison Wesley Longman, Inc.

Reading, Massachusetts • Harlow, England • Menlo Park, California
Berkeley, California • Don Mills, Ontario • Sydney
Bonn • Amsterdam • Tokyo • Mexico City

Library of Congress Cataloging-in-Publication Data

Winston, Patrick Henry
    On to Smalltalk / Patrick Henry Winston.
        p.   cm.
    Includes index.
    ISBN 0-201-49827-8
    1. Smalltalk (Computer program language)   I. Title.
QA76.73.S59W56   1998
005.13'3–dc21

                                                                97-15969
                                                                CIP

Reprinted with corrections, March 1998.

Reproduced by Addison-Wesley from film supplied by the author.

2 3 4 5 6 7 8 9 10-CRW-01009998

CONTENTS

ACKNOWLEDGMENTS

The cover photograph, the cover design, and the interior design are by Chiai Takahashi, with counsel from Karen A. Prendergast.

Eric Clayberg, Juanita Ewing, Richard Lyon, Steve Messick, Brian Wilkerson, and David Zeleznik all read the manuscript carefully, found many errors and blunders, and made copious suggestions. The author is extremely grateful for their expert advice.

Lyn Dupré was the developmental editor. She has a special gift for rooting out problems and suggesting improvements. The errors in this book were introduced—by an author who never stops writing—after Ms. Dupré finished her work. In particular, Robert K. Bonner found a number of such errors in the first printing.

If you write technical material, you should read *BUGS in Writing*, Ms. Dupré's book (Addison-Wesley, 1995).

1 HOW THIS BOOK TEACHES YOU THE LANGUAGE

1   The purpose of this book is to help you learn the essentials of Smalltalk programming. In this section, you learn why you should learn Smalltalk and how this book is organized.

2   **Object-oriented programming languages,** such as Smalltalk, encourage you to design programs around classes, such as the `Integer` class, along with classes that you define yourself. Typically, you define classes and class hierarchies that reflect important general properties of individual nails, horseshoes, horses, kingdoms, or whatever else happens to come up naturally in your application.

3   In the vernacular of Smalltalk programming, **messages** are sent to **receivers,** and receivers return **answers.** To do the necessary computation, Smalltalk finds the appropriate **method,** given the receiver and the message, and that method specifies exactly how the computation is to be performed.

For example, Smalltalk allows you to send a message, `sqrt`, to a receiver, 2, which is a member of the `Integer` class. To handle the message, Smalltalk finds the appropriate way to compute the required square root for receivers belonging to the `Integer` class; then, Smalltalk produces the answer, `1.41421`, which is an instance of the `Float` class.

4   Visually, the receiver has center stage; 2 is a receiver that provides access to a method that deals with the `sqrt` message.

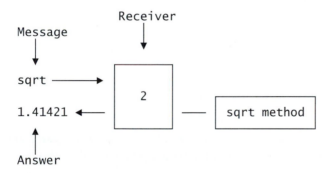

5   In contrast, **procedure-oriented programming languages,** such as C, encourage you to think in terms of **functions** and **procedures,**[1] instead of in terms of classes and class hierarchies.

Thus, to compute the square root of 2 using a procedure-oriented programming language, you must identify the appropriate **function,** which, when **applied** to 2—a datum of the integer **data type**—answers `1.41421`, the function's **value.** Visually, the function has center stage; 2 is just the function's **argument:**

---

[1] Strictly speaking, functions are procedures that lack side effects. Nevertheless, *function* and *procedure* are used interchangeably.

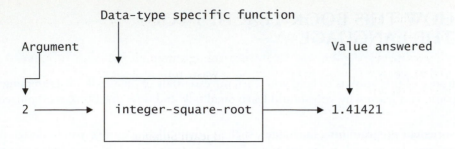

6   In this book, you learn what *object-oriented* means and why many programmers prefer object-oriented languages. For now, it suffices to know that Smalltalk is an object-oriented programming language, whereas most programs have been written by programmers using procedure-oriented programming languages.

7   Among the object-oriented programming languages, Smalltalk has attractive characteristics, such as the following:

- Smalltalk is object-oriented from the ground up, in contrast to other popular object-oriented languages, such as C++, which programmers created by pasting a veneer onto a preexisting language.

- Smalltalk programming is done in **powerful development environments**, which enable efficient program writing, editing, testing, debugging, and maintenance. Smalltalk development environments provide myriad built-in classes and methods.

- Smalltalk development environments encourage the development of gorgeous **graphical user interfaces**, liberally decorated with fancy graphical elements.

8   Smalltalk is said to be a pure object-oriented language because every entity in Smalltalk is an object and every object can receive and send messages. Being a pure object-oriented language is one of Smalltalk's distinguishing strengths.

9   The enormous power of Smalltalk development environments is derived from an unusual armamentarium of powerful tools:

- Smalltalk development environments provide powerful **browsers** that allow you to examine all class and method definitions—even the built-in classes and methods.

- Smalltalk development environments provide powerful **debugging tools**. Using these tools, you see the message sequences that lead to program interruption, you inspect parameter and variable values to zero in on errors, you modify method definitions, and you restart or resume your interrupted program.

- Smalltalk classes and methods are compiled as you write them, incrementally. You never have to waste time waiting for a compiler to translate an entire program or program module into machine instructions.

10   Also, Smalltalk provides for automatic memory recycling. When you use a language such as C++, you have to remember to free the memory allocated to program elements, such as class instances, once you are finished with them. Failing to free memory produces a

memory leak that may exhaust all the memory available to your program, leading either to erratic behavior or to a total crash.

Smalltalk frees memory automatically, by performing **automatic garbage collection,** so you never need to worry about memory leaks, or to waste time looking for one. Thus, you are more productive, and are less likely to be driven crazy by doing tedious, mind-numbing debugging.

11   There are two principal reasons why you should learn Smalltalk:

- Smalltalk's inherent characteristics ensure that your productivity using Smalltalk is likely to exceed your productivity in other programming languages.

- The supply of powerful Smalltalk software modules, provided by Smalltalk development environments, enables you to develop applications principally by gluing together existing software, rather than by writing new software from scratch.

12   Some Smalltalk implementations are expensive because they offer large graphics libraries and other productivity-promoting features for use by professional programmers. Fortunately, other Smalltalk implementations are available at no cost. Most of this book is based on Smalltalk Express™, because Smalltalk Express is free, yet offers all you need to learn the language and to enjoy its power. You can learn how to obtain a copy of Smalltalk Express on page 289.

Capabilities of a commercial Smalltalk, VisualWorks™, are explained in Section 38 through Section 42.

13   In this book, single-idea segments, analogous to slides, are arranged in sections that are analogous to slide shows. At the moment, you are reading Segment 13 of Section 1.

14   The segments come in several varieties: **basic segments** explain essential ideas; **sidetrip segments** introduce interesting, but skippable, ideas; **practice segments** provide opportunities to experiment with new ideas; and **highlights segments** summarize important points.

15   Four principles determined this introductory book's organization and style:

- The book should get you up and running in the language quickly.

- The book should answer your basic questions explicitly.

- The book should encourage you to develop a personal library of solutions to standard programming problems.

- The book should deepen your understanding of the art of good programming practice.

16   To get you up and running in Smalltalk quickly, the sections generally supply you with the most useful approach to each programming need, be it to display characters on your screen, to define a new method, or to read information from a file.

17   To answer your basic questions explicitly, the sections generally focus on one issue, which is plainly announced in the title of the section. Accordingly, you see titles such as the following:

- How to Write Arithmetic Expressions

- How to Define Simple Methods

- How to Create Classes and Instances

- How to Benefit from Data Abstraction

- How to Design Classes and Class Hierarchies

18 To encourage you to develop a personal library of solutions to standard programming problems, this book introduces many useful, productivity-increasing, general-purpose, templatelike patterns—sometimes called **idioms** by experienced programmers—that you can fill in to achieve particular-purpose goals.

Idioms are introduced because learning to program involves more than learning to use programming-language primitives, just as learning to speak a human language involves more than learning to use vocabulary words.

19 To deepen your understanding of the art of good programming practice, this book emphasizes the value of such ideas as data abstraction and procedure abstraction, along with principles such as the explicit-representation principle, the modularity principle, the no-duplication principle, the look-it-up principle, and the is-a versus has-a principle.

20 Finally, the book develops simple, yet realistic, Smalltalk programs, which you see in many versions as your understanding of the language increases. In its ultimate version, one of the programs rates foods according to their protein, carbohydrate, and fat content.

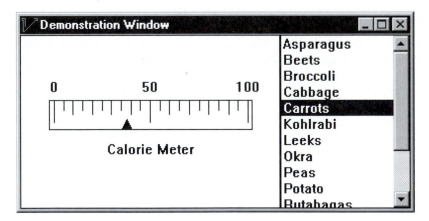

HIGHLIGHTS

- Smalltalk is an object-oriented programming language. Object-oriented programming languages emphasize user-defined classes and class hierarchies.

- In Smalltalk, receivers perform computations in response to messages, and return answers. Methods specify exactly how the computations are to be performed.

- Smalltalk is popular because it is an object-oriented language from the ground up, because Smalltalk development is done in a powerful development environment, and because Smalltalk facilitates the development of graphical user interfaces.

- This book gets you up and running in Smalltalk quickly; it answers your basic questions explicitly; it equips you with program patterns that you can adapt to your own purposes; and it deepens your understanding of the art of good programming practice.

2 HOW TO EXPERIMENT USING THE WORKSPACE

22 In this section, you learn how to perform simple arithmetic computations and to display the results of such computations. You also review the standard terminology used throughout the rest of this book.

23 When you work with many programming languages, you write a program using an **editor**, producing a **text file**. Next, you translate your program into machine instructions using a **compiler**, producing an **executable file**. Finally, you run your program.

When you work with Smalltalk, you work within a **development environment** that contains an integrated set of tools (including an editor, a compiler, and a debugger), as well as your program (in both text and compiled form). When you have finished your program, you generally strip out the editor, compiler, and perhaps the debugger, leaving only the **application image**.

24 To familiarize yourself with Smalltalk, you should enter your Smalltalk development environment by clicking the appropriate icon. Then, if you happen to be using Smalltalk Express, you see the **transcript window** or, more compactly, the **transcript**:

Once you see the transcript, you need to activate what is generally known as a **workspace window** or, more compactly, a **workspace**. To activate the workspace, you click on **File** and then on **New Workspace**. The following emerges:

25 Once you are in a workspace, you can type and edit expressions as though you were entering text with a word processor. For example, you can enter the following arithmetic expression:

```
2 sqrt
```

Once you have entered such an expression, you can **select** it; that is, you can cause the expression to be highlighted by moving the cursor to the left side of the expression, pressing down on a mouse button (usually the left one), dragging the mouse to the right side of the expression, and releasing the button.

```
2 sqrt
```

Having selected such an expression in a workspace, you cause it to be **compiled** and **evaluated,** with the resulting answer **displayed**, by clicking the right mouse button, and then clicking **Show It** with the left mouse button. The resulting answer is displayed in the workspace to the immediate right of the evaluated expression:

```
2 sqrt1.41421
```

To save space in this book, right clicking on selected text, followed by clicking on **Show It** with the left mouse button, is denoted by **right→Show It**.

26 When you evaluate the expression 2 `sqrt`, you are said to **send a message**, consisting of a **method selector**, `sqrt`, to the **receiver** of the message, 2. The receiver finds the **method** named by the method selector, uses the method to produce a value, and **answers** with that value.

27 In Smalltalk, every entity is an **object**. Accordingly, numbers, characters, arrays, and even files and windows are objects.

28 All objects can receive messages. In Section 5, you learn how to define methods that determine how objects behave in response to messages. Those methods generally arrange for messages to be sent to objects. Thus, via methods, objects can send as well as receive messages.

29 Because numbers, characters, arrays, and even files and windows are objects, all can receive and send messages.

30 Because every entity in Smalltalk is an object that can receive and send messages, Smalltalk is said to be a **pure object-oriented language**. Being a pure object-oriented language is one of Smalltalk's distinguishing strengths.

31 Objects that describe groups of individuals are called **classes**. Examples include the `Integer`, `Float`, and `Fraction` classes. Objects that describe individuals are called **instances**. Examples include 194, which is an instance of the `Integer` class; 1.41421, which is an instance the `Float` class; and 2/3, which is an instance of the `Fraction` class.

32 Class names always begin with an uppercase character.

33 Messages can include **arguments** as well as method selectors. In the following expression, for example, the message consists of a method selector, `raisedTo:`, and an argument, 10:

```
2 raisedTo: 10
```

Note that the colon is part of the `raisedTo:` method selector; the colon is there to indicate that an argument is expected. Note also that the T is in uppercase, in accordance with the Smalltalk method naming conventions explained in Segment 103.

34 Graphically, in the expression 2 `raisedTo:` 10, the second number, 10, is packaged with the method selector, `raisedTo:`, to form the message sent to the receiver:

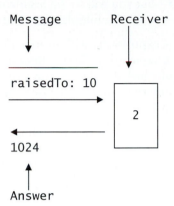

Thus, when you select 2 `raisedTo:` 10 and click **right→Show It**, you see the answer, 1024, displayed, because `raisedTo:` indicates that the receiver is to be raised to a power corresponding to the argument.

35 Multiplication also requires a message with a selector and an argument. In the following expression, the message consists of a method selector, *, and an argument, 9:

194 * 9

36 Graphically, in the expression 194 * 9, the second number, 9, is packaged with the method selector, *, to form the message sent to the receiver:

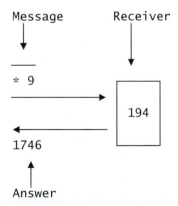

Thus, when you select 194 * 9 and click **right→Show It**, you see 1746 displayed.

37 You refer to messages by the names of the method selectors that appear in them. Thus, you refer to a message in which `sqrt` is the method selector as a `sqrt` message.

38   You have seen examples of three kinds of methods:

Methods such as `sqrt` are said to be **unary methods**, because they appear in messages that have no arguments. Thus, unary methods focus entirely on one object: the receiver.

Methods such as `raisedTo:` are said to be **keyword methods**, because their selectors include colons, which indicate that arguments are expected. The **raisedTo:** method happens to work on two objects—the receiver and the argument—but you will see (in Segment 147, for example) that some keyword methods are meant to work on multiple arguments.

Like keyword methods, methods such as `*` appear in expressions with arguments, but because their selectors include no colons, they are not keyword methods. Instead, their selectors consist of one or two special characters, most of which denote common arithmetic operations. Collectively, these methods are said to be **binary methods**, because they bring exactly two objects together: the receiver and one argument.

39
SIDE TRIP   Evidently, the designers of Smalltalk introduced binary messages because they thought that it would be excessively doctrinaire to require programmers to use keyword arguments in arithmetic expressions. Accordingly, you write 194 `*` 9 instead of the ugly 194 `*:` 9 or the long-winded 194 `multipliedBy:` 9.

40   Instead of displaying results in a workspace, you can arrange for Smalltalk to display results in the **transcript**, which is really just a special workspace. Conveniently, the transcript appears whenever you activate Smalltalk.

Before you can display a result in the transcript, however, you generally must use the `printString` method to produce an instance of the `String` class.

In a workspace, `String` instances are marked by surrounding quotation marks. Accordingly, when you select `1746 printString`, and click **right→Show It**, you produce the following result:

`1746 printString``'1746'`

41   Suppose, for example, that you want to display 1746 in the transcript. First, you send a `printString` message to the `Integer` instance, 1746, which answers the `String` instance, `'1746'`. Then, you combine `'1746'` with `show:`, producing a `show:` message to be sent to `Transcript`:

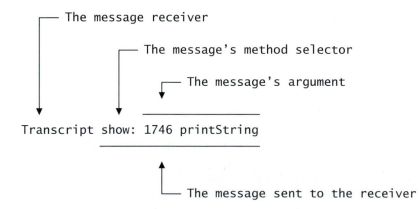

Having prepared an expression such as `Transcript show: 1746 printString` in a workspace, you cause it to be evaluated by selecting it and clicking **right**→**Do It**. Evaluating the expression causes Smalltalk to display 1746 in the transcript.

42   You click **right**→**Do It**, rather than **right**→**Show It**, because you only want the `show:` message to display the 1746 instance in the transcript. You are not interested in the answer produced by the `show:` message.

43   The `show:` message appears throughout the rest of this book because you will find it is helpful, when you are learning Smalltalk, to display the results of intermediate computations as well as final answers. Thus, you often see combinations that consist of an expression to be evaluated in a workspace, along with the result of evaluation, produced via **right**→**Do It**, in the transcript:

    Workspace
```
Transcript show: 1746 printString
```
     Transcript
```
1746
```

44   The expression `Transcript show: 1746 printString` includes both a unary and a keyword method. In general, expressions can include unary, binary, and keyword methods.

45   Whenever a Smalltalk expression contains multiple methods of mixed types, a few simple rules determine how the expression is to be evaluated:

- Unary messages are sent first.

- Then, binary messages are sent.

- Finally, keyword messages are sent.

Thus, unary messages are said to have the highest **precedence**; keyword messages have the lowest precedence; and binary messages have precedence in between.

Thus, `Transcript show: 1746 printString` produces the following event sequence:

- A unary `printString` message is sent to 1746.

- The `Integer` instance, 1746, answers a `String` instance, '1746'.

- A keyword `show:` message is sent to `Transcript`, with '1746' as the argument.

- The `show:` method causes a character sequence, 1746, to be displayed in the transcript.

46   Of course, you can use parentheses to circumvent the precedence rules by establishing subexpressions. In the following, for example, parentheses are needed, because the unary `printString` message is to be sent to the answer produced when the binary * message is sent:

    Workspace
```
Transcript show: (194 * 9) printString
```
     Transcript
```
1746
```

11

Without the parentheses, Smalltalk sends the printString message to 9, which answers with a String instance, '9', which cannot be an argument of the binary * message, inasmuch as you cannot multiply an Integer instance times a String instance.

47 Whenever a Smalltalk expression contains multiple messages of the same type, Smalltalk sends the messages in **left-to-right order**. Thus, arithmetic expressions are not handled according to the usual rules of arithmetic, as you learn in Segment 65.

48 You can send String instances to the transcript directly, without working on them with a printString message:

```
    Workspace
Transcript show: 'The number of calories is: '
    Transcript
The number of calories is:
```

49 You can start a new line in the transcript by sending a cr message, where cr is an acronym for carriage return:

```
    Workspace
Transcript cr
    Transcript
```

50 You can cause several expressions to be evaluated in sequence, with a single selection and mouse click, if you separate those expressions by periods:

```
    Workspace
Transcript show: 'The number of calories is '.
Transcript show: (194 * 9) printString.
Transcript cr
    Transcript
The number of calories is 1746
```

Each expression thus separated is called a **statement**.

51 Note that periods are **separators**; periods do not initiate or terminate statements. Thus, is no period before the first statement, and there is no period after the final statement.

52 In Segment 18, you learned that this book introduces many templatelike, general-purpose program patterns, called idioms, which you can fill in to suit your own specific purposes. In these patterns, each place to be filled in is identified by a box that contains a description of the item to be inserted, such as this .

The following, for example, is the pattern that you use when you want to display the answer produced by an expression in the transcript:

```
Transcript show: expression printString
```

When you fill in such a pattern, replacing descriptions with specific instances, you are said to **instantiate** the pattern.

53   When you decide to stop working, you must go through the ritual required to shut down your development environment. To perform it, you click the **close button** in the title bar of the transcript window. When you are asked whether you want to save the image, click **No**.

54   When you test programs, you encounter bugs; when you encounter a Smalltalk bug, you
SIDE TRIP   see a walkback window. Suppose, for example, that you forget to use `printString` to covert a number into a string before printing:

> Workspace
> `Transcript show: 1746`

Smalltalk responds by popping up a walkback window:

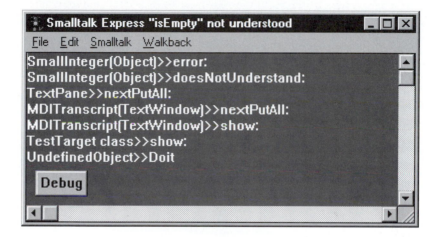

You learn about walkback windows and many other debugging aids in Section 28.

55   `Transcript` is the name of a global variable bound to an input–output stream. You
SIDE TRIP   learn about global variables in Section 19, and you learn about input–output streams in Section 22.

56   Create a workspace and write expressions that display in the transcript various strings,
PRACTICE   numbers, and products of numbers.

57
HIGHLIGHTS

- When you work with Smalltalk, unlike with most programming languages, you enter a development environment. The editor, compiler, and your programs all reside in the development environment.

- An **object** is an entity that receives and sends messages. In Smalltalk, every entity is an object, so every entity is capable of receiving appropriate messages.

- Smalltalk programmers speak anthropomorphically about objects—as though objects were people who can receives messages, find appropriate procedures for handling messages, and respond with answers.

- Smalltalk expressions may contain unary, binary, or keyword messages. The unary messages are sent first, followed by the binary messages, and then by the keyword messages. Thus, unary messages have the highest precedence and keyword messages have the lowest.

- Messages with the same precedence are sent in left-to-right order.

- **If** you want to display the answer produced by an expression in a workspace, **then** select that expression and click **right**→**Show It**.

- **If** you want to display the answer produced by an expression in the transcript, **then** construct a `show:` message:

  `Transcript show: expression printString`

  and then select the entire `show:` expression and click **right**→**Do It**:

- **If** you want to start a new line in the transcript, **then** use the `cr` message.

  `Transcript cr`

- **If** you want to evaluate several expressions in sequence, **then** separate those expressions into statements by periods.

3 HOW TO WRITE ARITHMETIC EXPRESSIONS

58   In Section 2, you saw sample expressions involving the keyword exponentiation method, raisedTo:; the binary multiplication method, *; and the unary square-root method, sqrt. In this section, you learn about additional arithmetic messages, and you learn how Smalltalk handles expressions with multiple arithmetic messages.

59   You arrange for basic arithmetic calculations using the +, -, *, and / messages for addition, subtraction, multiplication, and division:

```
6 + 3          ◄── Add 3, answering 9
6 - 3          ◄── Subtract 3, answering 3
6 * 3          ◄── Multiply by 3, answering 18
6 / 3          ◄── Divide by 3, answering 2
```

60   When an Integer instance does not divide evenly into another Integer instance, the division message produces a **rational number**, expressed as a Fraction instance, which is marked with surrounding parentheses:

```
5 / 3          ◄── Divide, answering (5/3), a Fraction instance
```

61   Of course, when an instance of the Float class is divided by another Float instance, Smalltalk produces a Float instance:

```
5.0 / 3.0      ◄── Divide, answering 1.66667, a Float instance
```

62   The // division message always produces an integer result, as in the following illustrations:

```
    Workspace
Transcript show: (22.0 / 7.0) printString.  Transcript cr.
Transcript show: (22.0 // 7.0) printString. Transcript cr.
Transcript show: (22 / 7) printString.       Transcript cr.
Transcript show: (22 // 7) printString.       Transcript cr.
    Transcript
3.14285714
3
22/7
3
```

63   The // division message truncates toward negative infinity:

```
    Workspace
Transcript show: (22 // 7) printString.  Transcript cr.
Transcript show: (22 // -7) printString. Transcript cr.
    Transcript
3
-4
```

64 Arithmetic expressions can contain more than one message:

```
6 + 3 + 2      ←— Two messages, answers 11
6 - 3 - 2      ←— Two messages, answers 1
6 * 3 * 2      ←— Two messages, answers 36
6 / 3 / 2      ←— Two messages, answers 1
```

65 Note that Smalltalk treats +, -, *, /, sqrt, and raisedTo: as methods that happen to appear in messages sent to numbers. Accordingly, to understand arithmetic expressions, you must forget about the **precedence** and **association** conventions of ordinary arithmetic. Instead, you must remember that unary methods have precedence higher than that of binary methods, and binary methods have precedence higher than that of keyword methods. You must also remember that methods of the same type are sent in left-to-right order.

66 As Smalltalk evaluates the expression 6 + 3 * 2, the message + 3 is sent to 6, which answers 9. Then, the message * 2 is sent to 9, which answers 18. Thus, Smalltalk takes 6 + 3 * 2 to be equivalent to (6 + 3) * 2, rather than to 6 +(3 * 2), even though the precedence of multiplication is higher than that of multiplication in ordinary arithmetic:

```
6 + 3 * 2      ←— Equivalent to (6 + 3) * 2, rather than 6 + (3 * 2)
```

67 Of course, you can use parentheses either to circumvent the precedence rules or to make your intentions clearer. In the following, for example, the parentheses are not essential: the result produced without parentheses is the same as the result with parentheses. Nevertheless, many programmers insert parentheses anyway, just to make the expression's meaning absolutely clear:

```
6 + 3 * 2      ←— Value is clearly 18
(6 + 3) * 2    ←— Value is even more clearly 18
```

68 The - message is a binary message. Accordingly, if you wish to calculate the negative of a number, you must use the unary negated method:

```
5 negated      ←— Negate 5, answer -5
```

Similarly, the / message is a binary message. If you wish to calculate the reciprocal of a number, you must use the unary reciprocal method:

```
5 reciprocal   ←— Reciprocate 5, answer (1/5)
```

69 When arithmetic expressions contain instances that belong to multiple classes, those expressions are called **mixed expressions**. The general rule about mixed expressions is that Smalltalk attempts to convert a number belonging to one class into a number belonging to another class in a way that does not lose information. Thus, when given a mixed expression that multiplies a Fraction instance by an Integer instance, Smalltalk creates a Fraction instance from the Integer instance in the course of producing an answer. Similarly, when given a mixed expression that multiplies a Float instance by an Integer instance, Smalltalk creates a Float instance from the Integer instance in the course of producing an answer:

```
6 * (2/5)            ◄── Multiply (6/1) times (2/5), answering (12/5)
6 * 3.1              ◄── Multiply 6.0 times 3.1, answering 18.6
```

70   If you want to tell Smalltalk to convert a number from one type to another explicitly, rather than relying on **automatic conversion**, you can use `asInteger` or `asFloat`. Note that `asInteger` rounds `Float` instances:

```
3.01 asInteger   ◄── Round 3.01 to an integer, answering 3
3.99 asInteger   ◄── Round 3.99 to an integer, answering 4
-3.01 asInteger  ◄── Round 3.01 to an integer, answering -3
-3.99 asInteger  ◄── Round 3.99 to an integer, answering -4
```

71   You can even convert numbers to strings using `asString`:

```
3 asString       ◄── Convert to string, answering '3'
3.14 asString    ◄── Convert to string, answering '3.14'
```

You need to convert numbers to strings when you want to produce formatted output, as you learn in Segment 460.

72   Conversion of one number type into another is called **casting** in some computer languages
SIDE TRIP   (such as C) and **coercion** in others (such as Lisp).

73   Typical Smalltalk implementations offer a host of arithmetic methods:

- Methods for basic arithmetic, such as +, -, *, /, `negated`, and `reciprocal`

- Methods for type conversion, such as `asInteger` and `asFloat`

- Methods for exponentiation, such as `raisedTo:`

- Methods for trigonometry, such as `sin`, `tan`, `arcSin`, and `arcTan`

- Methods for logarithms, such as `ln` (natural logarithm) and `log:` (base provided as argument)

- Methods for manipulating and dissecting floating-point numbers, such as `round` and `truncated`

74   You can easily determine exactly which of these arithmetic methods are available by using
SIDE TRIP   a **class-hierarchy browser**, as explained in Segment 85.

75   Write an expression that computes the number of millions of seconds in a year.
PRACTICE

76   Write an expression that determines the number of days occupied by 1 million seconds.
PRACTICE

77   Using the `raisedTo:` message, write an expression that computes the volume of Earth in
PRACTICE   cubic miles using Earth's radius.

78
HIGHLIGHTS   • Smalltalk offers negation, reciprocation, addition, subtraction, multiplication, division, and many other arithmetic methods.

```
```

- Smalltalk does *not* follow the precedence conventions of ordinary arithmetic; instead, Smalltalk handles arithmetic messages as it handles messages in general.

- **If** you want to alter the way an arithmetic expression is computed, **or if** you want to make your arithmetic expressions clearer, **then** use parentheses to create subexpressions.

- **If** you want to convert a number belonging to one class into a number belonging to another class, **then** use `asInteger` or `asFloat`.

4 HOW TO DEFINE SIMPLE METHODS

79   In this section, you learn how to define Smalltalk methods.

80   In Section 2, you learned you can multiply 194 by 9, hence computing the number of calories in 194 grams of fat, as follows:

```
194 * 9
```

Of course, if you propose to compute calorie content many times, you should arrange for the appropriate work done by a new method, as in the following expression, in which a `fatToCalories` message is sent to an instance of the `Integer` class:

```
194 fatToCalories
```

To respond to the `fatToCalories` message, the receiver, 194, must find the method identified by the `fatToCalories` selector and follow the instructions found in that method.

Accordingly, you must learn how to define a `fatToCalories` method appropriate for `fatToCalories` messages sent to instances of the `Integer` class.

81   To define the `fatToCalories` method, you have to find your way into the description of the `Integer` class. First, enter the **class-hierarchy browser** by clicking **File→Browse Classes**, at which point the class-hierarchy browser emerges:

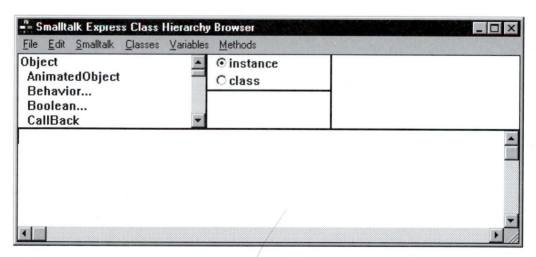

82   To understand what you see in the class-hierarchy browser, you need to know how the class hierarchy is displayed.

First, note that every class in Smalltalk is a subclass of some other class, except for the class named `Object`. Thus, the classes in Smalltalk form an treelike, hierarchical structure, rooted in the `Object` class. The following shows a small portion of the **class hierarchy**:

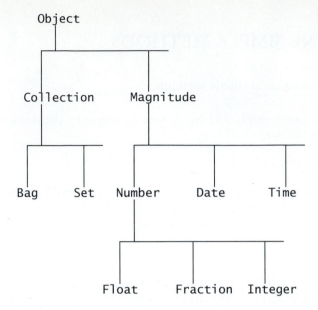

Now, think of turning the class-hierarchy diagram on its side:

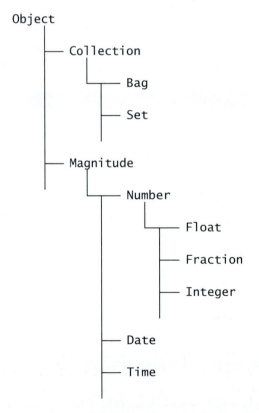

Then, think of deleting all empty lines and indenting classes on each level by just one space per level:

```
Object
 Collection
  Bag
  Set
  ...
 Magnitude
  Number
   Float
   Fraction
   Integer
   ...
  Date
  Time
  ...
 ...
```

83 Finally, when you first enter the class-hierarchy Browser, only the Object class and the classes immediately under the Object class are shown, with ellipses indicating that there are unseen subclasses:

```
Object
 AnimatedObject
 Behavior...
 Boolean...
 CallBack
 ClassReader
 ClipboardManager
 Collection ...
 Compiler
 CursorManager
 DeletedClass
 ...
```

Because the classes are shown alphabetically, you do not see classes such as the Collection class until you scroll down.

84 Note that the word *object* is used in two ways. Written with a capital O, Object is the name of the highest-level class. Written with a lowercase o, *object* is an entity that receives and sends messages.

85 To see the subclasses of a particular class, you double click on that class. Thus, to find the Integer class, you scroll down to the Magnitude class and double click on that class; then, you double click on the Number class.

Then, if you click once on the Integer class, you see a list of the methods defined for the Integer class in the right column:

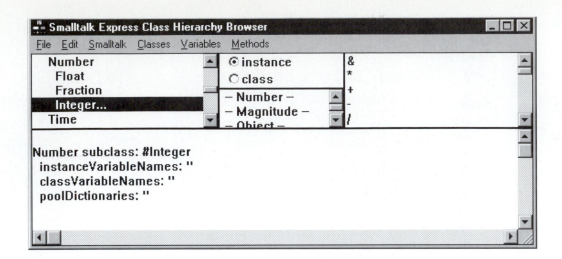

86   Now, you can define your own method by clicking **Methods→New Method**.

Then, you see a template for defining a new method in the lower half of the class-hierarchy browser:

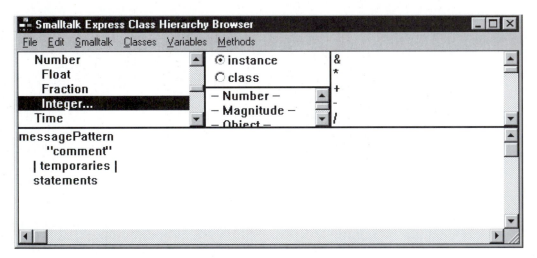

87   The `fatToCalories` method is to be sent to *instances* of the `Integer` class. Accordingly, be sure that the `instance` button is selected, rather than the `class` button, in the **instance–object window**, so that you will define an **instance method**. You learn about the role of the `class` button in Segment 253.

88   You learn about the **variables window**, which lies under the instance–object window, in Segment 207.

89   To define the new `fatToCalories` method, you enter the following in the lower half of the class-hierarchy browser:

```
fatToCalories
   "Answer the calories in the receiver, viewed as grams of fat"
   ^ self * 9
```

You can enter the method definition by replacing portions of the template provided by Smalltalk; alternatively, you can replace the template as a whole.

90 The following diagram shows what each part of the method definition does:

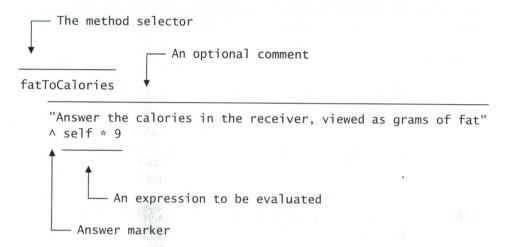

91 Note that self always refers to the receiver. If you send the fatToCalories message to 194, then inside the fatToCalories method, self refers to 194.

92 The **answer marker**, ^, is an important part of the definition of fatToCalories, because the answer marker identifies the expression, self * 9, that produces the answer when fatToCalories messages are sent to integers. Such an expression is called an **answer expression**.

93 You can include **comments** in Smalltalk methods, using double-quotation marks, at any point. Whenever Smalltalk encounters a double-quotation mark, Smalltalk ignores both the double-quotation mark and all other characters up to and including the next double-quotation mark, as in the following examples:

```
" A short comment "
"
   A comment ...
   that just goes on ...
   and on ...
   and on ...
"
```

Traditionally, a comment explaining what the method does appears immediately inside the definition, as shown in Segment 90.

94 If you wish to test how a method works without certain fragments, you can hide those fragments in a comment, instead of deleting them. In the following, for example, the method definition specifies that `self` is answered, because `* 9` has been hidden in a comment:

```
fatToCalories
  ^ self "* 9 "
```

95 You cannot place a comment inside another comment. If you try, you find that the inner comment's first double-quotation mark terminates the outer comment, and your Smalltalk compiler misconstrues your intentions, and sees the inner comment uncovered:

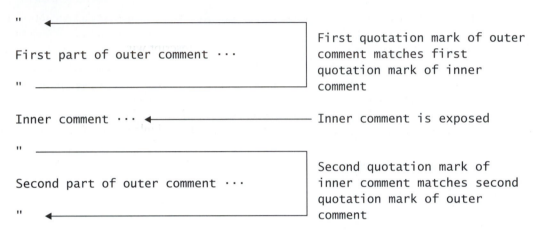

96 The method defined in Segment 90 lacks the portion between vertical bars shown in Segment 86, because the method has no local variables. You learn about local variables in Section 9.

97 To tell Smalltalk that you have finished defining `fatToCalories`, click **right→Save** in the lower half of the class-hierarchy browser. Your new method's selector appears in the third column:

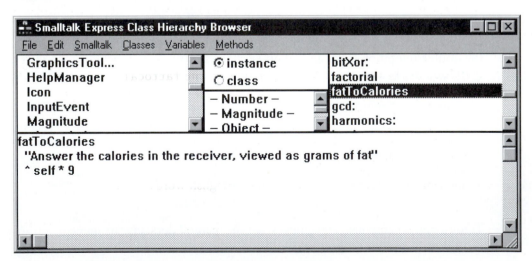

98 To keep the size of this book manageable, the information displayed in the class-hierarchy browser shown in Segment 97 is rerepresented in the following form:

Integer method definition	• instance

```
fatToCalories
  "Answer the calories in the receiver, viewed as grams of fat"
  ^ self * 9
```

When you see such a definition representation, you are to assume that Smalltalk has accepted the definition in response to your clicking **right→save**.

99 If you want to preserve the methods that you define, you must save your development environment when you stop working. To save your environment, you click the **close button**—the one in the upper-right corner of the transcript window. When you are asked whether you want to save the image, click **yes**.

100 Spaces, tabs, and carriage returns are called **whitespace characters**. Smalltalk is **blank insensitive** because Smalltalk treats all sequences of whitespace characters—other than those in character strings—as though there were just a single space. Thus, the following are equivalent:

Integer method definition	• instance

```
fatToCalories
  ^ self * 9
```

Integer method definition	• instance

```
fatToCalories    ^    self    *    9
```

Neither of these layout options can be said to be "best" or "official." In fact, experienced Smalltalk programmers argue heatedly about how to arrange methods to maximize transparency and to please the eye. In this book, the methods are written in a style that both uses paper efficiently and lies within the envelope of common practice.

101 The definitions given in Segment 100 do not have comments. Good programming practice dictates that every method should have a comment explaining what kind of arguments that method expects and what kind of answer it produces. This book omits such comments only to save space.

102 Smalltalk is **case sensitive**; for example, if you write `fattocalories` or `fatToCALORIES` when you mean `fatToCalories`, Smalltalk cannot understand your intent.

103 Most Smalltalk programmers would never define a method with a method selector such as `fattocalories` or `fatToCALORIES`, because most Smalltalk programmers adhere to the following **naming conventions**:

- Method selectors consist of one or more English words.

- None of the words are abbreviated.

- The first character of each word, except the first, is an uppercase character; all the other characters are lowercase characters.

- There are no separator characters, such as _, between the words.

- The combination of words explains what the method does.

Your Smalltalk programs will look silly and amateurish to many Smalltalk programmers if you fail to adhere to the conventions.

104 The `fatToCalories` method, as defined in Segment 89, contains only one expression, `∧ self * 9`. Most Smalltalk methods contain multiple expressions, divided into statements by periods. In the following definition of `displayFatCalories`, for example, there are three statements, each of which displays a string in the transcript:

```
Integer method definition        • instance
displayFatCalories
   Transcript show: 'There are '.
   Transcript show: (self * 9) printString.
   Transcript show: ' calories in the fat'
      Workspace
194 displayFatCalories
      Transcript
There are 1746 calories in the fat
```

105 Because `displayFatCalories` does not contain any expression marked by ∧, the method is said to **fall off its end**, answering `self` by default.

106 Rather than allowing a method to fall off its end, answering `self` by default, you can
SIDE TRIP include an equivalent, explicit answer of `self` by concluding the method definition with `∧ self`. Generally, you should include `∧ self` only when you wish to indicate to yourself or other programmers that you expect the answered `self` to be used.

107 Another way to define `displayFatCalories` is to use Smalltalk's string-concatenation method, which is written as a comma. The concatenation method is sent to a string with another string as an argument. The answer is a string in which the two strings are concatenated.

```
Integer method definition        • instance
displayFatCalories
   Transcript show:
      'There are ' , (self * 9) printString , ' calories in the fat'
```

108 Still another way to define `displayFatCalories` is to use Smalltalk's **cascading** feature. To use cascading, you write out an expression, followed by a semicolon, followed by an expression with an implied receiver:

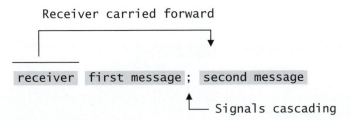

26

109 The answer produced by a cascaded expression is the answer produced by the final message in the cascade.

110 Cascading works for any kind of message and any number of expressions. In the following, for example, cascading is used to combine three `show:` keyword messages:

```
Integer method definition          • instance
displayFatCalories
  Transcript
    show: 'There are ';
    show: (self * 9) printString;
    show: ' calories in the fat'
```

Note that aligning the `show:` selectors in display expressions makes those statements easier to read.

111 In this section, you learned that you can use the class-hierarchy browser to define new methods. You can also use the class-hierarchy browser to examine the definitions of all methods, both those you define and those provided by Smalltalk.

You learn in Section 11 that you also can use the class-hierarchy browser to examine the definitions of all classes—both those that you define and those provided by Smalltalk.

112 Providing access to the definitions of predefined methods is one of the great—and unusual—strengths of the language. That access both deepens your understanding of the language and facilitates method and class reuse. Frequently, you can copy and adapt an existing method or class definition to suit a new purpose, rather than writing a new method or class from scratch.

113 The class-hierarchy browser is not the only tool for finding and looking at definitions. You learn, for example, about the method-selector window in Section 28.

114 **PRACTICE** Define a method for the `Integer` class that computes the volume of a sphere, given that the receiver is the radius. Use your method to compute the volume of Earth in cubic miles.

115 **PRACTICE** Define a method for the `Integer` class that computes how long it takes an object to fall, in seconds, given that the distance to be covered, in meters, is the receiver. Use the formula $s = \frac{1}{2}at^2$, where $a = 9.8m/sec^2$. Use your method to determine how long a cannon ball takes to drop to the ground from the top of a 10-story building.

116 **HIGHLIGHTS**

- If you want to define a method with neither arguments nor local variables, **then** instantiate the following pattern in the class-hierarchy browser:

```
method selector
  comment
  statement 1
  statement 2
  ...
  statement n
```

- If you want to refer to the receiver of a message in a method, **then** use `self`.

- If you want the value of an expression to be a method's value, **then** mark that expression with a answer marker, $\wedge$.

- Smalltalk is blank insensitive.

- Smalltalk is case sensitive. By convention, method names consist of English words run together, with all but the first capitalized.

- If you want to insert a comment into a method, **then** mark both ends of the comment with double-quotation marks.

  `"` `a comment` `"`

- If you want to send multiple messages to one receiver, **then** cascade the messages, separating them with semicolons.

- If you want to concatenate two `String` instances, **then** deploy a concatenation message, written as a comma.

5 HOW TO DEFINE METHODS WITH PARAMETERS

117 In this section, you learn how to introduce parameters into Smalltalk methods, so that messages can include arguments. You also learn that a parameter is accessible only via expressions that lie within the same method within which the parameter lies.

118 Suppose, for example, that you want to define `covertToCaloriesWith:`, a keyword method called when a `covertToCaloriesWith:` message is sent to an integer with an argument:

> Workspace
> ```
> Transcript show: (194 convertToCaloriesWith: 4) printString
> ```
> Transcript
> ```
> 776
> ```

To define such a method, you must learn how to incorporate parameters into method definitions.

119 **Parameters** are names that serve as handles for objects that are supplied as message arguments, such as 4 in the expression `194 convertToCaloriesWith: 4`.

Accordingly, whenever a `convertToCaloriesWith:` message appears, Smalltalk must arrange for the following to be done:

- Identify the argument object, 4, with a parameter—say `caloriesPerGram`—specified by you when you define the `convertToCaloriesWith:` method.

- Evaluate the expression `self * caloriesPerGram`.

- Answer the value of `self * caloriesPerGram` for use in other computations.

120 Identifying an argument object with a parameter is called **parameter assignment**. Whenever Smalltalk makes such a connection, the parameter is said to be **assigned a value** and the value is said to be **assigned to the parameter**.

121 You define the `convertToCaloriesWith:` method in basically the same way that you learned to define the `fatToCalories` method in Section 5. The only difference is the addition of a parameter:

> Integer method definition   • instance
> ```
> convertToCaloriesWith: caloriesPerGram
>   ^ self * caloriesPerGram
> ```

The following diagram shows what each part of the method definition does:

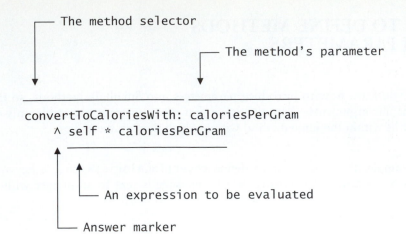

The method selector

The method's parameter

```
convertToCaloriesWith: caloriesPerGram
    ∧ self * caloriesPerGram
```

An expression to be evaluated

Answer marker

122 It is important to know that parameter values established when a method is entered are available only inside the method. It is as though Smalltalk builds an isolating fence to protect any other uses of the same parameter name outside of the method.

123 Consider the convertToCaloriesWith: method, as defined in Segment 121, for example. When the convertToCaloriesWith: method is called, any existing values for other parameters that happen to be named caloriesPerGram are protected:

```
convertToCaloriesWith: fence
   The value of caloriesPerGram
   inside the fence is isolated
   from values outside

   The Method computes the value
   of self * caloriesPerGram using
   the value of caloriesPerGram
   inside this fence
```

The values of caloriesPerGram outside the fence, if any, are isolated from the value inside

124 The **scope** of a parameter is that portion of a program that can get at the value of the parameter. A method's parameter is said to have **local scope** because the value of that parameter is available in only those expressions that appear in the definition of the method itself.

Thus, **local scope** is the technical term for parameter fencing, and Smalltalk is said to be a **locally scoped language**.

125 Suppose that you define three methods: the outerParameterDisplay: method calls the middleParameterDisplay: method, which, in turn, calls the innerParameterDisplay: method. All three methods happen to use aParameter as a parameter.

As shown in the following illustration, each use of aParameter is fenced. Also, none of the methods happen to use self, so all the receiver integers are ignored:

```
outerParameterDisplay: aParameter
  Transcript show: 'Value inside outerParameterDisplay: ';
            show: aParameter printString;
            cr.
    self middleParameterDisplay: 2.
  Transcript show: 'Value inside outerParameterDisplay: ';
            show: aParameter printString;
            cr
```

Integer method definition   • instance

```
middleParameterDisplay: aParameter
  Transcript show: 'Value inside middleParameterDisplay: ';
            show: aParameter printString;
            cr.
    self innerParameterDisplay: 1.
  Transcript show: 'Value inside middleParameterDisplay: ';
            show: aParameter printString;
            cr
```

Integer method definition   • instance

```
innerParameterDisplay: aParameter
  Transcript show: 'Value inside innerParameterDisplay: ';
            show: aParameter printString;
            cr
```

Workspace

```
4 outerParameterDisplay: 3
```

Transcript

```
Value inside outerParameterDisplay: 3
Value inside middleParameterDisplay: 2
Value inside innerParameterDisplay: 1
Value inside middleParameterDisplay: 2
Value inside outerParameterDisplay: 3
```

126   Although parameter values are fenced, changes to the internal structure of a parameter
SIDE TRIP   value do propagate outside. If, for example, the value of a parameter is an array, and you
change the value of an array element inside a method, then the change to the value of the
array element persists after the method returns.

127   Smalltalk programmers generally use long, descriptive parameter names. Some names,
such as `caloriesPerGram`, indicate the role of the parameter. Others, such as `anInteger`,
indicate the expected type of the parameter. Such names tend to improve readability, but
Smalltalk does not force you to adhere to any particular naming convention. Smalltalk is
happy to work with more conventional parameter names, such as x and y.

128   You may, of course, write methods that involve multiple keywords. Those multiple keywords introduce multiple parameters in method definitions and identify multiple arguments
in messages.

Whenever a method involves multiple keywords, the method selector is taken to be the
concatenation of all the keywords. For example, in Segment 147, you learn about the

`ifTrue:ifFalse:` method selector.

129
PRACTICE

The energy of a moving mass is given by the formula $\frac{1}{2}mv^2$. Write a method that answers the energy ratio of a car moving at two speeds, with one speed supplied as the receiver and the other speed supplied as an argument. Use your method to determine how much more energy a car has when moving at 80 miles per hour than when it is moving at 55 miles per hour.

130
HIGHLIGHTS

- **If** you want to define a method with parameters, **then** click into the class-hierarchy browser to the appropriate place **and then** instantiate the following pattern:

```
selector part 1  parameter 1
  selector part 2  parameter 2
  ...
  selector part m  parameter m
    comment
    statement 1
    statement 2
    ...
    statement n
```

- Whenever a message is sent, the message's arguments are evaluated, and the resulting answers are assigned to the method's parameters. Then, the statements in the method are evaluated.

- Parameters in Smalltalk methods have local scope. Identically named parameters in multiple methods cannot interfere with one another, and a parameter established in one method cannot be evaluated in another method.

6 HOW TO PERFORM TESTS USING PREDICATES

131　In this section and in the next several sections, you learn how to do routine testing and branching. You see that Smalltalk's mechanisms for accomplishing such tasks differ from those that you would find in other programming languages, because, in Smalltalk, all such mechanisms reflect Smalltalk's receiver–message–answer paradigm.

In particular, in this section, you learn how number testing can be cast in the receiver–message–answer paradigm.

132　A **predicate** is a method that answers with either of two special objects, `true` or `false`. Smalltalk offers several binary predicates that test the relationship between pairs of numbers:

Predicate	Purpose
=	Are the receiver and the argument equal?
~=	Are the receiver and the argument not equal?
>	Is the receiver greater than the argument?
<	Is the receiver less than the argument?
>=	Is the receiver greater than or equal to the argument?
<=	Is the receiver less than or equal to the argument?

133　For example, the value of the expression 6 = 3, in which the equality message appears, is `false`. The value of the expression 6 ~= 3, in which the inequality message appears, is `true`. Thus, the value answered by predicates, such as the = and ~= predicates, may be either `true` or `false`.

134　Note that `not` is a unary message that answers `true` when sent to `false` and `false` when sent to `true`:

```
   Workspace
Transcript show: false not printString; cr;
          show: true not printString; cr
   Transcript
true
false
```

135　In addition to predicates for testing numbers, Smalltalk offers other predicates, such as `isInteger` and `isString`, that test instances to determine whether those instances belong to particular classes:

```
Transcript show: 4 isInteger printString; cr;
          show: 4 isString printString; cr;
          show: 'four' isInteger printString; cr;
          show: 'four' isString printString; cr
```

Transcript

```
true
false
false
true
```

136
PRACTICE

You are too heavy if your weight in kilograms divided by the square of your height in meters exceeds 30. Write a method to be sent to a number, denoting weight, along with another number, denoting height, as an argument. Your method is to answer true if the weight is too ponderous for the height.

137
HIGHLIGHTS

- A *predicate* is a method that answers true or false.

- The not message answers false when sent to true, and true when sent to false.

- If you want to compare two numbers, then use predicates such as =, ~=, >, <, >=, or <=.

- If you want to determine whether an instance is a member of a particular class, then use predicates such as isInteger and isString.

7 HOW TO WRITE CONDITIONAL EXPRESSIONS

139   In this section, you learn what to do when the computation that you want to perform depends on whether the value of an expression is `true` or `false`.

140   An expression that evaluates to either `true` or `false` is a **Boolean expression**. The Boolean expressions include, for example, `true`, `false`, and expressions in which the message is one of the binary predicates described in Section 6.

141   Note that `true` and `false` must be objects, because all entities in Smalltalk are objects. Accordingly, `true` and `false`, like all other objects, can receive messages.

142   For example, in a **conditional expression**, a message, such as the `ifTrue:` message, is sent to a receiver, `true` or `false`, that is produced by a Boolean expression. Following the `ifTrue:` selector in the `ifTrue:` message, you find one or more statements surrounded by brackets:

`Boolean expression` `ifTrue: [ statements ]`

Whenever `ifTrue:` is sent to `true`, the `ifTrue:` method evaluates the statements between the brackets. Whenever `ifTrue:` is sent to `false`, `ifTrue:` ignores the statements between the brackets.

143   Suppose, for example, that you want to define a method that displays a message that depends on the number of calories consumed in a day. Specifically, if the number of calories is greater than 1600, you want your method to display `You have had enough`; if the number is less that 1200, you want your method to display `You need more`.

One solution is to write a method that uses `ifTrue:` statements in which the embedded statements display a string in the transcript:

```
Integer method definition        • instance
analyzeCalories
  self > 1600 ifTrue: [Transcript show: 'You have had enough'; cr].
  self < 1200 ifTrue: [Transcript show: 'You need more'; cr]
        Workspace
1700 analyzeCalories.
1100 analyzeCalories
        Transcript
You have had enough
You need more
```

144   Whenever a set of statements is delimited by brackets, that set of statements constitutes a **block**. Thus, `[Transcript show: 'You have had enough'; cr]` is a block consisting of a single statement, which contains only a single cascaded expression.

Thus, in `ifTrue:` expressions, the receiver is `true` or `false`, the selector is `ifTrue:`, and the argument is a block.

145　Of course, blocks are objects, just as all other entities in Smalltalk are objects. In this section, you see examples of blocks used as message arguments. In Section 16, you see examples of blocks used as message receivers.

146　Smalltalk permits conditional expressions with `ifFalse:` messages instead of `ifTrue:` messages. Whenever an `ifFalse:` message is sent to `true`, the block argument is ignored; whenever an `ifFalse:` message is sent to `false`, the statements in the block are evaluated. Thus, you can redefine the **analyzeCalories** method defined in Segment 143 as follows:

```
Integer method definition        • instance
analyzeCalories
  self <= 1600 ifFalse: [Transcript show: 'You have had enough'; cr].
  self >= 1200 ifFalse: [Transcript show: 'You need more'; cr]
     Workspace
1700 analyzeCalories.
1100 analyzeCalories
     Transcript
You have had enough
You need more
```

147　You can combine `ifTrue:` and `ifFalse:` into a two-argument message with two keywords:

```
Boolean expression
  ifTrue:  if-true block
  ifFalse: if-false block
```

If the Boolean expression evaluates to `true`, the first block is evaluated, and the second is ignored. Conversely, the second block is evaluated, and the first is ignored, if the Boolean expression evaluates to `false`.

148　When `ifTrue:` and `ifFalse:` are combined, `ifTrue:ifFalse:` is said to be the method selector. Whenever multiple keywords are used to call up a method, the method selector is taken to be the keywords run together, as in the `ifTrue:ifFalse:` combination.

149　Smalltalk also permits you to send `ifFalse:ifTrue:` messages:

```
Boolean expression
  ifFalse: if-false block
  ifTrue:  if-true block
```

150　Because order matters in Smalltalk, you should not think of the `ifFalse:ifTrue:` message
SIDE TRIP　as a reordering of the keywords and arguments in an `ifTrue:ifFalse:` message. Instead, you should understand that the `ifTrue:ifFalse:` selector and the `ifFalse:ifTrue:` selectors are distinct selectors, both of which happen to label methods that do the same work.

151　You can embed a conditional expression inside another conditional expression. Yet another solution to the calorie-testing problem is as follows:

```
analyzeCalories
  self > 1600
    ifTrue: [Transcript show: 'You have had enough'; cr]
    ifFalse: [self < 1200
                ifTrue: [Transcript show: 'You need more'; cr]
                ifFalse: [Transcript show: 'You have eaten wisely'; cr]]
```

Workspace

```
1700 analyzeCalories.
1400 analyzeCalories.
1100 analyzeCalories
```

Transcript

```
You have had enough
You have eaten wisely
You need more
```

Note that the ifTrue:ifFalse: expression's second argument is an ifTrue:ifFalse: expression. This embedded ifTrue:ifFalse: expression is evaluated only if the number of calories is 1600 or less.

152   The answer produced by an ifTrue:, ifFalse:, ifTrue:ifFalse:, or ifFalse:ifTrue: message is the value produced by the evaluated block. The value produced by an evaluated block is the value of the expression that constitutes the final statement in the block. Accordingly, you can move the show: message out of the block in analyzeCalories as defined in Segment 151:

Integer method definition   • instance

```
analyzeCalories
  Transcript show:
    (self > 1600
       ifTrue: ['You have had enough']
       ifFalse: [(self < 1200)
                   ifTrue: ['You need more']
                   ifFalse: ['You have eaten wisely']]);
            cr
```

Workspace

```
1700 analyzeCalories.
1400 analyzeCalories.
1100 analyzeCalories
```

Transcript

```
You have had enough
You have eaten wisely
You need more
```

Note that the entire conditional expression is surrounded by parentheses; otherwise, Smalltalk would look for a show:ifTrue:ifFalse method, and, failing to find one, Smalltalk would complain.

153 Blocks may contain answer expressions. If an answer expression is encountered during block evaluation, the value of the answer expression immediately becomes the answer produced by the method in which the block is embedded; nothing else in the method is evaluated. Accordingly, you can move the show: message entirely out of analyzeCalories as defined in Segment 152:

```
Integer method definition          • instance
analyzeCalories
  self > 1600
    ifTrue: [^ 'You have had enough']
    ifFalse: [(self < 1200)
               ifTrue: [^ 'You need more']
               ifFalse: [^ 'You have eaten wisely']]
    Workspace
Transcript show: 1700 analyzeCalories; cr.
Transcript show: 1400 analyzeCalories; cr.
Transcript show: 1100 analyzeCalories; cr
    Transcript
You have had enough
You have eaten wisely
You need more
```

154 Write a method that displays a message such as The weight change is 1 kilogram or
PRACTICE The weight change is 2 kilograms when sent to a number representing a change in weight. Be sure that the word *kilogram* is in the singular only if the receiver is 1.

155 Write a method that displays one of three comments when sent to a number representing
PRACTICE an athlete's resting pulse rate: if the rate is less than 50, the value answered by the method is to be Wow; if the rate is more than 80, the value answered is to be Too High; otherwise, the value answered is to be Ok.

Next, write a method that displays one of three comments when sent to a number representing an athlete's body fat as a percentage of weight: if the athlete's body-fat percentage is less than 10, the value answered is to be Wow; if it is more than 20, the value answered is to be Too High; otherwise, the value answered is to be Ok.

156
HIGHLIGHTS

- A Boolean expression is an expression that evaluates to true or false.

- A block is a sequence of statements delimited by brackets. The value produced when a block is evaluated is the value produced by the final statement in the block.

- If you want to evaluate an expression only when a Boolean expression evaluates to true, then use an ifTrue: message:

```
Boolean expression ifTrue: if-true block
```

- **If** you want to evaluate an expression only when another expression evaluates to `false`, **then** use an `ifFalse:` message:

  ```
  Boolean expression ifFalse: if-false block
  ```

- **If** you want to evaluate one expression when a predicate expression evaluates to `true`, and a second expression, when the predicate expression evaluates to `false`, **then** use an `ifTrue:ifFalse:` or an `ifFalse:ifTrue:` message:

  ```
  Boolean expression
    ifTrue:  if-true block
    ifFalse: if-false block
  Boolean expression
    ifFalse: if-false block
    ifTrue:  if-true block
  ```

- **If** you want to a method to answer with a value produced inside a block, **then** include an answer expression in that block.

8 HOW TO COMBINE BOOLEAN EXPRESSIONS

157   In this section, you learn how to combine Boolean expressions to form larger Boolean expressions.

158   The **and message, &,** and the **or message,** |, do what they sound like they should do. The and message answers `true` if *both* the receiver and the argument evaluate to `true`. The or message answers `true` if *either* the receiver or the argument evaluates to `true`.

```
receiver expression  &  argument expression
receiver expression  |  argument expression
```

159   The following method, for example, answers `true` only if the value of `self` is between 1200 and 1600, inclusively:

```
Integer method definition        • instance
inRange
  ^ (1200 <= self) & (self <= 1600)
      Workspace
Transcript show: 1700 inRange printString; cr;
          show: 1400 inRange printString; cr;
          show: 1100 inRange printString.
      Transcript
false
true
false
```

Similarly, the `show:` message in the following method is sent only if the value of `self` is in the 1200-to-1600 range:

```
Integer method definition        • instance
analyzeCalories
   (1200 <= self) & (self <= 1600)
     ifTrue: [Transcript show: self printString; show: ' is reasonable';
cr]
      Workspace
1700 analyzeCalories.
1400 analyzeCalories.
1100 analyzeCalories
      Transcript
1400 is reasonable
```

160   The `show:` message in the following method is sent only if the value of `self` is outside the 1200-to-1600 range:

```
Integer method definition          • instance
analyzeCalories
  (self < 1200) | (self > 1600)
    ifTrue: [Transcript show: self printString;
                        show: ' is unreasonable';
                        cr]
```

```
          Workspace
1700 analyzeCalories.
1400 analyzeCalories.
1100 analyzeCalories
          Transcript
1700 is unreasonable
1100 is unreasonable
```

161   When evaluating & and | expressions, Smalltalk evaluates both the receiver expression and the argument expression.

162   Note that, whenever the receiver of an & message is false, the computation required to evaluate the argument is wasted, because the answer must be false no matter what the argument's value may be. Similarly, whenever the receiver of an | message is true, the computation required to evaluate the argument is wasted, because the answer must be true no matter what the argument's value may be.

To avoid wasting the computation required to evaluate arguments, many Smalltalk programmers avoid & and | altogether, using the and: and or: messages instead.

163   Both the and: and or: methods take blocks as arguments:

```
receiver expression  and:  argument block
receiver expression  or:  argument block
```

If the receiver of an and: message is false, the argument block is ignored, and the value of the expression is false.

If the receiver of an or: message is true, the argument block is ignored, and the value of the expression is true.

Thus, for the and: message, the argument block is evaluated only if the receiver is true, and the value of the expression is the value of the block. For the or: message, the argument block is evaluated only if the receiver is false, and the value of the expression is the value of the block.

164   In the following example, the argument block in the and: expression is evaluated only if self is greater than 1200. The argument block in the or: expression is evaluated only if self is not greater than 1200.

Note that the parentheses are mandatory; without them, Smalltalk would think you were trying to use and:ifTrue: and or:ifTrue: messages:

```
analyzeCalories
  (1200 <= self and: [self <= 1600])
    ifTrue:
      [Transcript show: self printString; show: ' is reasonable'; cr].
  (self < 1200 or: [self > 1600])
    ifTrue:
      [Transcript show: self printString; show: ' is unreasonable'; cr]
```

Workspace
```
1700 analyzeCalories.
1400 analyzeCalories.
1100 analyzeCalories
```

Transcript
```
1700 is unreasonable
1400 is reasonable
1100 is unreasonable
```

165
SIDE TRIP

You can use the `and:` message to ensure that a parameter has been assigned a value before you evaluate an expression that depends on an assignment. For example, the following expression uses `isNumber` to ensure that the `>` test is evaluated only if a number has been assigned to `x`:

```
x isNumber and: [x > 1600]
```

166
SIDE TRIP

It is possible to use an `and:` message instead of an `ifTrue:` message by exploiting the property that the argument block in an `and:` expression is evaluated only if the receiver is `true`.

Note, however, that most programmers object to the use of `and:` and `or:` messages to only allow or prevent evaluation. They argue that, when an `and:` or `or:` message is included in an expression anyone—other than the original programmer—naturally expects the value produced by the expression to be used. If the value is not used, the person who looks at the program may wonder whether the original programmer left out a portion of a method definition unintentionally.

167
PRACTICE

Write a method that analyzes an athlete's condition when sent to a number representing an athlete's resting pulse rate with an argument representing that athlete's body-fat percentage. Your method is to display `The athlete appears to be in great shape` if both the athlete's pulse rate and body fat are low. Use the work you performed in response to the problem posed in Segment 155,

168
HIGHLIGHTS

- If you want to combine two Boolean expressions, **and** the result is to be `true` if the values of *both* expressions are `true`, **then** send the first Boolean expression the & message with the second Boolean expression as an argument.

- If you want to combine two Boolean expressions, **and** the result is to be `true` if the value of *either* expression is `true`, **then** send the first Boolean expression the | message with the second Boolean expression as an argument.

43

- **If** you want to combine two Boolean expressions, **and** the result is to be `true` if the values of *both* expressions are `true`, **and** you want to prevent wasted computation, **then** send the first Boolean expression the `and:` message with the second Boolean expression embedded in a block argument.

- **If** you want to combine two Boolean expressions, **and** the result is to be `true` if the value of *either* expression is `true`, **and** you want to prevent wasted computation, **then** send the first Boolean expression the `or:` message with the second Boolean expression embedded in a block argument.

9 HOW TO INTRODUCE LOCAL VARIABLES

169   In this section, you learn how to introduce local variables into Smalltalk methods.

170   A **variable** is a name that **refers to** an object. The object referred to by a variable is said to be that variable's **value**. As it may in all programming languages, a variable's value may change, but in contrast to the conventions of many programming languages, such as C, a variable's value may change not only to another instance of the same class, but also to an instance of another class.

171   Establishing the connection between a variable and its value is called doing **variable assignment**. Accordingly, whenever Smalltalk makes such a connection, the variable is said to be **assigned a value** and the value is said to be **assigned to the variable**.

172   You introduce **local variables** into a method by listing those variables between vertical bars in front of the first statement in the method. In the following method, three variables `multiplier` and `multiplicand`, and `result` are introduced, but are not used:

```
Integer method definition          • instance
fatToCalories
  | multiplier multiplicand result |
  ^ self * 9
```

173   Smalltalk assigns an object named `nil` to all a method's local variables on entry to that method. Thus, a value of `nil` generally means *not yet assigned* or *unassigned*.

174   Because `nil` is the initial assignment of all local variables, all local variables are said to be **initialized** to `nil`.

You can test a variable with the `notNil` predicate to determine if that value of that variable has been changed.

175   To change the value of a variable, you use the **assignment operator**, `:=`. Three assignment-operator containing statements appear in the following method definition:

```
Integer method definition          • instance
fatToCalories
  | multiplier multiplicand result |
  multiplier := self.
  multiplicand := 9.
  result := multiplicand * multiplier.
  ^ result
     Workspace
Transcript show: 194 fatToCalories printString
     Transcript
1746
```

Of course, this method is defined awkwardly—the only reason to split the computation into multiple statements is to demonstrate variable assignment.

176   The **scope** of a variable is that portion of a program in which that variable can be evaluated or changed. The local variables in Smalltalk are **locally scoped**: those variables are available for evaluation or assignment in only the method itself.

- A variable value assigned in one method cannot interfere with a variable assignment or parameter assignment in another method, even if the names are the same.

- The value of a variable established in one method cannot be determined in another method.

177   Assignment expressions, like all expressions in Smalltalk, have values. By convention, the value is the same as the value assigned. Thus, the value produced by the expression y := 9 is 9.

Accordingly, assignment expressions can appear as subexpressions nested inside larger expressions.

In the following, for example, the assignment expression, y := 9, which assigns a value to y, appears inside a larger assignment expression, which assigns a value to x as well:

```
x := (y := 9)
```

When the assignment expression is evaluated, 9 is assigned to y first; then, the value of the subexpression, which is also 9, is assigned to x.

178   In Smalltalk methods, local variables act as though they were parameters with nil val-
SIDE TRIP   ues. However, although you can change the value of a local variable using an assignment statement, you cannot change the value of a parameter using an assignment statement. For example, you *cannot* amend the convertToCaloriesWith: method, defined in Segment 121, as follows:

Integer method definition   • instance
```
convertToCaloriesWith: x
   "The following assignment statement does not work"
   x := self * x.
   ^ x
```

179   A Smalltalk variable refers to a chunk of memory that holds the address for data, rather
SIDE TRIP   than the data themselves. In some implementations, the chunk of memory that holds the address also holds a few data-type–identifying bits; in other implementations, type-identifying bits are held in the same chunk of memory as the data.

Either way, data are typed, but variables are not. Accordingly, there are no variable declarations of the sort found in languages such as C.

180   Implement an Integer method, powers, that displays the powers of the receiver, from
PRACTICE   the first to the fifth power, in the transcript, without any unnecessary multiplication. For example, when sent to 2, powers should answer the following:

```
2 4 8 16 32
```

- Variables are names that serve has handles for objects.

- **If** you wish to introduce a local variable into a method, **then** you must list that variable between vertical bars in the method's definition before the first statement:

```
method selector
  | variable 1 ··· variable n |
  ...
```

- Local variables have local scope. Accordingly, a variable value assigned in one method cannot interfere with a variable assignment or parameter assignment in another method, even if the names happen to be the same, and a variable established in one method cannot be evaluated in another method.

- All local variables are initialized to `nil`.

- **If** you wish to assign a local variable, **then** use an assignment statement:

```
variable := expression
```

10 HOW TO BENEFIT FROM PROCEDURE ABSTRACTION

182 In this section, you learn how procedure abstraction increases your efficiency and makes your programs easier to maintain.

183 When you move computational detail into a method, you are said to be doing **procedure abstraction**, and you are said to be hiding the details of how a computation is done behind a **procedure-abstraction barrier**.

184 The key virtue of procedure abstraction is that *you make it easy to reuse your programs*. Instead of trying to copy particular lines of a program, you—or another programmer— arrange to call a previously defined method.

185 A second virtue of procedure abstraction is that *you push details out of sight and out of mind*, making your programs easier to read and enabling you to concentrate on high-level steps.

186 A third virtue of procedure abstraction is that *you can debug your programs more easily*. By dividing a program into small, independently debuggable pieces, you exploit the powerful divide-and-conquer problem-solving heuristic.

187 A fourth virtue of procedure abstraction is that *you can augment repetitive computations easily*. For example, you saw the `fatToCalories` method defined this way in Segment 89:

```
Integer method definition        • instance
fatToCalories
   ^ self * 9
```

You can add a line that displays the calories in fat every time that such calories are computed:

```
Integer method definition        • instance
fatToCalories
   Transcript show: 'The number of fat calories computed is ';
             show: (self * 9) printString;
             cr.
   ^ self * 9
    Workspace
194 fatToCalories
    Transcript
The number of fat calories computed is 1746
```

Thus, to add the display capability, you do not need to find all the places where calories are computed from fat grams, because you need to change only the definition of the `fatToCalories` method.

188 A fifth virtue of procedure abstraction is that *you can improve how a computation is done*. You might decide, for example, that it is wasteful for your `fatToCalories` method

to multiply out `self` and 9 twice. Accordingly, you might decide to do the computation just once, using a variable, named `result`, to hold onto the value:

```
Integer method definition          • instance
fatToCalories
  | result |
  result := self * 9.
  Transcript show: 'The number of fat calories computed is ';
            show: result printString;
            cr.
  ^ result
```

Again, you do not need to find all the places where calories are computed from fat grams; you need to change only the definition of the `fatToCalories` method.

189 A sixth virtue of procedure abstraction is that *you can change the way a computation is done*. If you find a way to reduce by one-third your body's ability to metabolize fat, for example, you could adjust your computation of fat calories to account for your marvelous discovery. Yet again, you would not need to find all the places where calories are computed from fat grams; you would need to change only the definition of the `fatToCalories` method.

190 If you write a program that is littered with places where fat grams are converted to calories by multiplication by 9, you will have to make many changes if you want to augment, improve, or change the way fat-to-calories conversion is done. On the other hand, if you write a program in which the multiplication by 9 is confined to a `fatToCalories` method, you will need to make only one change.

191 Write a method for `Integer` instances named `celsiusToFahrenheit` that, when sent to
PRACTICE a number representing temperature in Celsius answers twice that number plus 30.

Next, amend your `celsiusToFahrenheit` method such that it displays "Performing an approximate temperature conversion" every time that it is entered.

Next, improve your `celsiusToFahrenheit` method by having it add 40 to the argument, multiply by 9/5, and subtract 40. Be sure that your method answers with an integer.

Finally, change your `celsiusToFahrenheit` method such that the receiver is in Celsius degrees relative to absolute zero and the result answered is in Fahrenheit degrees relative to absolute zero. Absolute zero is −273 degrees Celsius.

For each change, comment on the corresponding benefit provided by procedure abstraction.

192
HIGHLIGHTS
• *Procedure abstraction* hides the details of computations inside methods, thus moving those details behind an abstraction barrier.

• You should practice procedure abstraction to take advantage of the following benefits:

- Your programs become easier to reuse.

- Your programs become easier to read.

- Your programs become easier to debug.

- Your programs become easier to augment.

- Your programs become easier to improve.

- Your programs become easier to change.

11 HOW TO CREATE CLASSES AND INSTANCES

193   To describe a particular food, while dieting, you think naturally in terms of its protein, carbohydrate, and fat content.

Thus, the numbers that describe a particular food constitute a natural bundle—a bundle of three numbers for each individual food.

In this section, you learn that one of Smalltalk's great virtues is that Smalltalk offers programming-language mechanisms that enable you to describe, construct, and manipulate bundles of descriptive data items that mirror real-world **individuals** and **groups of individuals**. These special mechanisms set Smalltalk apart from most other programming languages.

194   Smalltalk encourages you to define Smalltalk **classes**, such as the `Vegetable` class, that correspond to naturally occurring groups. Once you have defined a class, you can construct any number of **instances** that belong to that class, each of which corresponds to an individual that belongs to the corresponding group.

When you define the `Vegetable` class, for example, you indicate that each serving has a protein, carbohydrate, and fat content. Then, you can construct `Vegetable` instances with particular per-serving protein, carbohydrate, and fat content.

Thus, the employment of classes enables you to create information bundles in your programs, in the form of class instances, that describe naturally occurring individuals. Consequently, classes help you to produce clearer, easier-to-understand programs.

195   Many basic classes—such as `Integer`, `Float`, and `Fraction`—are **built-in classes**.

196   When you define a class, you tell Smalltalk about **instance variables**, which are variables that describe the instances of the class.

Thus, in the following diagram, the `Vegetable` class description contains instance variable names, whereas the descriptions of particular `Vegetable` instances contain instance variable values.

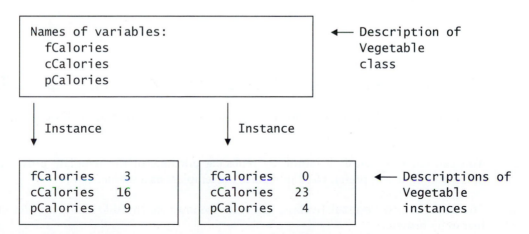

```
Names of variables:          ← Description of
   fCalories                    Vegetable
   cCalories                    class
   pCalories
```

```
        Instance                      Instance

   fCalories    3            fCalories    0        ← Descriptions of
   cCalories    16           cCalories    23         Vegetable
   pCalories    9            pCalories    4          instances
```

197   In Segment 196, *fat*, *carbohydrate*, and *protein* are abbreviated to f, c and p in fCalories, cCalories, and pCalories. But as you learned in Segment 103, the names really should be fatCalories, carbohydrateCalories, and proteinCalories, because Smalltalk programmers generally avoid abbreviations. In this book, however, names must fit into programs that fit into the dimensions of the page. Accordingly, some names depart from standard Smalltalk programming practice.

198   To define the Vegetable class, you must first enter the class-hierarchy browser by clicking **File→Browse Classes**, as you learned in Segment 81.

199   Now, assuming that your new Vegetable class is to be a subclass of the Object class, you first select the Object class by clicking the left mouse button while the cursor is over Object in the class window.

       Then, you click **Classes→Add Subclass...**, whereupon a popup window appears, soliciting the name for your new subclass of the object class.

       Finally, type Vegetable as the name of the new subclass.

200   Now, you see the Vegetable class highlighted in the first column of the class-hierarchy browser, along with a template for defining the Vegetable class:

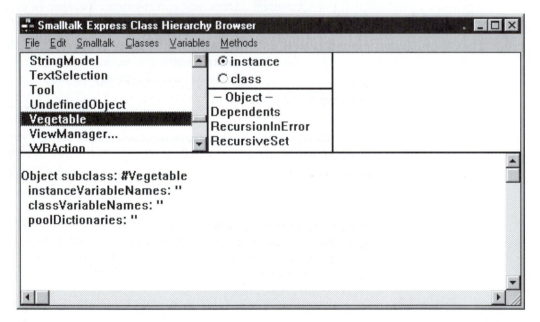

       At this point, Smalltalk is ready for you to enter a class definition in the lower half of the class-hierarchy browser.

201   You can enter the class definition by replacing portions of the template provided by Smalltalk, or, if you prefer, you can replace the template as a whole.

202   To define the new Vegetable class, you enter the instance-variable names into the class-hierarchy browser:

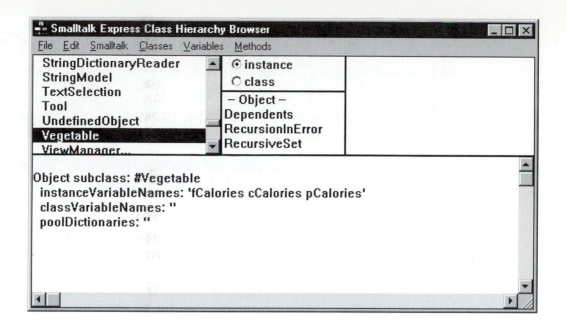

203 Note that a class definition, in contrast to a method definition, is expressed as a message sent to a class. The following diagram explains:

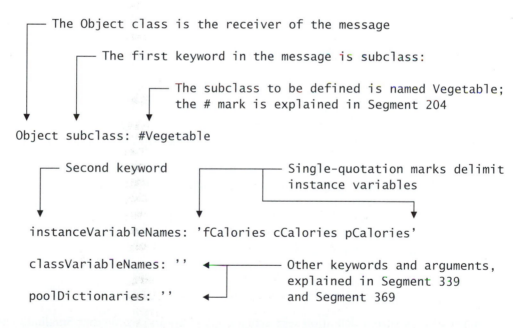

204 The **hash mark**, or **pound sign**, #, in #Vegetable tells Smalltalk that Vegetable *is not a variable to be evaluated*, but rather *is a string to be used as is*. Thus, a hash mark introduces a **literal symbol**. In every class definition, you use a literal symbol to name the class that you wish to define.

205 All numbers and strings are literals because numbers and strings are always used as is; numbers and strings never are used as variables.

206 When you have finished defining the Vegetable class, you click **right→save** in the lower half of the class-hierarchy browser.

207 Once you have saved your definition of the Vegetable class, the variables defined in the class appear in the **variables window**, which lies just under the **instance–object window**:

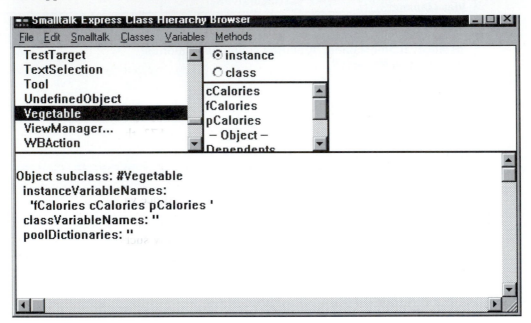

Note that the variables window shows not only the variables defined in the Vegetables class, but also all the variables that appear in superclasses. In the figure, for example, you see a hint that variables are defined for the Object class. The particular variable that you see part of, Dependents, happens to be a class variable. You learn about class variables in Section 18.

208 To keep the size of this book manageable, class definitions displayed in the class-hierarchy browser shown are rerepresented in the following form:

Vegetable class definition
```
Object subclass: #Vegetable
   instanceVariableNames: 'fCalories cCalories pCalories'
   classVariableNames: ''
   poolDictionaries: ''
```

When you see such a definition representation, you are to assume that Smalltalk has accepted the definition in response to your clicking **right→save**

209 In other programming languages, instance variables are called **member variables, fields,** or **slots**. The virtue of alternative terms, such as *slots*, is that they encourage you to think

of class definitions as patterns and to think of instances as filled-in patterns. Bowing to convention, however, this book uses the term *instance variable* throughout.

210   Note that instance-variable names, by convention, start with lowercase characters.

211   Once a class is defined, you can create new instances of the class by sending a new message to the class. For example, once the Vegetable class is defined, you can create new Vegetable instances as follows:

> Workspace

```
Vegetable new
```

Note that, although most messages are sent to instance objects, new messages are sent to class objects.

212   Whenever you create an instance, that instance's instance variables are initially assigned values of nil, which means, as you learned in Segment 173, that the variables are *not yet assigned* or *unassigned*.

213   Once you have created a Vegetable instance, you will want to assign and refer to that instance's fCalories, cCalories, and pCalories instance variables.

To assign an instance variable in a Vegetable instance, you must use a method that is known to instances of the Vegetable class, because only such methods have access to a Vegetable instance's instance variables. You can, for example, define a keyword method, fCalories:, for instances of Vegetable:

> Vegetable method definition   • instance

```
fCalories: aNumber
  fCalories := aNumber
```

Because fCalories: is defined for instances of Vegetable, fCalories: is free to assign an instance variable, fCalories, in a Vegetable instance.

214   A method whose primary purpose is to assign instance variables is called a **writer** or **setter**. In this book, the word *setter* is used because many programmers use the word *writer* to refer to methods that write information into files.

215   Most Smalltalk programmers do not include answer expressions in setters, as illustrated
SIDE TRIP by the setter defined in Segment 213. Such setters answer self, by default, as explained in Segment 105.

216   To get the assigned value of a Vegetable instance's instance variable, you must use a method that is known to instances of the Vegetable class, again because only such methods have access to instance variables. You can, for example, define a unary message, fCalories, for instances of Vegetable:

> Vegetable method definition   • instance

```
fCalories
  ^ fCalories
```

Because fCalories is defined for instances of Vegetable, fCalories is free to refer to—and to answer the value of—the instance variable, fCalories, in a Vegetable instance.

217 A method whose primary purpose is to get at instance variables is called a **getter** or **reader**. In this book, the word *getter* is used because many programmers use the word *reader* to refer to methods that read information from files.

218 Both setters and getters are called **accessors**, because they provide access to instance variables.

219 The convention in Smalltalk is to use setter and getter names based on instance variable names. Thus, fCalories: and fCalories are the setter and getter of the fCalories instance variable, with the colon of the setter distinguishing the setter from the colon-free getter. If you wish to express more clearly that a method is a setter or a getter, you can use names such as setFCalories: and getFCalories; if you do, however, many Smalltalk programmers will consider your code oafish.

220 You can, of course, include additional computation in your setters and getters. For example, if you are interested in how often your program accesses the value of the fCalories instance variable, you can have fCalories display informative text in the transcript each time that fCalories is sent to a Vegetable instance:

```
Vegetable method definition        • instance
fCalories: aNumber
   fCalories := aNumber.
   Transcript show: 'The calorie content of a food changed to ';
             show: self fCalories printString;
             cr.
   ^ fCalories
```

221 Linking fCalories setters and getters to displays is extremely popular in Smalltalk programs. In Section 35, you learn to connect setters to meterlike displays, rather than to textual displays.

222 You may wish to use getters to provide access to **derived attributes** that exist only in the sense that their values can be computed from instance variables that do exist. For example, you can create fGrams, which seems to refer to the contents of an fGrams instance variable, but which actually refers to the contents of the fCalories instance variable:

```
Vegetable method definition        • instance
fGrams
   ^ fCalories / 9
```

From the **behavior perspective**, fGrams provides the answers you want, and you do not need to concern yourself with how those answers are produced.

223 You may also wish to use setters that seem to set derived attributes, but that actually set instance variables. For example, you can create a fGrams: setter, which seems to set the fGrams derived attribute, but which actually sets the fCalories instance variable:

```
Vegetable method definition        • instance
fGrams: aNumber
  fCalories := aNumber * 9
```

224   In Section 5, you learned that you can use the class-hierarchy browser to define new methods. In this section, you learned that you can use the class-hierarchy browser to define new classes as well. You can also use the class-hierarchy browser to examine the definition of all methods and classes provided by Smalltalk. Provision of access to the definitions of predefined methods classes and classes is one of the great, and unusual, strengths of the language.

225   The class-hierarchy browser is just one of several browsers that enable you to find and look at definitions. You learn about other browsers in Section 28.

226   Devise a class, JunkFood, for junk food.

PRACTICE

227   Write getters and setters for the JunkFood class.

PRACTICE

228

HIGHLIGHTS

- Smalltalk classes correspond to groups, and Smalltalk instances correspond to individuals.

- Class definitions generally include instance variables, also known as member variables, fields, or slots.

- If you want to define a simple class, with instance variables only, **then** click on that class's superclass in the class-hierarchy browser and instantiate the following pattern:

```
superclass name  subclass: #class name
  instanceVariableNames: 'instance variables'
  classVariableNames: ''
  poolDictionaries: ''
```

- If you want to create an instance of a class, **then** instantiate the following pattern:

```
class name  new
```

- Setter and getter methods provide a route to instance-variable assignment and reference. Collectively, setters and getters are called accessors.

- If you want to be able to assign an instance-variable value using a setter, **then** instantiate the following definition in the class-hierarchy browser:

```
variable name: aValue
  ^variable name := aValue
```

- If you want to be able to refer to a instance-variable value using a getter, **then** instantiate the following definition in the class-hierarchy browser:

```
variable name
   ^variable name
```

- You can define setter and getter methods for derived attributes.

12 HOW TO DEFINE CLASSES THAT INHERIT INSTANCE VARIABLES AND METHODS

229   In this section, you learn that instance variables that you list in a class definition appear automatically in all that class's subclasses. Thus, you begin to learn about **inheritance**, one of the key concepts that distinguish object-oriented programming from traditional programming.

230   So far, you have learned how you can define a `Vegetable` class. Now suppose that you want to add three more specific classes for dairy products, meats, and grains.

You could, of course, repeat what you have defined for the `Vegetable` class, including `fCalories`, `cCalories`, and `pCalories` instance variables, along with corresponding setters and getters.

However, maintaining multiple copies of instance variables and methods makes software development and maintenance difficult as you try to correct bugs, to add features, to improve performance, and to change behavior. Adding multiple programmers and multiple years to the mix turns mere difficulty into certain failure.

231   Fortunately, Smalltalk encourages you to cut down on duplication, thereby easing program writing, debugging, and maintenance, by allowing you to arrange class definitions in a way that reflects **natural hierarchies**.

232   You can introduce a `Food` class and define the `Vegetable`, `Dairy`, `Meat`, and `Grain` classes to be subclasses of the `Food` class.

Note that the `fCalories`, `cCalories`, and `pCalories` instance variables appear in the `Food` class definition alone, but the effect is equivalent to placing those variables in all the subclass definitions as well. The four subclasses are said to **inherit** instance variables from the `Food` class:

```
Food class definition
Object subclass: #Food
  instanceVariableNames: 'fCalories cCalories pCalories'
  classVariableNames: ''
  poolDictionaries: ''
Vegetable class definition
Food subclass: #Vegetable
  instanceVariableNames: ''
  classVariableNames: ''
  poolDictionaries: ''
Dairy class definition
Food subclass: #Dairy
  instanceVariableNames: ''
  classVariableNames: ''
  poolDictionaries: ''
```

Meat class definition

```
Food subclass: #Meat
    instanceVariableNames: ''
    classVariableNames: ''
    poolDictionaries: ''
```

Grain class definition

```
Food subclass: #Grain
    instanceVariableNames: ''
    classVariableNames: ''
    poolDictionaries: ''
```

233 Because the Vegetable class is directly under the Food class in the class hierarchy, with no other class in between, the Vegetable class is said to be a **direct subclass** of the Food class, and the Food class is said to be the **direct superclass** of the Vegetable class.

234 Note that the Food class must be defined before you define the Vegetable, Dairy, Food, or Grain classes as subclasses of the Food class. You cannot define a class until its direct superclass has been defined.

235 Once you have indicated that the Vegetable, Dairy, Meat, and Grain classes are subclasses of the Food class, you can send messages defined for the Food class to instances of the Vegetable, Dairy, Meat, and Grain classes.

In particular, the following setters and getters, moved from the Vegetable class to the Food class, are accessible not only to Food instances, but also to Vegetable, Dairy, Food, and Grain instances as well:

Food method definition   • instance
```
fCalories ^ fCalories
```
Food method definition   • instance
```
fCalories: aNumber fCalories := aNumber
```
Food method definition   • instance
```
cCalories ^ cCalories
```
Food method definition   • instance
```
cCalories: aNumber cCalories := aNumber
```
Food method definition   • instance
```
pCalories ^ pCalories
```
Food method definition   • instance
```
pCalories: aNumber pCalories := aNumber
```

236 Of course, you can also define methods for the Food class that are not setters and getters. For example, tCalories uses the fCalories, cCalories, and fCalories instance variables to compute the total number of calories in a serving of a particular food:

Food method definition   • instance
```
tCalories
  ^ fCalories + cCalories + pCalories
```

237　In general, when you send a message to a receiver, Smalltalk finds a method with a name that matches the message selector. To find a method, Smalltalk first determines whether a matching method is defined for the receiver's class. Next, if no matching method is defined for the receiver's class, Smalltalk determines whether a matching method is defined for the receiver's direct superclass. Then, if no matching method is found in the direct superclass, Smalltalk continues up the class hierarchy, class by class, until Smalltalk finds a matching method or reaches the end of the superclass chain. If no matching method is found, Smalltalk reports an error.

238　Sometimes, multiple methods with the same name show up in a subclass–superclass chain. In such situations, the method-finding algorithm described in Segment 237 dictates that Smalltalk uses the method found closer to the message receiver. The other methods—the ones found higher in the subclass–superclass chain—are said to be **overridden** or **shadowed**.

239　Suppose, for example, that you want to define isVegetable, a predicate that determines whether a Food instance is also instance of the Vegetable class. First, you capture the fact that most Food instances are not instances of the Vegetable class by defining isVegetable for the Food class:

```
Food method definition        • instance
isVegetable
  ^ false
```

Next, you capture the fact that Vegetable instances are instances of the Vegetable class:

```
Vegetable method definition        • instance
isVegetable
  ^ true
```

240　With an isVegetable method defined for both the Vegetable and Food classes, the method defined for the Vegetable class will override the one defined for the Food class if, and only if, isVegetable is sent to a Vegetable instance.

On the other hand, whenever isVegetable is sent to a Food instance that is not a Vegetable instance, there is no overriding, and the instance makes use of the isVegetable method defined for Food, which answers false:

```
    Workspace
Transcript show: Food new isVegetable printString; cr;
          show: Vegetable new isVegetable printString; cr;
          show: Dairy new isVegetable printString; cr;
          show: Meat new isVegetable printString; cr;
          show: Grain new isVegetable printString; cr
    Transcript
false
true
false
false
false
```

241 You could, of course, define `isVegetable` for the `Object` class, rather than for the `Food` class. Generally, however, you should define such a predicate for the lowest class in the class hierarchy that is a superclass of all classes whose instances are possible receivers of the predicate; otherwise, you clutter up the definition of the `Object` class and confound your use of the file-out mechanism, described in Section 30.

242 A method defined for more than one class is said to be **polymorphic**. Thus, `isVegatable` is an example of a polymorphic method.

243 To gain insight into how classes, instance variables, and methods work together, you should draw a **class-hierarchy diagram**, such as the following:

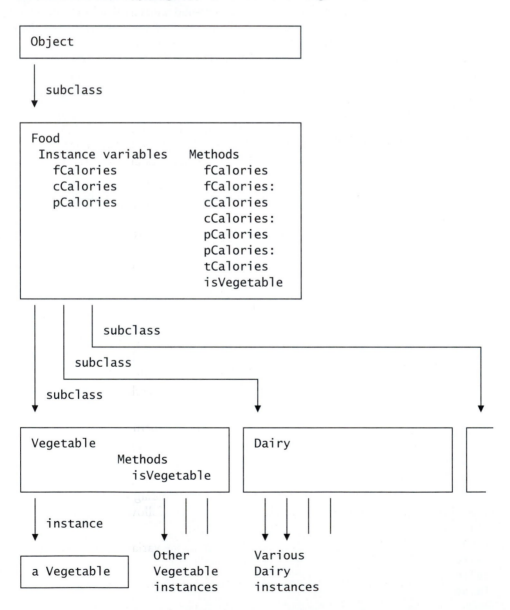

Such a class-hierarchy diagram helps you to see how to distribute instance variables and methods among the classes in the hierarchy.

244 As a general rule, you should place instance variables and define methods such that two criteria are satisfied:

- There is no unnecessary duplication of instance variables or method definitions.

- Each method defined in a class is useful in all that class's subclasses.

For example, the fCalories, cCalories, and pCalories instance variables are all placed in the Food class, because they are useful for all Food subclasses, although they are not useful for classes that are not Food subclasses, such as the Integer, Float, and Fraction classes. Similarly, various accessors and the tCalories method are defined for the Food class, because they are useful for all Food subclasses.

245 A class can have many subclasses; the Food class has four subclasses.

No class can have more than one direct superclass, however. Accordingly, Smalltalk is said to support **single inheritance** only. Some other programming languages, such as C++, allow classes to have multiple superclasses; such languages are said to support multiple inheritance.

246 Ordinarily, the existence of sibling classes is justified by differing behavior with respect to a
SIDE TRIP variety of polymorphic methods. As defined in this section, the Vegetable, Dairy, Meat, and Grain differ in behavior only with respect to the illustrative isVegetable method.

247 Define an isFood predicate. Try your predicate on instances of the Object, Vegetable,
PRACTICE and Food classes.

248
HIGHLIGHTS

- Class hierarchies reflect subclass–superclass relations among classes.

- An instance can inherit instance variables and methods not only from the class to which it belongs, but also from all that class's superclasses.

- When a subclass–superclass chain contains multiple methods with the same name, the one closest to the receiver in the subclass–superclass chain is the one that is employed. All others are overridden.

- If you want to create a class hierarchy, **then** draw a diagram that reflects natural categories, **and** use the diagram to help ensure the following:

  - There is no unnecessary duplication of instance variables or methods.

  - Each instance variable and each method defined in a class is useful in all that class's subclasses.

- **If** you want to define a predicate that tests instances for class membership, **then** instantiate the following method pattern for the lowest class in the class hierarchy that is a superclass of all classes whose instances are possible receivers of the predicate:

  `predicate name`
  ```
    ^ false
  ```

  and then instantiate the following method pattern for the class itself:

  `predicate name`
  ```
    ^ true
  ```

13 HOW TO DEFINE INSTANCE-CREATION METHODS

249   In this section, you learn about **instance-creation methods**, which are methods that create instances.

250   In Segment 211, you learned that the new message creates new instances when sent to class objects. The new method is therefore an **instance-creation method**. In other languages, instance-creation methods are called **constructors**.

251   Suppose that you want to announce the creation of every Food instance. You could define an instance method for, say, the Food class, so as to make the required announcement. The method is, of course, inherited by the Vegetable class:

```
Food method definition          • instance
announce
   Transcript show: 'Creating a new class instance: '
                    , self printString; cr.
      Workspace
Vegetable new announce
      Transcript
Creating a new class instance: a Vegetable
```

252   Alternatively, you can define new for the Food class so that new:

- Uses the new method associated with the superclass of Food, to create a new instance of the Food class.

- Sends the announce message to the new instance to announce the creation of the instance.

- Answers the new instance.

253   Because you want to define new to be a method that is to be sent to the Food class, rather than to Food instances, you click the **class** button, rather than the **instance** button, thereby defining new as a **class method**.

254   Inside your definition of new for the Food class, you need to tell Smalltalk to send new to Food, the value of self, to create a new food instance. However, you do not want Smalltalk to use the new method that you are defining, because that would lead to unbounded recursion. Instead, you want Smalltalk to use the new method associated with the direct superclass of the Food class, rather than with the Food class itself.

Fortunately, whenever a message is sent to super in a method definition, Smalltalk acts as though the message were sent to self, except that Smalltalk initiates method search in the direct superclass of the class for which the method is defined.

Thus, you use super in the definition of a new method for the Food class:

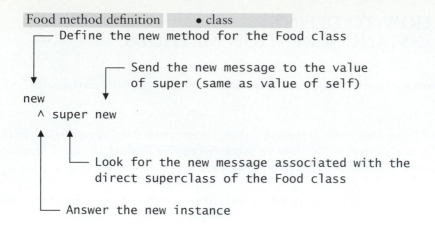

```
Food method definition          • class
          ┌── Define the new method for the Food class



new
  ^ super new
```

255 Of course, nothing is gained by the new version of the new class method defined in Segment 254. In the following revision, however, the announce message is sent to the new instance. Because the new instance is an instance of the Food class, the announce message activates the announce instance method associated with the Food class:

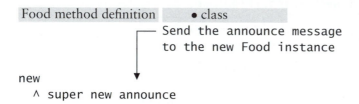

```
Food method definition          • class
                        ┌── Send the announce message
                        │   to the new Food instance

new
  ^ super new announce
```

256 Class methods, like ordinary methods, are inherited. In particular, the newly defined new class method is inherited by all subclasses of Food, such as the Vegetable class:

```
        Workspace
Food new.
Vegetable new
        Transcript
Creating a new class instance: a Food
Creating a new class instance: a Vegetable
```

257 Note carefully that super is a signal to initiate method search in the direct superclass of the class for which the super-containing method is defined. Thus, super is not a signal to initiate search in the direct superclass of the class of the message receiver that activates the super-containing method.

258 A full understanding of class methods requires you to understand the concept of **metaclass**
SIDE TRIP and a bit of behind-the-scenes Smalltalk magic.

When a class is defined, Smalltalk defines a companion metaclass. Each class is an instance—the sole instance—of its metaclass. Metaclasses have no names.

Thus, the Food class is not only a direct subclass of the Object class, but also the instance of an automatically generated metaclass:

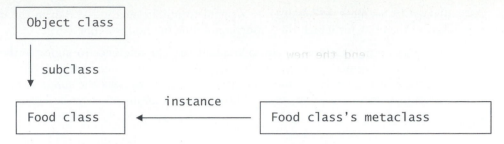

259
SIDE TRIP Smalltalk links together the metaclasses in a class hierarchy. Those links form a meta-class hierarchy that parallels that of the corresponding classes. The metaclass hierarchy terminates in a class named `Class`, which is a subclass of the `Behavior` class:

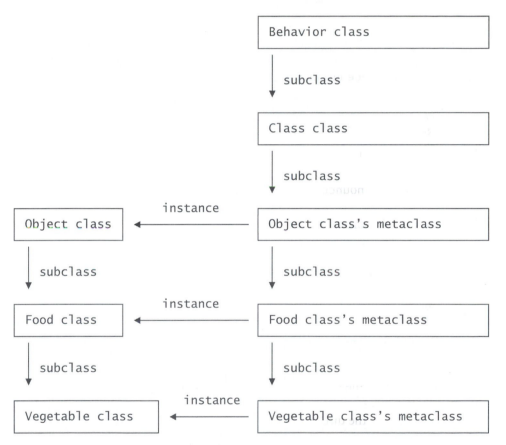

260
SIDE TRIP When you define a new class method, you actually define an instance method for the class's metaclass. The definition given in Segment 255, for example, actually defines an instance method for the Food class's metaclass.

261
SIDE TRIP When you send a class method, Smalltalk treats the receiver as an instance of its metaclass, and finds a corresponding instance method in the metaclass hierarchy using the method-finding algorithm described in Segment 237. Frequently, the search continues up to the `Behavior` class, which offers both `new` and `new:` methods.

As explained in Segment 257, super is a signal to initiate method search in the direct superclass of the class for which the super-containing method is defined.

Suppose, for example, that new is sent to Vegetable. The reference to super in the new method defined in Segment 255 signals that search is to be initiated in the Object class's metaclass, the direct superclass of the Food class's metaclass, because the super-containing new method is defined as a Food class method, which is an instance method of the Food class's metaclass.

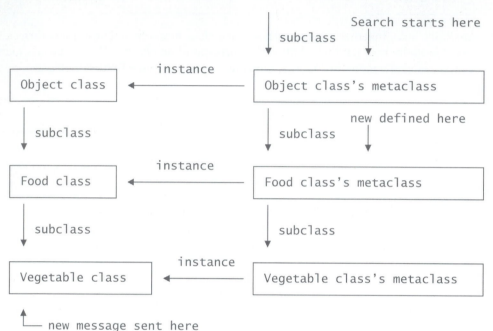

Initialization can be done in instance-method initializors that are incorporated into the new class method. For example, suppose that you want the initial value of each Food instance variable to be 0, rather than nil. You first define an initializor instance method that sets values to 0:

Food method definition   • instance
```
initialize
  self fCalories: 0; cCalories: 0; pCalories: 0.
```

Next, you incorporate the initialize instance method into the new class method:

Food method definition   • class
```
new
  ^ super new initialize
```

Then, all new Food instances have instance variables set to 0:

Workspace
```
Transcript show: Vegetable new tCalories printString
```
Transcript
```
0
```

Explain the result of using the following definition for new, as contrasted to the definition provided in Segment 255:

Food method definition	• class

```
new
  ∧ self new announce
```

In Segment 114, you defined an instance method for the Integer class that computes volumes. That method is sent to receivers that are instances of the Integer class.

Another approach is to create a Volume class and to define class methods for that class that computes volumes. Such methods resemble functions in standard programming languages, inasmuch as the receiver does not enter into the computations performed inside the method.

Define sphere: to be a Volume class method, with an argument representing a sphere's radius. Use your method to calculate the volume of Earth in cubic miles.

Define new for the Vegetable class, such that, whenever a new Vegetable is created, the fCalories instance variable is set to 1, a value that happens to approximate the fat calories found in one serving of a vegetable.

- Instance-creation methods are class methods that create new instances.

- Initializors perform initialization work, such as assigning values to the instance variables of new instances.

- **If** you want to incorporate a variable-initializing initializor into an instance-creation method for a given class, **then** instantiate the following class-method pattern:

```
new
  ∧ super new initialize
```
and then instantiate the following instance-method pattern:
```
initialize
    instance variable := initial value .
    .
    .
    .
```

14 HOW TO BENEFIT FROM DATA ABSTRACTION

268   In Section 11, you learned about setters and getters, and you learned how you can define setters and getters for derived attributes. In Section 13, you learned about instance-creation methods. In this section, you learn how instance-creation methods, setters, and getters help you to practice data abstraction, thereby increasing your efficiency and making your programs easier to maintain.

269   Suppose that you develop a program around a Food class definition; getters and setters for fCalories, cCalories, pCalories instance variables; and a tCalories method, such as those you already have seen in Segment 232, Segment 235, and Segment 236:

```
Food class definition
Object subclass: #Food
  instanceVariableNames: 'pCalories cCalories fCalories'
  classVariableNames: ''
  poolDictionaries: ''
```
```
Food method definition          • instance
fCalories
  ^ fCalories
```
```
Food method definition          • instance
fCalories: f
  fCalories := f
```
```
Food method definition          • instance
cCalories
  ^ cCalories
```
```
Food method definition          • instance
cCalories: c
  cCalories := c
```
```
Food method definition          • instance
pCalories
  ^ pCalories
```
```
Food method definition          • instance
pCalories: p
  pCalories := p
```
```
Food method definition          • instance
tCalories
  ^ fCalories + cCalories + pCalories
```

270   The defect of the definition of tCalories, as presented, is that, if you decide to use instance variables for gram content—fGrams, cGrams, and pGrams—instead of for calorie content, then you have to rewrite the tCalories definition, and perhaps many others, to use the new instance variables:

```
Food method definition          • instance
tCalories
  ^ fGrams * 9 + cGrams * 4 + pGrams * 4
```

271   On the other hand, suppose that you make a habit of using access procedures. You would define `tCalories`, and perhaps many other methods, to send getters to `self`:

Food method definition   • instance

```
tCalories
  ^ self fCalories + self cCalories + self pCalories
```

272   Then, if you decide to switch to gram-based instance variables, you need to make no change to `tCalories`; instead, you redefine the getters such that they access the new gram-based instance variables. From the **behavior perspective**, the altered getters provide the same answers as the original getters:

Food class definition
```
Object subclass: #Food
  instanceVariableNames: 'pGrams cGrams fGrams'
  classVariableNames: ''
  poolDictionaries: ''
```
Food method definition   • instance
```
fCalories ^ fGrams * 9
```
Food method definition   • instance
```
cCalories ^ cGrams * 4
```
Food method definition   • instance
```
pCalories ^ pGrams * 4
```

273   Thus, if you use setters and getters, you need to make no changes outside the setters and getters to accommodate a switch from calorie-based instance variables to gram-based instance variables. Both before and after the switch, you still send `fCalories`, `cCalories`, and `pCalories` messages.

274   You might wonder why you would ever want to replace calorie-based instance variables by gram-based instance variables. One answer is to increase efficiency. Suppose, for example, that you discover, on program testing, that fast access to gram information is more important than fast access to calorie information. You might then decide to switch from calorie-based instance variables to gram-based instance variables for faster access.

Of course, in a small program, you could manage changes similar to the replacement of calorie-based instance variables by gram-based instance variables without the benefit of access methods. In large programs, such changes would be extremely difficult without the benefit of access methods.

275   In general, instance-creation methods, setters, and getters have the power to isolate you from the details of how a class is implemented. Once you have written those methods, you can forget about how they set and get values; none of the details, such as whether you have a `fCalories` or a `fGrams` instance variable, clutter programs that use Food instances.

276   When you move representation details into instance-creation methods, setters, and getters, you are said to be practicing **data abstraction**, and you are said to be hiding behind a **data-abstraction barrier** the details of how data are represented.

Good programmers carefully design into their programs appropriate data-abstraction barriers.

277 Because the virtues of data abstraction parallel those of procedure abstraction, the following discussion of the virtues of data abstraction is much like the previous discussion, in Section 10, of the virtues of procedure abstraction.

278 The key virtue of data abstraction is that *you make it easy to reuse your work*. You can develop a library of class and method definitions and transfer the entire library to another programmer with little difficulty.

279 A second virtue of data abstraction is that *you push details out of sight and out of mind*, making your methods easier to read and enabling you to concentrate on high-level steps.

280 A third virtue of data abstraction is that *you can augment what a class provides*. You can, for example, add information-displaying statements to your setters and getters, as you saw in Segment 220.

281 A fourth virtue of data abstraction is that *you can improve the way information is stored*. In this section, you have seen an example in which there is a switch from a `fCalories` instance variable to a `fGrams` instance variable.

282 Many good programmers provide access methods for some instance variables, but do not do so for others. The choice is a matter of taste and style. Until you have developed your own taste and style, you should rely on the following heuristic:

- Whenever the detailed implementation of a class may change, use instance-variable access methods to insulate your programs from the potential change.

283
PRACTICE

Define the `Sphere` class. Include a `radius` instance variable, with a setter and getter. Then, use the setter and getter to define a `volume` method for instances of the `Sphere` class.

Next, alter the class definition such that the instance variable is `diameter`, rather than `radius`. Write a getter and setter for the `diameter` variable. Write a getter and setter for the `radius` derived attribute. Check your `volume` method to be sure that it still provides correct answers, without change, even though the detailed representation for sphere instances has changed.

284
HIGHLIGHTS

- Getters, setters, and instance-creation methods are called access methods. When you move instance-variable evaluations and assignments into access methods, you are practicing data abstraction.

- Data abstraction has many virtues, including the following:

  - Your programs become easier to reuse.

  - Your programs become easier to read.

- You can augment what a class provides.

- You can improve the way information is stored.

- **If** you anticipate that the detailed definition of a class may change, **then** you should provide access methods for the instance variables to isolate the effects of the potential changes.

15 HOW TO DESIGN CLASSES AND CLASS HIERARCHIES

285   At this point, you have learned how to *define* classes and class hierarchies. In this section, you learn how to *design* classes and class hierarchies by observing several principles of representation design.

286   The **explicit-representation principle**: Whenever there is a natural category with which your program needs to work, there should be a class in your program that corresponds to that category.

In the food domain, for example, there are natural categories corresponding to vegetables, dairy products, meats, and grains.

287   The **modularity principle**: Generally, you should divide your programs into units that you can develop and maintain independently. Programs so divided are said to be **modular**.

One way to achieve modularity is to define your classes such that they reflect naturally occurring categories, exploiting the tendency of human language to divide the world into coherent, relatively independent concepts.

Thus, you define a `Vegetable` class to reflect the category identified by the word *vegetable*; Similarly, you define the `Diary` class to reflect the category identified by the phrase *dairy product*.

288   The **no-duplication principle**: Instance variables and instance methods should be distributed among class definitions so that there is no needless duplication. Otherwise, duplicate copies are bound to become gratuitously different.

For example, in Segment 269, the `fCalories`, `cCalories`, and `pCalories` instance variables reside in the `Food` class, rather than in the `Vegetable`, `Diary`, `Meat`, and `Grain` classes, making those instance variables more generally available.

289   The **look-it-up principle**: Whenever practicable, a program should look up a frequently needed answer, rather than computing that answer.

For example, in Segment 269, the `fCalories`, `cCalories`, and `pCalories` instance variables reside in the `Food` class, whereas in Segment 272, the `fGrams`, `cGrams`, and `pGrams` instance variables appear. The right choice depends on whether you are more likely to be interested in calories or in grams.

290   The **is-a versus has-a principle**: You learned in Section 11 that instances mirror real-world individuals and classes mirror read-world categories. Accordingly, when you decide to implement a class, you are building a **model** of an aspect of the real world.

Many programmers new to object-oriented programming find it difficult to decide between implementing a new class and installing a new instance variable, because the **subclass–superclass relation** is easily confused with the **part–whole relation**.

Generally, if you find yourself using the phrase *an X is a Y* when describing the relation between two classes, *X* and *Y*, then the first class is a subclass of the second. On the other hand, if you find yourself using *X has a Y*, then instances of the second class, *Y*, appear as parts of instances of the first class, *X*.

For example, a human is an animal. Accordingly, the **is-a rule** dictates that, if you define a Human class, that class should be a subclass of the Animal class. Similarly, a box car is a railroad car, and the BoxCar class should be a subclass of the RailroadCar class.

On the other hand, humans have arms and legs, so the **has-a rule** dictates that the Human class should have arms and legs instance variables. Similarly, a box car has a box, and the BoxCar class therefore should have a box instance variable.

291 Deciding between a subclass–superclass relation and a part–whole relation is not always straightforward, however. For example, you may decide to model a piano as an instrument that has a keyboard, or you may decide to model a piano as a keyboard instrument. If you follow the has-a rule, you implement the Piano class as a subclass of the Instrument class; if you follow the is-a rule, you implement the Piano class as a subclass of the KeyboardInstrument class, and you implement the KeyboardInstrument class as a subclass of the Instrument class.

The rule that you should follow is the one that seems to make the most sense in light of those aspects of the real world that you are modeling. If your program is to deal with many types of keyboard instruments, and if the types share behavior, then following the is-a rule, rather than the has-a rule, is the better choice, and you should define a KeyboardInstrument class

292 The subclass–superclass versus part–whole issue is mercurial, in part, because different applications may view the same objects from different perspectives. For applications that deal with railroads, a box car is best viewed as a railroad car that has a box; for applications that deal with containers, a box car is best viewed as a box that has wheels that run on tracks. Thus, there is no universal right answer to the decision between modeling with the subclass–superclass relation and with the part–whole relation.

293
PRACTICE
Design a class hierarchy for a dozen buildings. At the highest level, define getters for squareFeet and age and locationMultiplier. Write an instance method, appraise, for the classes in your hierarchy. Include classes such as Bungalow, Mansion, Skyscraper, and Warehouse.

294
PRACTICE
Design a class hierarchy for a dozen occupations. At the highest level, define getters for yearsOfExperience and locationMultiplier. Write estimatedSalary, an instance method for the classes in your hierarchy. Include classes such as Physician, Lawyer, Engineer, Athlete, Ornithologist, Astrologer, Programmer, and Editor.

295
HIGHLIGHTS

- Programs should obey the explicit-representation principle: classes should reflect natural categories.

- Programs should obey the modularity principle: program elements should be divided into coherent classes.

- Programs should obey the no-duplication principle: variables and methods should be situated among class definitions to facilitate sharing.

- Programs should obey the look-it-up principle: class definitions should include instance variables for frequently requested information.

- **If** you find yourself using the phrase *an X is a Y* when describing the relation between two classes X and Y, **then** the first class is a subclass of the second.

- **If** you find yourself using *X has a Y* when describing the relation between two classes, X and Y, **then** instances of the second class appear as parts of instances of the first class.

16 HOW TO WRITE ITERATION STATEMENTS

296   In this section, you learn how to tell Smalltalk to repeat a computation with Smalltalk's `whileTrue:`, `whileFalse:`, and `timesRepeat:` messages.

297   Smalltalk's **iteration messages** enable methods to do computations over and over until a test has been satisfied. Smalltalk's `whileTrue:` message, for example, consists of a receiver, the `whileTrue:` selector, and an argument. The receiver and argument are both blocks:

```
receiver block  whileTrue:  argument block
```

298   As you learned in Segment 145, blocks, like all other entities in Smalltalk, are objects. A receiver block is an object that responds to the `whileTrue:` message by evaluating itself, noting whether the answer produced by the receiver block is `true`, and if so, evaluating the argument block. The evaluate-receiver-block–evaluate-argument-block cycle continues as long as the receiver block evaluates to `true`.

299   For example, the following method fragment repeatedly decrements an integer, n, by 1 until n is 0:

```
[n ~= 0] whileTrue: [n = n - 1]
```

300   Suppose, for example, that you have become overweight, and you fear that your excess weight will double every year. Plainly, your excess weight after n years will be proportional to 2^n. To determine your excess weight after n years, you need to develop a method that computes the nth power of 2.

One way to do the computation is to count down the parameter, n, to 0, multiplying a variable, `result`, whose initial value is 1, by 2 each time that you decrement n:

```
Integer method definition        • instance
powerOfTwo
  | n result |
  n := self.
  result := 1.
  [n ~= 0] whileTrue: [n := n - 1.  result := 2 * result].
  ^ result
     Workspace
Transcript show: 4 powerOfTwo printString
     Transcript
16
```

Evidently, if you are 1 pound overweight now, and your fears are realized, you will be 16 pounds overweight in 4 years.

301   As you would expect, Smalltalk also offers the `whileFalse:` message. You can rewrite `powerOfTwo` to test for n equal to zero, rather than n not equal to zero:

```
Integer method definition        • instance
powerOfTwo
  | n result |
  n := self.
  result := 1.
  [n = 0] whileFalse: [n := n - 1.  result := 2 * result].
  ^ result
     Workspace
Transcript show: 4 powerOfTwo printString
     Transcript
16
```

302 The defect of many `whileTrue:` and `whileFalse:` expressions is that the details that govern the iteration appear in three places: the place where the counting variable is initialized, the place where it is tested, and the place where it is altered. Such distribution makes complex iteration difficult to understand.

303 Thus, you need to know about the `timesRepeat:` message:

> `integer number of repeats` `timesRepeat:` `argument block`

An integer, n, receiving the `timesRepeat:` message knows that it must evaluate the argument block n times.

304 Now, you can define the `powerOfTwo` method using a `timesRepeat:` message instead of a `whileTrue:` or `whileFalse:` message:

```
Integer method definition        • instance
powerOfTwo
  | result |
  result := 1.
  self timesRepeat: [result := result * 2].
  ^ result
     Workspace
Transcript show: 4 powerOfTwo printString
     Transcript
16
```

305 Next, suppose that you want to define `factorial`, a method that answers $n!$, where the receiver is to be an integer, n, and $n! = n \times n-1 \times \ldots \times 1$. As in the calculation performed by `powerOfTwo`, repeated multiplication is involved, but this time the multipliers are not all the same.

You could define `factorial` using `timesRepeat`, albeit awkwardly:

```
Integer method definition          • instance
factorial
   | result multiplier |
   result := 1.
   multiplier := self.
   self timesRepeat: [result := result * multiplier.
                        multiplier := multiplier - 1].
   ^ result
```
      Workspace
```
Transcript show: 4 factorial printString
```
      Transcript
```
24
```

306 A more elegant definition of `factorial` uses a `to:do:` message.

The first argument of a `to:do:` message, with the receiver, determines an inclusive integer range.

The second argument is a block that contains a **block parameter**. The block parameter is identified by a prefixing colon, and the parameter is separated from the statements in the block by a bar:

```
[: parameter name  |  statements ]
```

When an `Integer` instance receives a `to:do:` message, that integer evaluates the `do:` argument, a block, once for each integer in the inclusive integer range. Each evaluation is done with one of the integers in the range assigned to the parameter.

For example, to display all the numbers from 1 to 4 in the Transcript, you deploy `to:do:` as follows:

      Workspace
```
1 to: 4 do:
   [:anInteger | Transcript show: anInteger printString; space]
```
      Transcript
```
1 2 3 4
```

307 Now you can redefine `factorial` to use a `to:do:` message. All the multipliers are supplied by the `to:do:` method; there is no need to produce those multipliers yourself:

```
Integer method definition          • instance
factorial
   | result |
   result := 1.
   1 to: self do: [:n | result := result * n].
   ^ result
```
      Workspace
```
Transcript show: 4 factorial printString
```
      Transcript
```
24
```

308   Any `Number` instance can receive a `to:do:` message. You are not limited to ranges that are bounded by 1 on the low end—you are not limited even to ranges bounded by integers on the low end.

309   You also can send `to:by:do:` messages, which produce results for numbers separated by the third argument, rather than by 1, as in the following example:

Workspace
```
1 to: 4 by: 2 do: [:anInteger | Transcript show: anInteger printString;
space]
```
Transcript
1 3

310   The number of positions at the bottom of a game tree with depth d and b choices at each
PRACTICE   position is b^d. The total number of positions in that game tree is $1 + b + b^2 + \cdots + b^d$. Write an iterative method, using the `timesRepeat:` message, to be sent to a number representing b with an argument representing d, that computes the total number of positions. Use your program to compute the total number of positions in a game tree with $b = 2$ and $d = 10$. Repeat with $b = 15$ and $d = 100$.

311   Resolve the problem posed in Segment 310 using the `to:do:` message instead of the
PRACTICE   `timesRepeat:` message.

312
HIGHLIGHTS

- If you want to repeat a calculation for as long as a Boolean expression's value is **true, then** use a `whileTrue:` expression:

  `receiver block` `whileTrue:` `argument block`

- If you want to repeat a calculation for as long as a Boolean expression's value is **false, then** use a `whileFalse:` expression:

  `receiver block` `whileFalse:` `argument block`

- If you want to repeat a calculation for a specified number of times, **then** use a `timesRepeat:` expression with a block parameter:

  `integer number of repeats` `timesRepeat:` [`statements`]

- If you want to repeat a calculation a given number of times **and** you want to use a range of integers in the calculation, **then** use a `to:do:` expression:

  `lowest integer` `to:` `highest integer`
  `do:` [: `parameter name` | `statements`]

84

17 HOW TO WRITE RECURSIVE METHODS

313   In Section 16, you learned how to repeat a computation by using iteration messages. In this section, you learn how to perform a computation over and over by using recursive messages.

314   If you are not yet familiar with recursion, it is best to see how recursion works through an example involving a simple mathematical computation that you already know how to perform using iteration. Suppose, for example, that you want to write a method, recursivePowerOfTwo, that computes the nth power of 2 recursively.

To define recursivePowerOfTwo, you can take advantage of the powerOfTwo method already provided in Section 16, because one way to define recursivePowerOfTwo is to hand over the real work to powerOfTwo:

```
Integer method definition          • instance
recursivePowerOfTwo
  ^ self powerOfTwo
      Workspace
Transcript show: 4 recursivePowerOfTwo printString; cr
        Transcript
16
```

315   Once you see that you can define recursivePowerOfTwo in terms of powerOfTwo, you are ready to learn how to turn recursivePowerOfTwo into a recursive method that does not rely on powerOfTwo.

First, note that you can eliminate the need to call powerOfTwo in the simple case in which the value of recursivePowerOfTwo's receiver is 0:

```
Integer method definition          • instance
recursivePowerOfTwo
  self = 0
    ifTrue: [^ 1]
    ifFalse: [^ self powerOfTwo]
      Workspace
Transcript show: 4 recursivePowerOfTwo printString; cr
        Transcript
16
```

316   Next, note that you can arrange for recursivePowerOfTwo to hand over a little less work to powerOfTwo by performing one of the multiplications by 2 in recursivePowerOfTwo itself, and subtracting 1 from powerOfTwo's argument:

```
Integer method definition        • instance
recursivePowerOfTwo
  self = 0
    ifTrue: [^ 1]
    ifFalse: [^ 2 * (self - 1) powerOfTwo]
      Workspace
Transcript show: 4 recursivePowerOfTwo printString; cr
       Transcript
16
```

Clearly, recursivePowerOfTwo must work as long as one of the following two situations holds:

- The value of self is 0; in this situation, the recursivePowerOfTwo answers 1.

- The value of self is not 0, but the powerOfTwo method is able to compute the power of 2 that is 1 less than the value of self.

317 Now for the recursion trick: you replace powerOfTwo in recursivePowerOfTwo by recursivePowerOfTwo itself.

```
Integer method definition        • instance
recursivePowerOfTwo
  self = 0
    ifTrue: [^ 1]
    ifFalse: [^ 2 * (self - 1) recursivePowerOfTwo]
      Workspace
Transcript show: 4 recursivePowerOfTwo printString; cr
       Transcript
16
```

318 The new version works for two reasons:

- If the value of self is 0, the recursivePowerOfTwo method answers 1.

- If the value of self is not 0, the recursivePowerOfTwo method first computes the result of the expression self - 1. Next, the recursivePowerOfTwo method sends the recursivePowerOfTwo message to that result to compute the power of 2 for a number that is 1 less than the value of self. Then, the recursivePowerOfTwo method may send another recursivePowerOfTwo message to ask itself to compute the power of 2 for a number that is 2 less than the original value of self, and so on, until the recursivePowerOfTwo method needs to deal with only 0.

319 Whenever a method, such as recursivePowerOfTwo, is used in its own definition, the method is said to be **recursive**. When a method makes use of itself, the method is said to **recurse**.

Given a positive, integer argument, there is no danger that recursivePowerOfTwo will recurse forever—sending an infinite number of messages—because eventually the receiver is counted down to 0, which handles the recursivePowerOfTwo message directly, without further recursion.

320 There is also no danger that the values taken on by the `self` parameter will get in each other's way. Each time `recursivePowerOfTwo` is entered, Smalltalk sets aside a private storage place to hold the value of `self` for that entry:

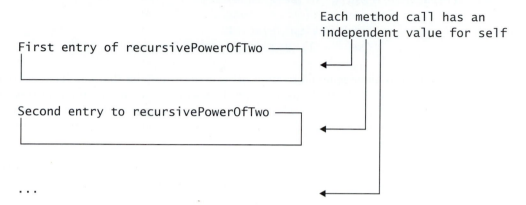

Each method call has an
independent value for self

First entry of recursivePowerOfTwo

Second entry to recursivePowerOfTwo

...

321 Note that the simple case—the one for which the result is computed directly—is handled by the **base part** of the method definition.

The harder case—the one in which the result is computed indirectly, via a solution to another problem—is handled by the **recursive part** of the method definition.

322 Here is a look at the four method evaluations performed when 3 is the receiver of the `recursivePowerOfTwo` method:

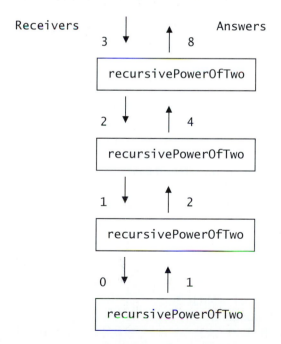

323 The `recursivePowerOfTwo` method is an instance of the **recursive countdown** pattern:

```
Integer method definition            ● instance
method selector
  self = 0
    ifTrue: [^ result for self equal 0 ]
    ifFalse: [^ combination receiver
              combination selector
              (self - 1) method selector ]
```

324 For another, more interesting illustration of recursion, suppose that you have discovered a miraculous diet that always leads to weight loss without any negative side effects. Your publisher tells you to write a book, and assures you that the sales will multiply "like rabbits" each month for at least 2 years. You wonder if that remark is fantastic news, or just a silly metaphor.

Fortunately, Fibonacci figured out long ago how fast rabbits multiply, deriving a formula that gives the number of female rabbits after n months, under the following assumptions:

- Female rabbits mature 1 month after birth.

- Once they mature, female rabbits have one female child each month.

- At the beginning of the first month, there is one immature female rabbit.

- Rabbits live forever.

- There are always enough males on hand to mate with all the mature females.

325 The following diagram shows the number of female rabbits at the end of every month for 6 months:

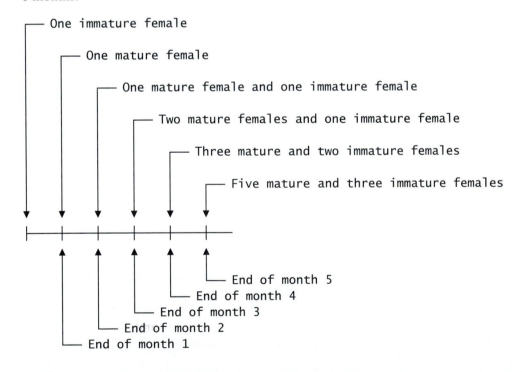

Clearly, the number of female rabbits there are at the end of the *n*th month is the number of females there were at the end of the previous month plus the number of females that gave birth during the current month.

Of course, the number of females that gave birth during the current month is the number of mature female rabbits at the end of the previous month, which is same as the number of females there were all together at the end of the month before that.

Thus, the following formula holds:

$$\text{Rabbits}(n) = \text{Rabbits}(n - 1) + \text{Rabbits}(n - 2)$$

326 Capturing the rabbit formula in the form of a Smalltalk method, you have the following definition for `rabbits`:

```
Integer method definition        • instance
rabbits
  (self = 0 or: [self = 1])
    ifTrue: [^ 1]
    ifFalse: [^ (self - 1) rabbits + (self - 2) rabbits]
        Workspace
Transcript
  show: 'After month 1, there is '  ;
  show: 1  rabbits printString; cr;
  show: 'After month 2, there are '  ;
  show: 2  rabbits printString; cr;
  show: 'After month 3, there are '  ;
  show: 3  rabbits printString; cr;
  show: 'After month 4, there are '  ;
  show: 4  rabbits printString; cr;
  show: 'After month 5, there are '  ;
  show: 5  rabbits printString; cr;
  show: 'After month 24, there are '  ;
  show: 24 rabbits printString; cr
        Transcript
After month 1, there is 1
After month 2, there are 2
After month 3, there are 3
After month 4, there are 5
After month 5, there are 8
After month 24, there are 75025
```

Evidently, at the end of 2 years, your book sales will be extremely healthy if those sales grow like rabbits.

327 Here is a look at the `rabbits` method at work on 3, the same argument used previously with `recursivePowerOfTwo`. The value answered is the number of rabbits at the end of the third month.

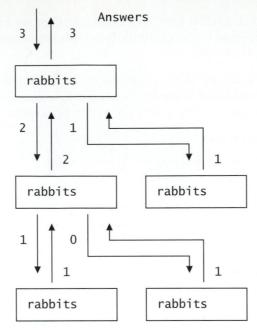

328   Now, to illustrate the concept of **mutually recursive methods**, suspend disbelief, and suppose that you have decided that the rabbits method is too big. Accordingly, you rewrite the rabbits method in terms of two auxiliary methods:

Integer method definition   • instance
```
rabbits
  (self = 0 or: [self = 1])
    ifTrue: [^ 1]
    ifFalse: [^ self previousMonth + self penultimateMonth]
```

Realizing that previousMonth must answer the number of rabbits at the end of the previous month, you see that you can define previousMonth as follows:

Integer method definition   • instance
```
previousMonth
  ^ (self - 1) rabbits
```

Analogous reasoning leads you to the following definition for penultimateMonth:

Integer method definition   • instance
```
penultimateMonth
  ^ (self - 2) rabbits
```

329   Note that rabbits, previousMonth, and penultimateMonth are **mutually recursive methods** because they all call themselves by way of one another.

330   Note that, no matter in what order you define mutually recursive methods, at least one method is referred to before it is defined. Fortunately, such forward references cause no problems in Smalltalk.

331 The following diagram shows `rabbits` and two `rabbits` auxiliaries working to determine how many rabbits there are at the end of 3 months.

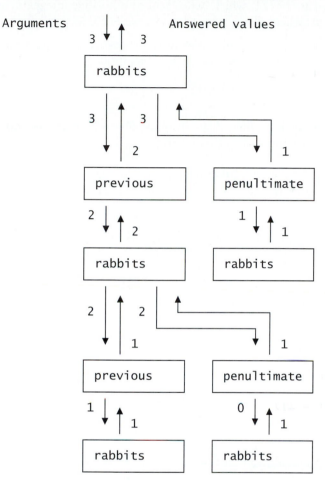

Each of the three cooperating methods can initiate a chain of calls that ends in a call to itself. Thus, the cooperating methods exhibit indirect, rather than direct, recursion.

332 You have seen two recursive definitions: one for `powerOfTwo` and one for `rabbits`. Many
SIDE TRIP mathematically oriented programmers prefer such recursive definitions to iterative definitions, when both are possible, believing that there is inherent elegance in defining a method partly in terms of itself.

Other, practically oriented programmers dislike recursive definitions for one or both of two reasons: first, the recursive approach usually produces much slower programs, because each send operation takes time; and second, the recursive approach may have problems with large arguments, because the number of send operations in a recursive chain of sends is usually limited to a few hundred. Recursion aficionados counter by creating compilers that handle certain recursive methods in sophisticated ways that avoid such limits.

333 Write a recursive method, `raisedToRecursively:`, which, when sent to a positive integer,
PRACTICE m, with a positive-integer argument, n, answers m^n.

Write a recursive method, `factorial`, which, when sent to a positive integer, n, answers the factorial of n, written $n!$, where $n! = n \times n - 1 \times \ldots \times 1$.

Convert the method that you wrote in Segment 334 into a program consisting of two cooperating methods, `factorial` and `recurse`. The `recurse` method is to call the `factorial` method.

- Recursive methods work by calling themselves to solve subproblems until the subproblems are simple enough to solve directly.

- The portion of a recursive method that handles the simplest cases is called the base part; the portion that transforms more complex cases is called the recursion part.

- If you want to solve a difficult problem, **then** try to break it up into simpler subproblems that can be solved recursively.

- If you are writing a recursive method, **then** your method must handle the simplest cases, **and** must break down every other case into the simplest cases.

- If your recursive method is to count down a number, **then** you may be able to instantiate the following recursive countdown pattern in the definition of an `Integer` instance method:

```
method selector
   self = 0
     ifTrue: [^ result for self equal to 0 ]
     ifFalse: [^ combination receiver
                 combination selector
               (self - 1) method selector ]
```

18 HOW TO STORE VALUES IN CLASS VARIABLES

337 In this section, you learn about class variables, which are accessible from any method defined for the same class in which the class variable is defined.

338 In Section 11, you learned that each instance of a class contains its own set of instance-variable values, so each Food instance, for example, contains its own values for the fCalories, cCalories, and pCalories' variables.

Because each instance maintains its own values for all instance variables, you would not want to use an instance variable for a value that does not vary from one instance to another.

For example, the number of calories contributed to a food by a gram of fat does not vary from food to food.

339 According, you could choose to store the ratio of fat calories to fat grams in a **class variable**. Unlike instance variables, there is but one value for a class variable for the entire class, and for all that class's subclasses, yet the value of that variable, like values for instance variables, is available to all methods defined for the class and that class's subclasses.

340 For example, the following revision of the Food class definition contains class variables for the ratios of calories to fat grams, to carbohydrate grams, and to protein grams:

Food class definition
```
Object subclass: #Food
   instanceVariableNames: 'fCalories cCalories pCalories'
   classVariableNames: 'FatRatio CarbohydrateRatio ProteinRatio'
   poolDictionaries: ''
```

341 Note that class variable names must start with an uppercase character.

342 Ordinarily, class variables are initialized by **class methods**. For example, the class variables of the Food class can be initialized as follows:

Food method definition   • class
```
initializeClassVariables
   FatRatio := 9.
   CarbohydrateRatio := 4.
   ProteinRatio := 4
```

343 You can set or get the Food class variables in any Food class or instance method. For example, the instance method, fGrams, provides the number of fat grams in a serving of food by dividing the number of fat calories in a serving of the food (the value of an instance variable) by the ratio of fat grams to fat calories (the value of a class variable):

Food method definition   • instance
```
fGrams
   ^ fCalories / FatRatio
```

344　Now suppose that you want to set or get the fat ratios elsewhere in your program, in methods that are not defined for the Food class and subclassess of the Food class.

Under these circumstances, you can define class setter and getter methods for the class variables. Then, you can set and get the values for the class variables using those setters and getters:

Food method definition	• class

```
fatRatio
  ∧ FatRatio
```

Food method definition	• class

```
fatRatio: aNumber
  FatRatio := aNumber
```

Food method definition	• class

```
carbohydrateRatio
  ∧ CarbohydrateRatio
```

Food method definition	• class

```
carbohydrateRatio: aNumber
  CarbohydrateRatio := aNumber
```

Food method definition	• class

```
proteinRatio
  ∧ ProteinRatio
```

Food method definition	• class

```
proteinRatio: aNumber
  ProteinRatio := aNumber
```

345　Data abstraction, explained in Section 14, provides another reason for using setter and getter methods for class variables. You might determine, for example, that the value of ProteinRatio must be equal to the value of CarbohydrateRatio. If you have used setters and getters for the class variables, you can enforce the equality constraint by storing just one number accessed by both setter–getter pairs:

Food class definition
```
Object subclass: #Food
  instanceVariableNames: 'fCalories cCalories pCalories'
  classVariableNames: 'FatRatio CommonRatio'
  poolDictionaries: ''
```

Food method definition	• class

```
carbohydrateRatio
  ∧ CommonRatio
```

Food method definition	• class

```
carbohydrateRatio: aNumber
  CommonRatio := aNumber
```

Food method definition	• class

```
proteinRatio
  ∧ CommonRatio
```

Food method definition	• class

```
proteinRatio: aNumber
  CommonRatio := aNumber
```

Define `MathematicsClass` to be a class. Define `Pi` to be a class variable. Define `pi` and `pi:` to be the getter and setter for `Pi`. Use the setter to set the value equal to `1 arcTan * 4`. Use the getter to redefine the `volume` method originally requested in Segment 114.

- **If** you need to store information that is useful to all instances of a class, but that does not vary from instance to instance, **then** you can store that information in class variables.

- **If** you store information in class variables, **then** you need to initialize those class variables with a class method.

- **If** you wish to use the value of a class variable inside a class or instance method defined for that class, or for one of its subclasses, **then** just use the variable name.

- **If** you wish to set or get the value of a class variable inside a method defined for a class that is not the one in which the class variable is defined, or one of that class's subclasses, **then** define class setters and getters.

19 HOW TO STORE VALUES IN DICTIONARIES

348 In this section, you learn about dictionaries. In particular, you learn about the Smalltalk dictionary, whose variables are universally accessible, and you learn about pool dictionaries, whose variables are available only in specific classes.

349 The Smalltalk environment contains a tablelike object called the **Smalltalk dictionary**. In the Smalltalk dictionary, **keys** are associated with **values**.

350 Suppose, for example, that you want to store 9 as the value associated with the key, #FatRatio, in the Smalltalk dictionary. You simply send a `at:put:` message as follows:

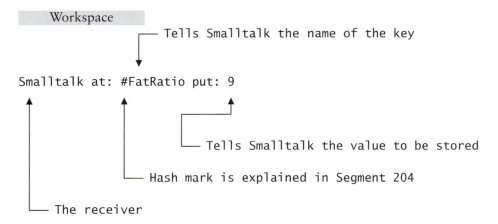

Workspace

Tells Smalltalk the name of the key

Smalltalk at: #FatRatio put: 9

Tells Smalltalk the value to be stored

Hash mark is explained in Segment 204

The receiver

351 The keys and values stored in the Smalltalk dictionary are referred to more commonly as **global variables** and **global-variable values**.

352 The values of global variables, unlike the values of class variables, are available for evaluation or assignment in any method defined for any class.

353 Note that global-variable names must begin with an uppercase character.

354 You can tell Smalltalk to look up the value of a global variable using an `at:` message, with a key, or you can use the key as a variable reference, as in the following examples:

Workspace
```
Transcript show: (Smalltalk at: #FatRatio) printString;
        cr;
        show: FatRatio printString
```
Transcript
```
9
9
```

355 Similarly, you can set the value of a global variable using an `at:put:` message, with a literal key, or you can use an assignment expression, as in the following examples:

```
Smalltalk at: #FatRatio put: 8.
FatRatio := 8.
```

356   You can redefine fGrams, previously defined in Segment 343 and in Segment 345, such that fGrams uses the FatRatio global variable.

Food method definition   • instance
```
fGrams
  ^ fCalories / FatRatio
```

357   Note that the implementation of fGrams looks the same in Segment 356 and Segment 343, because the global variable here happens to have the same name as the class variable there.

358   If you use Smalltalk Express, you can avoid the at:put: message altogether, relying
SIDE TRIP   instead on assignment to create and initialize global variables:

Workspace
```
TestVariable := 8.
```

Note, however, that other versions of Smalltalk issue a warning if you use assignment to create and initialize global variables, and still others report an error.

359   If a method happens to have a parameter or local variable that has the same name as a global variable, that global variable is said to be **overridden**. Inside such a method, the overridden global variable cannot be evaluated or assigned.

360   Because global variables can be evaluated and assigned at any point in a program after they are established, unless overridden, global variables are said to have **universal scope**.

361   Even if a global variable is overridden by a parameter or local variable, you can still get and set the global variable using the at: and at:put: messages.

362   Global variables are useful as handles for holding on to values as you experiment in a workspace. Their broader use as program elements is discouraged, however. One reason is that the Smalltalk dictionary contains not only the global variables that you define, but also all class names. There is a serious danger of an accidental name conflict if you use many global variables.

363   Instead of using global variables that reside in the Smalltalk dictionary, you can create a new dictionary to hold key–value pairs and assign that new dictionary to just one global variable in the Smalltalk dictionary.

364   To create a new dictionary, you simply send new to the Dictionary class:

```
Dictionary new
```

To assign the new dictionary to a global variable, such as CalorieGramRatios, in the Smalltalk dictionary, you use an at:put: message:

```
Smalltalk at: #CalorieGramRatios put: Dictionary new
```

365 To add a new key–value pair to the new dictionary, or to change an existing value, you use at:put: again:

```
CalorieGramRatios at: 'FatRatio' put: 9
```

366 Note that the key used in Segment 365 is a string, rather than a literal symbol. Although you can use literal symbols as dictionary keys, Smalltalk Express requires you to use strings in any dictionary that is used, as explained in Segment 369, as a pool dictionary.

367 To access information in the CalorieGramRatios dictionary, you use the at: method, along with a key:

```
CalorieGramRatios at: 'FatRatio'
```

368 The following, for example, defines fGrams to use an entry in the CalorieGramRatios dictionary:

Food method definition   • instance
```
fGrams
  ^ fCalories / (CalorieGramRatios at: 'FatRatio')
```

369 You can avoid the awkward (CalorieGramRatios at: 'FatRatio') expression, replacing it with FatRatio, by inserting CalorieGramRatios into the poolDictionaries: portion of the Food class definition. That way, you tell Smalltalk that you want all Food methods to have direct access to the CalorieGramRatios dictionary:

Food class definition
```
Object subclass: #Food
  instanceVariableNames: 'fCalories cCalories pCalories'
  classVariableNames: ''
  poolDictionaries: 'CalorieGramRatios'
```

370 Once the methods of the Food class have direct access to the CalorieGramRatios dictionary, the definition of fGrams returns to the familiar form shown in Segment 343 and Segment 356:

Food method definition   • instance
```
fGrams
  ^ fCalories / FatRatio
```

371 In some versions of Smalltalk, pool dictionaries are inherited; in other versions they are not. Accordingly, if you want to be sure that the variables in a dictionary are available by name, you should include an explicit reference to that dictionary in every class for which there are methods that need access to the dictionary. For example, you should identify the CalorieGramRatios dictionary as a pool dictionary in the Vegetable class if you wish to use values from that dictionary in Vegetable methods, even if you have already identified the CalorieGramRatios dictionary as a pool dictionary in the Food class.

Define `MathematicsDictionary` to be a global variable with a value that is an instance of the `Dictionary` class. Use Pi as a key in that new dictionary. Set the value associated with the key to `1 arcTan * 4`. Use Pi to redefine the `volume` method originally requested in Segment 114.

- If you need to store information that is useful throughout your application, **then** you can store that information in the Smalltalk dictionary. Key–value pairs stored in the Smalltalk dictionary are often called global-variable–global-variable-value pairs.

- If you want to create and assign a global variable, **then** instantiate the following pattern:

  `Smalltalk at: #global-variable name put: value`

- If you want to access the value of a global variable, **then** use the global variable's name.

- If you want to reassign a global variable, **then** instantiate one of the following patterns:

  `Smalltalk at: #global-variable name put: new value`
  `global-variable name := new value`

- If you want to create a new dictionary that is assigned to a global variable, **then** instantiate the following pattern:

  `Smalltalk at: #dictionary name put: Dictionary new`

- If you want to add a new key–value entry to a dictionary, **then** instantiate the following pattern:

  `dictionary name at: 'key name' put: initial value`

- If you want to know the value of a key–value entry in a dictionary, **then** instantiate the following pattern:

  `dictionary name at: 'key name'`

- If you need to store information that is needed in several parts of your application, **then** you should store that information in a dictionary, **and then** you should include that dictionary in the pool dictionaries of the classes for which methods are defined that need access to the dictionary.

- If you have installed a dictionary as a pool dictionary in a class, **then** you can set and get the values stored in that dictionary using assignment expressions to set values and keys to get values.

20 HOW TO WORK WITH ARRAYS

374   In this section, you learn how to store objects in arrays and how to retrieve those objects, once stored.

375   A one-dimensional **array** is a collection of objects in which the objects are stored and retrieved via an integer **index**. Each object in an array is called an **element** of that array. In Smalltalk, the first element is indexed by 1; hence, Smalltalk is said to have **1-based arrays**.

The following, for example, is a diagram of a one-dimensional array with integer elements:

1	2	3	4	← Index
570	720	640	720	

376   Note that a Smalltalk array can hold elements of one class in some locations and elements of another class in other locations. The objects in a Smalltalk array do not all have to belong to the same class.

377   To create an instance of an array, you send the `new:` message to the `Array` class, with the number of elements in the array supplied as the argument.

The following, for example, creates a four-location `Array` instance, and assigns that instance to a global variable, `Calories`:

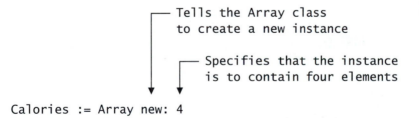

```
                    ┌─ Tells the Array class
                    │  to create a new instance
                    │
                    │    ┌─ Specifies that the instance
                    │    │  is to contain four elements
                    ▼    ▼
Calories := Array new: 4
```

378   To use an array, once it is created, you need to know how to **store into** the array and to **retrieve from** the array at locations identified by an integer index.

To store data into an `Array` instance, you use the `at:put:` message with the `at:` argument providing the integer index and the `put:` argument providing the value. The following expression, for example, stores an integer into the array assigned to `calories` at the location indexed by the value of another variable, named `counter`:

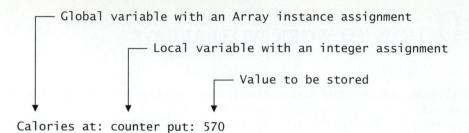

```
Calories at: counter put: 570
```

To retrieve data from an array, once the data have been stored, you send the `at:` message with an integer. The following expression, for example, yields the data stored in the location indexed by the value of the `counter` variable:

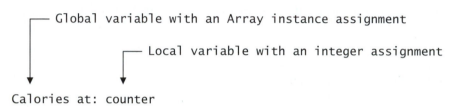

```
Calories at: counter
```

379 The following defines an array of four elements, assigns that array to a global variable, stores data in the array, and retrieves the stored data:

Workspace
```
Smalltalk at: #Calories put: (Array new: 4).
```
Workspace
```
Calories at: 1 put: 570;
         at: 2 put: 720;
         at: 3 put: 640;
         at: 4 put: 720.
Transcript
  show: 'The total calorie count is ';
  show: ((Calories at: 1)
         + (Calories at: 2)
         + (Calories at: 3)
         + (Calories at: 4))
       printString
```
Transcript
```
The total calorie count is 2650
```

380 Instead of using `new:` and `at:put:`, you can create and initialize small arrays, with one to four elements, by using one of four methods: `with:`, `with:with:`, `with:with:with:` or `with:with:with:with:`. In the following, for example, a `with:with:with:with:` message creates and initializes a four-element `Array` instance:

```
Array with: 570 with: 720 with: 640 with: 720
```

381   If an array is to contain only literals, you can create a **literal array** by arranging the array elements between a #(prefix and a) suffix. Because numbers are literals, you can create the array produced by the expression in Segment 380 as follows:

```
#(570 720 640 720)
```

382   One way to add up the elements in an `Array` instance is to send the array the `do:` message with a block as an argument. The following shows what the appropriate block looks like, given that the array is assigned to `Calories`, a global variable, and that `sum`, a local variable, is initially assigned to 0:

```
Calories do: [:element | sum := sum + element].
```

Observe that blocks sent along with the `do:` message have a parameter reminiscent of the parameter blocks involved in `to:do:` messages, which you learned about in Segment 307. The receiver, an array, handles such a block by evaluating the block as many times as there are elements in the array. Each such evaluation is done with a different array element assigned to the parameter. Thus, `do:` expressions perform computations that center on **enumeration**.

383   You can, of course, insert the expression shown in Segment 382 into a method such that messages based on that method, when sent to `Array` instances containing numbers, add up the numbers in the array. There is no need for a variable, such as `Calories`, however; `self` names the array:

Array method definition   • instance
```
sumUp
   | sum |
   sum := 0.
   self do: [:element | sum := sum + element].
   ^ sum
```
Workspace
```
Transcript show: (Array with: 570 with: 720 with: 640 with: 720)
                  sumUp printString
```
Transcript
```
2650
```

384   In the example in Segment 383, the parameter, `element`, is assigned successively to 570, 720, 640, and 720 with the statement in the block evaluated each time:

Iteration	Value of element	New value assigned to sum
1	570	0 + 570 = 570
2	720	570 + 720 = 1290
3	640	1290 + 640 = 1930
4	720	570 + 720 = 2650

385   You can also add the numbers in an `Array` instance by arranging for integers between 1 and the size of the array to be assigned to a parameter. Then you can use the parameter as an array index inside a block.

Thus, you have the following alternative to the approach in Segment 383 for adding up the numbers in an array. Note that the size message determines the size of the array:

```
Array method definition     • instance
sumUp
  | sum |
  sum := 0.
  1 to: self size
    do: [:index | sum := sum + (self at: index)].
  ^ sum
        Workspace
Transcript show: (Array with: 570 with: 720 with: 640 with: 720)
                sumUp printString
        Transcript
2650
```

386 In the example in Segment 385, the value of the parameter, index, becomes 1, 2, 3, and 4, with the statement in the block evaluated each time:

Iteration	Value of index	New value assigned to sum
1	1	0 + 570 = 570
2	2	570 + 720 = 1290
3	3	1290 + 640 = 1930
4	4	1290 + 640 = 2650

You may be more comfortable with the index-based approach, because the principal feature of Array instances is that you can get at them using a parameter as an index. On the other hand, using a parameter as an index, rather than as an element, produces a bulkier program, and hence a more error-prone program.

387 Yet another, much more elegant way to add up the numbers in an array is to use the powerful inject:into: method, inherited from the Collection class, with a two-argument block:

```
an Array instance
  inject: initial value
  into: [:previousResult :nextElement | statements ]
```

Here is what happens when you send a inject:into: method:

• The initial value is assigned to previousResult, and the first element in the array is assigned to nextElement.

• The statements are evaluated to produce a value for the block.

• The value of the block is assigned to previousResult, and the second element in the array is assigned to nextElement.

• The statements are evaluated again.

• The previous steps are repeated for all the elements in the array. The answer of the overall inject:into: is the value produced by the final evaluation of the block.

388 The following illustrates how you can use `inject:into:` to add the values in an array:

```
      Workspace
Transcript show: ((Array with: 570 with: 720 with: 640 with: 720)
                  inject: 0
                  into: [:sum :element| sum + element])
                  printString; cr.
      Transcript
2650
```

389 The following diagram explains what happens in Segment 388 as the `inject:into:` method marches down the receiver `Array` instance, combining the `Array` instance's elements with the `inject:` argument or with the previous result:

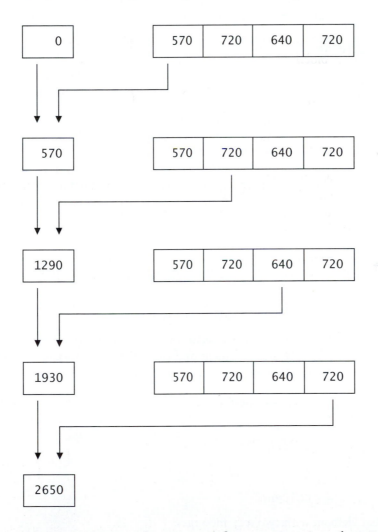

390 Of course, if you wish, you can define a new version of `sumUp` using the `inject:into:` method:

```
sumUp
  ^ self inject: 0
          into: [:sum :element | sum + element]
```

```
Transcript show: (Array with: 570 with: 720 with: 640 with: 720)
                  sumUp printString
```

```
2650
```

391 So far, for simplicity, the sample arrays contain Integer instances. You can just as easily create and use arrays of instances of other classes. The following, for example, contrasts the creation of an array of Integer instances with the creation of an array of Food instances:

```
Array with: 570 with: 720 with: 640 with: 720
```

```
Array with: Vegetable new
      with: Dairy new
      with: Meat new
      with: Grain new
```

Neither array cares what you put into it, and you need not put instances of the same class at every location in the array. The second array has instances of four different classes in it.

392 You easily can define arrays with more than one dimension by using arrays as array elements. For example, to define weekOfCalories with seven rows (for the days of the week) and three columns (for breakfast, lunch, and dinner calories), you first create an array of seven elements, assigned, say, to Calories:

```
Calories := Array new: 7
```

Next, you arrange for each element in the array to be an array of three elements:

```
(Interval from: 1 to: 7)
  do: [:index | Calories at: index put: (Array new: 3)]
```

To retain 850 as the number of calories in the second meal of the fourth day, you send one at: message to get the correct array element and one at:put: message to set the appropriate element in that array element:

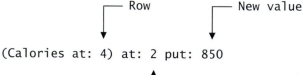

```
(Calories at: 4) at: 2 put: 850
```

Later, you recover that element with two at: messages:

```
(Calories at: 4) at: 2
```

393
SIDE TRIP
A more elegant way to implement a two-dimensional arrays is to create a new class, as suggested in Segment 397.

394
PRACTICE
Write sumOfSquares, a method that computes the sum of the squares of the numbers in an array. Use the method shown in Segment 383 as a guide. Then repeat this assignment, using the method shown in Segment 390 as a guide.

395
PRACTICE
Write squares, a method that answers an array in which each element is the square of the corresponding element in the receiver array.

396
PRACTICE
Write oddElements, a method that answers an array that contains only the odd-numbered elements of the receiver array. Use the to:by:do: message explained in Segment 309.

397
PRACTICE
Define Matrix, a class that is to store a two-dimensional array. Next, define a class method, rows:columns:, which creates locations for all matrix values. Then, define the row:column:put: and row:column: methods for setting and getting values from Matrix instances.

398
HIGHLIGHTS

- If you want to create a one-dimensional array, **then** instantiate the following pattern:

  ```
  Array new: number of elements
  ```

- If you have an array, **and** you want to store an expression's value in the array, **then** instantiate the following pattern:

  ```
  array name at: index put: expression
  ```

- If you have values stored in an array, **and** you want to retrieve one of those values, **then** instantiate the following pattern:

  ```
  array name at: index
  ```

- If you want to iterate over the elements in an array, **then** instantiate one of the following patterns:

  ```
  array name do: [:element | ··· element ···]

  1 to: array name size
     do: [:index | ··· (array name at: index) ···]
  ```

- If you want to iterate over the elements in an array, **and** you want to include the results of a previous iteration in each computation, **then** instantiate the following pattern:

  ```
  an Array instance
    inject: initial value
    into: [:previousResult :nextElement | statements]
  ```

- **If** you want to create a two-dimensional array, **then** create an array in which the elements are themselves arrays.

21 HOW TO WORK WITH ORDERED COLLECTIONS AND SORTED COLLECTIONS

399   In Section 20, you learned about the `Array` class. In this section, you learn about several other classes that you will find useful when you need to store objects.

400   The classes that you learn about in this section are all subclasses of the `Collection` class. The power offered by these subclasses is one of Smalltalk's distinguishing strengths.

401   An **ordered collection** is a collection of objects into which objects generally are added at the front or back, are retrieved from the front or back, or are removed from the front or back. Each object in an ordered collection is called an **element** of that ordered collection, just as each object in an array is called an element of that array.

The following, for example, is a diagram of an ordered collection that contains integer elements:

570	720	640	720

402   Ordered collections are instances of the `OrderedCollection` class. An instance of the `OrderedCollection` class can hold elements of one type in some locations and elements of another type in other locations.

403   To create an instance of `OrderedCollection`, you send the `OrderedCollection` class the `new` message.

The following, for example, creates an `OrderedCollection` instance and assigns that instance to a global variable named `CaloriesCollection`:

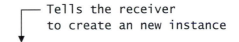
Tells the receiver
to create an new instance

```
CaloriesCollection := OrderedCollection new
```

404   To use an ordered collection, once it is created, you need to know how to store into the ordered collection and retrieve from the ordered collection.

Consider `CaloriesCollection`. To store data into the `CaloriesCollection`, you use the `addFirst:` message. The following expression, for example, stores an integer into the front.

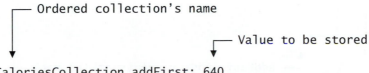
Ordered collection's name

Value to be stored

```
CaloriesCollection addFirst: 640
```

405 To retrieve data from the front of the `CaloriesCollection` ordered collection, once the data have been stored, you send the `first` message:

```
CaloriesCollection first
```

406 To remove data from the front of the `CaloriesCollection` ordered collection, once the data have been stored, you send the `removeFirst` message:

┌── Ordered collection's name
│
▼
```
CaloriesCollection removeFirst
```

407 Note that the answer produced by `removeFirst` is the element removed:

Workspace
```
Transcript show: CaloriesCollection removeFirst printString.
```
Transcript
```
640
```

408 You can work equally easily with either the front or the back of an ordered collection. To store an element at the back, you use the `addLast:` message; to retrieve an element from the back, you use the `last` message; to remove an element from the back, you use the `removeLast` method.

409 You can also send the `add:` message to an ordered collection. The `add:` message is handled as though it were an `addLast:` message; unlike `addLast:`, however, `add:` is polymorphic. That is, `add:` is defined for other classes, as you see in Segment 420, Segment 425, and Segment 429.

410 To determine whether an ordered collection is empty, you send it the `isEmpty` message, which answers `true` or `false`.

411 Using the `addLast:`, `first`, and `removeFirst` methods, you can use ordered collections to represent **first-in, first-out (FIFO) queues**:

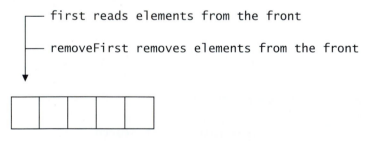

Similarly, you can use ordered collections to represent **last-in, first-out (LIFO) push-down stacks** by using the addFirst:, first, and removeFirst methods:

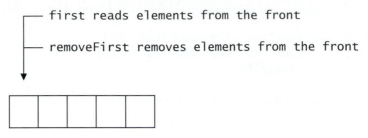

first reads elements from the front

removeFirst removes elements from the front

addFirst: adds elements to the front

412 Once an element of an ordered collection is in place, you can, if you wish, get that element
SIDE TRIP with an at: message and an integer index, and you can set that element with an at:put: message and an integer index.

Thus, ordered collections act as though they were expandable arrays, and ordered collections are therefore handy when you want to be able to access elements by integer indexes, but you are not sure how many elements there will be in advance.

413 The answer produced by addFirst: is the object added; it is not the receiver. Thus, the answer produced by the following cascaded expression is 720—the answer produced by the final addFirst: message in the cascade; it is not the new ordered collection:

```
Workspace
Transcript show:
  (OrderedCollection new
      addFirst: 570; addFirst: 720; addFirst: 640; addFirst: 720)
   printString; cr
   Transcript
720
```

414 If you send the yourself message to an object, the answer produced is the object itself.

Thus, if you want the answer produced by such a cascaded expression to be the receiver, then send a yourself message at the end of the cascade:

```
Workspace
Transcript show:
  (OrderedCollection new
    addFirst: 570;
    addFirst: 720;
    addFirst: 640;
    addFirst: 720;
    yourself)
   printString; cr
   Transcript
OrderedCollection(720 640 720 570)
```

415   You can iterate over the elements in an `OrderedCollection` instance by using a `do:` message exactly like the `do:` message used to iterate over the elements in arrays:

> Workspace
> ```
> (OrderedCollection new addFirst: 570; addFirst: 720;
>                        addFirst: 640; addFirst: 720;
>                        yourself)
>   do:
>   [:element | Transcript show: element printString; space]
> ```
> Transcript
> ```
> 720 640 720 570
> ```

An `OrderedCollection` instance, acting as a receiver, handles blocks just as an `Array` instance would: both evaluate the block as many times as there are elements in the ordered collection. Each such evaluation is done with a different ordered-collection element assigned to the parameter. Thus, the `do:` expression performs **ordered-collection iteration**.

416   You learned in Segment 380 that you can create and initialize `Array` instances by using `with:`, `with:with:`, `with:with:with:`, and `with:with:with:with:` messages. You can also create and initialize `OrderedCollection` instances with those same messages.

417   You easily can create and use `OrderedCollection` instances that contain any kind of class instances. Ordered collections do not care what you put into them, and you do not need to put instances of the same class at every place.

418   A **bag** is like an ordered collection, except that the elements are in no particular order.

419   Bags are instances of the `Bag` class. A `Bag` instance can hold elements of one type in some locations and elements of another type in other locations.

420   To create a bag, you send a `new` message to `Bag`. To add an element, you send `add:` with an argument.

Because the elements are in no particular order, you cannot use methods such as `addFirst:`, `first`, and `removeFirst`.

421   You can iterate over the elements in a `Bag` instance by using a `do:` message exactly like the `do:` message used with arrays or ordered collections:

> Workspace
> ```
> (Bag new add: 570; add: 720; add: 640; add: 720; yourself)
>   do:
>   [:element | Transcript show: element printString; space]
> ```
> Transcript
> ```
> 570 640 720 720
> ```

Note that in the bag in Segment 421, the two instances of 720 seem to have been brought together into adjacent positions. Actually, 720 is stored just once in the bag, with a count of how many times it is to be viewed as appearing in the bag. Smalltalk records duplicate entries in this way to save memory and to increase access speed.

423 A **set** is like a bag, except that there are no duplicate elements in a set.

424 Sets are instances of the `Set` class. A `Set` instance can hold elements of one type in some locations and elements of another type in other locations.

425 To create a set, you send a `new` message to `Set`. To add an element, you send `add:` with an argument. If there is already an element in the set that is equal to the element that you are trying to add, the set remains unchanged.

426 You can iterate over the elements in a `Set` instance by using a `do:` message exactly like the `do:` message used with arrays, ordered collections, or bags:

```
    Workspace
(Set new add: 570; add: 720; add: 640; add: 720; yourself)
  do:
  [:element | Transcript show: element printString; space]
    Transcript
640 720 570
```

Evidently, the set contains only three numbers: 640, 720, and 570. The attempt to add the second 720 comes to nothing, because sets contain no duplicates.

427 A **sorted collection** is like an ordered collection, except that the order of the elements is determined by what the sorting criterion is, rather than by how the elements are added.

Accordingly, you do not add an element to the front or the back of a sorted collection; instead, you add the element, and the sorted-collection instance takes care of placing the element properly.

428 Sorted collections are instances of the `SortedCollection` class. A `SortedCollection` instance can hold elements of one type in some locations and elements of another type in other locations.

429 To create a sorted collection in which the elements are sorted in ascending numerical order, you send a `new` message to `SortedCollection`. To add an element, you send `add:` with an argument.

430 You can iterate over the elements in a `SortedCollection` instance by using a `do:` message exactly like the `do:` message used with arrays, ordered collections, bags, or sets:

> **Workspace**
> ```
> (SortedCollection new add: 570; add: 720; add: 640; add: 720; yourself)
>   do:
>   [:element | Transcript show: element printString; space]
> ```
> **Transcript**
> 570 640 720 720

431   To create a sorted collection in which the elements are sorted in other than ascending numerical order, you send a `sortBlock:` message to `SortedCollection`. The block following the `sortBlock:` selector is a two-parameter block that answers `true` if and only if the first element is to appear before the second. Thus, if `[:x :y | x < y]` is the sort block, you might as well create the sorted collection using `new`; if `[:x :y | x > y]` is the sort block, the elements are sorted in descending order.

> **Workspace**
> ```
> ((SortedCollection sortBlock: [:x :y | x > y])
>   add: 570; add: 720; add: 640; add: 720; yourself)
>   do:
>   [:element | Transcript show: element printString; space]
> ```
> **Transcript**
> 720 720 640 570

432   Smalltalk comes with many methods that allow you to **convert** an instance of one class into an instance of another class. For example, if you create and populate an array, and then wish it were a set, you can arrange a conversion by sending an `asSet` message:

> **Workspace**
> ```
> #(570 720 640 720)
>   asSet do: [:element | Transcript show: element printString; space]
> ```
> **Transcript**
> 640 720 570

433   You can perform conversions with `asArray`, `asOrderedCollection`, `asBag`, `asSet`, and `asSortedCollection`.

434   The `Array`, `OrderedCollection`, `Bag`, `set`, and `SortedCollection` classes all are subclasses of the `Collection` class.

435   To determine the number of elements in a collection-class instance, you send it the `size` message.

436   To iterate over the elements in a collection-class instance, you send the `do:` message, as described in Segment 382 for `Array` instances, and in this section for `OrderedCollection`, `Bag`, `Set`, and `SortedCollection` instances.

437   You can also send the `collect:` message to any instance of a collection class. The `collect:` message answers with a new collection instance in which the elements are the values produced by the final statement in the argument block.

The following example illustrates. Each value in the ordered collection is assigned, successively, to the `element` variable. For each assignment, `1 + element` is evaluated, producing an element of the ordered collection produced by the `collect:` message:

Workspace

```
((OrderedCollection new addFirst: 570; addFirst: 720;
                       addFirst: 640; addFirst: 720;
                       yourself)
   collect: [:element | 1 + element])
  do: [:element | Transcript show: element printString; space].
```
Transcript
```
721 641 721 571
```

438
SIDE TRIP
The instance answered by the `collect:` method usually belongs to the same class as the receiver, but there are exceptions. In the following, for example, the receiver is an instance of the `Interval` class, but the answer is an instance of the `Array` class, as demonstrated by the `class` method, which identifies the class to which an instance belongs.

```
Transcript show: (1 to: 5) class printString; cr.
Transcript show: ((1 to: 5) collect: [:x | x * x]) class printString
```
Transcript
```
Interval
Array
```

439 The following `decision tree` will help you to choose the appropriate collection class from the alternatives:

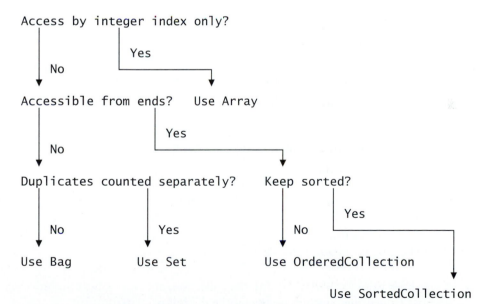

440 The powerful `inject:into:` method, about which you learned in Segment 390, is inherited by all subclasses of the `Collection` class. You can use it to perform all sorts of

computations on collections, such as adding up all the element in a collection filled with numbers or finding the maximum value in such a collection.

441
PRACTICE Implement a method for the `Collection` class that answers the average of the elements of the collection.

442
PRACTICE The standard deviation of a collection of numbers is the square root of the average of the squared differences between the numbers and the average of the numbers. Implement a method for the `Collection` class that answers the standard deviation of the elements of the collection.

443
PRACTICE Implement NumberCollection, a subclass of the `OrderedCollection` class. Define `include:` for the `NumberCollection` class such that the argument is added to the class instance only if the argument is a number; otherwise, `include:` is to ignore the argument. Use the `isNumber` predicate.

444
HIGHLIGHTS

- If you want to create a collection, **then** instantiate one of the following patterns:

  ```
  Array new: size
  OrderedCollection new
  Bag new
  Set new
  SortedCollection new
  ```

- If you want to iterate over the elements in a collection, **then** instantiate the following pattern:

  ```
  collection do: [:element | ··· element ···]
  ```

- If you have an ordered collection, **and** you want to store an expression's value into the ordered collection, **then** instantiate one of the following patterns:

  ```
  ordered collection addFirst: expression
  ordered collection addLast: expression
  ```

- If you have values stored in an ordered collection, **and** you want to retrieve one of those values, **then** instantiate one of the following patterns:

  ```
  ordered collection first
  ordered collection last
  ```

- If you have values stored in an ordered collection, **and** you want to remove one of those values, **then** instantiate one of the the following patterns:

  ```
  ordered collection removeFirst
  ordered collection removeLast
  ```

- **If** you have a bag, set, or sorted collection, **and** you want to store an expression's value into the collection, **then** instantiate the following pattern:

  `ordered collection` `add:` `expression`

- **If** you want to convert one kind of collection into another, **then** send `asArray`, `asOrderedCollection`, `asBag`, `asSet`, or `asSortedCollection`.

22 HOW TO CREATE FILE STREAMS FOR INPUT AND OUTPUT

445 Having learned how to create collections, such as arrays, you now learn about Smalltalk Express methods that allow you to fill collections with information stored in files, and to move the information stored in collections into files. In particular, you learn how to obtain `String`, `Integer`, and `Float` instances from files.

Note, however, that file access tends to be implementation specific. Segment 783 explains how to use VisualWorks to work with information stored in files.

446 A **stream** is a sequence of data objects. To read data from a file, you create an **input file stream** that flows from an input file to your program. Similarly, to write data into a file, you create an **output file stream** that flows from your program to the output file.

```
                    file stream                 file stream
Input file ─────────────────────> Your program ─────────────────────> Output file
```

447 To create a file stream, which is an instance of the `FileStream` class, you send a `pathName:` message to the `File` class with a file-specifying string. Unlike most instance-creation methods, `pathName:` creates an instance of a class different from that of the receiver:

```
          ┌─ File-specifying string
          ▼
          ─────────────
File pathName: 'vtbls.dta'
─────────────────────────────
  ▲
  └─ FileStream instance
```

448 Typically, you assign the file stream to a variable so you can access the file stream whenever you want to read information from the file or write information into the file. The following is an example in which the stream happens to be assigned to a local variable named `inputStream`:

```
inputStream := File pathName: 'vtbls.dta'
```

449 Of course, the file specification may include a file-directory path, as in the following example:

```
inputStream := File pathName: 'c:\test\vtbls.dta'
```

450 Once you have created a stream for reading, you can read information from the corresponding file. For example, to read an alphanumeric string from a file, bounded by nonalphanumeric characters, you send a `nextWord` message to the stream. Assuming that `inputStream` is a local variable with an input-stream assignment, the following reads a string from the corresponding file, and converts that string into an `Integer` instance.

```
inputStream nextWord asInteger
```

451 If `asInteger` is sent to strings that cannot be interpreted as numbers, the message answers with 0.

452 If there are no more strings in a stream, `nextWord` answers `nil`.

453 Once you have finished reading information from a file, you should so indicate by sending a `close` message to the stream:

```
inputStream close.
```

454 Now, suppose that you have a file, `vtbls.dta`, that contains descriptions of foods in the following format:

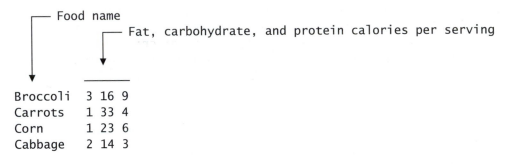

```
          ┌─ Food name
          │        ┌─ Fat, carbohydrate, and protein calories per serving
          │        │
          ▼        ▼
                 ─────
Broccoli   3 16 9
Carrots    1 33 4
Corn       1 23 6
Cabbage    2 14 3
```

455 Using what you have learned previously from Segment 447 and Segment 450, you can write `initializeFrom:`, which initializes a Food instance (the receiver) with information from a file (the argument). The Food class is the same as that shown in Segment 232, except that an extra instance variable, `name`, is added.

Food class definition
```
Object subclass: #Food
   instanceVariableNames: 'name fCalories cCalories pCalories'
   classVariableNames: ''
   poolDictionaries: ''
```
Food method definition   • instance
```
name ^ name.
```
Food method definition   • instance
```
name: aString name:= aString.
```
Food method definition   • instance
```
fCalories ^ fCalories
```
Food method definition   • instance
```
fCalories: aNumber fCalories := aNumber
```
Food method definition   • instance
```
cCalories ^ cCalories
```
Food method definition   • instance
```
cCalories: aNumber cCalories := aNumber
```

120

Food method definition ● instance

```
pCalories ^ pCalories
```

Food method definition ● instance

```
pCalories: aNumber pCalories := aNumber
```

Food method definition ● instance

```
initializeFrom: aFile
  | inputStream |
  inputStream := File pathName: aFile.
  self name: inputStream nextWord.
  self fCalories: inputStream nextWord asInteger.
  self cCalories: inputStream nextWord asInteger.
  self pCalories: inputStream nextWord asInteger.
  inputStream close.
  ^ self.
```

Workspace

```
Test := (Food new initializeFrom: 'c:\test\vtbls.dta').
Transcript show: Test name printString; cr;
          show: Test fCalories printString; cr;
          show: Test pCalories printString; cr;
          show: Test cCalories printString; cr.
```

Transcript

```
'Asparagus'
3
9
16
```

456 Once you know how to read one calorie description, you can, of course, write a method that reads a whole file full of calorie descriptions and stores them in an `OrderedCollection` instance. You know that every description has been read when the `nextWord` message, sent to the stream, answers `nil`.

Food method definition ● class

```
collectFrom: aFile
  |inputStream collection food|
  inputStream := File pathName: aFile.
  collection := OrderedCollection new.
  [(food := inputStream nextWord) notNil]
    whileTrue:
      [collection add:
          (Food new name: food;
            fCalories: inputStream nextWord asInteger;
            cCalories: inputStream nextWord asInteger;
            pCalories: inputStream nextWord asInteger)].
  inputStream close.
  ^ collection
```

457 Just as `pathName` creates an instance of the `FileStream` class that enables you to read from a file, `newFile:` creates a file stream that enables you to write into a new file or to

overwrite an existing file. In the following method fragment, the stream is assigned to a local variable, outputStream:

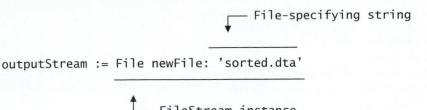

```
outputStream := File newFile: 'sorted.dta'
```

458 Once you have opened a file for output, you can write information into that file by sending nextPutAll: and cr messages to the stream. For example, the following writes the string 'Carrots', followed by a carriage return, into a file via outputStream:

```
outputStream nextPutAll: 'Carrots'; cr
```

459 Once you have finished writing information into a file, you should so indicate by sending a close message to the stream:

```
outputStream close.
```

460 Now, suppose that you have read information into an OrderedCollection instance using the method defined in Segment 456. You can convert that OrderedCollection instance into a SortedCollection instance in which the food descriptions are sorted by name. Then, you can arrange for each food to be written into a file, using asString, introduced in Segment 71, to convert calorie numbers into strings. Finally, you send a cr message to terminate the line:

Food method definition   • instance
```
printFoodLine: aStream
  aStream nextPutAll:
    name , ' ' ,
    fCalories asString , ' ' ,
    cCalories asString , ' ' ,
    pCalories asString ;
    cr
```

Food method definition   • class
```
outputFoods: foodCollection to: aFile
  | outputStream |
  outputStream := File newFile: aFile.
  foodCollection do:
    [:element | element printFoodLine: outputStream].
  outputStream close
```
Workspace
```
Food outputFoods: ((Food collectFrom: 'c:\test\vtbls.dta')
                  asSortedCollection: [:x :y | x name <= y name])
      to: 'c:\test\foods.srt'
```

122

The result, in the file \test\foods.srt, is as follows:

```
Broccoli 3 16 9
Cabbage 2 14 3
Carrots 1 33 4
Corn 1 23 6
```

461   You also can read and write individual characters using streams. To read a character, you send the **next** message to the stream:

```
inputStream next
```

To write a character into a file, you send the **nextPut:** message with a character argument:

```
outputStream nextPut: a character
```

462   In Smalltalk, **literal characters** are denoted by a $ prefix. Thus, to insert the character X into a stream, you send the following message:

```
outputStream nextPut: $X
```

463
SIDE TRIP   Of course, you need a way to denote the $ when you really want a $, rather than the escape character. Accordingly, Smalltalk allows you to mark the $ with the $ itself to denote $. That is, if you want to denote the $ character, you type $$.

464
SIDE TRIP   You cannot use the **nextWord** message to read floating-point numbers, because **nextWord** stops reading when it encounters a decimal point. Fortunately, you can define **nextNumber**, which reads numbers whether they are **Integer** instances or **Float** instances.

The following simple version of the **nextNumber** method uses **peek** to determine whether the first part of the number is followed by a decimal point; if so, it reads the rest, and uses **asFloat** to convert the concatenated parts:

```
Stream method definition          • instance
nextNumber
  | number fraction |
  number := self nextWord.
  self peek = $.
    ifTrue: [fraction := self nextWord.
              ^ (number , '.' , fraction) asFloat]
    ifFalse: [^ number asInteger]
```

465
SIDE TRIP   The simple version of **nextNumber** shown in Segment 464 is limited, because the numbers read cannot have either a sign or an exponent. You can, however, compose fancier number-reading methods using **peek** and **next** to read numbers character by character.

You need to know one trick to handle character-by-character reading. To determine the digit associated with a character, you send the **digitValue** message to that character, as in the following illustration:

```
         Workspace
Transcript show: $5 printString; cr;
          show: $5 digitValue printString; cr
         Transcript
$5
5
```

466
SIDE TRIP Other versions of Smalltalk include methods that do all the work for you. In VisualWorks, for example, you send readFrom: to the Number class with a stream argument. Then, readFrom: reads all the characters constituting the number from the stream, answering a number of the appropriate class.

467
PRACTICE Sometimes, names consist of multiple words, making it impracticable to rely entirely on nextWord to do all the reading that you need to do. Often, names are marked by **delimiters** on both ends, as in the following example, so that multiple words cause no problems:

```
'Raw Carrots' 1 33 4
'Broccoli' 3 16 9
'Corn on the Cob' 1 23 6
'Cooked Cabbage' 2 14 3
```

To deal with files containing such information, you need the upTo: message, which, when sent to a stream, answers with a string containing all the characters up to the next occurrence of the character provided as the argument. The argument character is absorbed, but is not included with the answer string. If the argument character does not exist in the rest of the stream, upTo: answers the remaining elements in the stream.

Define nextMarkedWord: using upTo: such that nextMarkedWord: answers the next sequence of characters delimited by the character provided as the argument. If there are no such marked characters, nextMarkedWord: is to answer nil.

468
PRACTICE Use nextMarkedWord:, which you defined in Segment 467, to rewrite the method shown in Segment 456 such that it reads files in which all food names are delimited with single quotation marks.

You can check to see whether there are any more characters in a stream by sending the stream the atEnd message, which answers true or false.

469
HIGHLIGHTS

- You communicate with files via input streams and output streams.

- **If** you want to open an input file for reading, **then** instantiate the following pattern:

  File pathName: 'file specification'

- **If** you want to open an output file for writing, **then** instantiate the following pattern:

  File newFile: 'file specification'

- **If** you are finished with an input or output stream, **then** you should close it by instantiating the following pattern:

  `stream close`

- **If** you want to read a whitespace-delimited `String` instance from a stream, **then** instantiate the following pattern:

  `stream nextWord`

- **If** you want to read an `Integer` instance from a stream, **then** instantiate the following pattern:

  `stream nextWord asInteger`

- **If** you want to read from a stream as long as it has wordlike strings to be read, **then** instantiate the following pattern:

  ```
  [(variable := stream nextWord) notNil]
     whileTrue: [appropriate statements].
  ```

- **If** you want to read a single character from a stream, **then** send the `next` message to the stream.

- **If** you want to write a string to a stream, **then** instantiate the following pattern:

  `stream nextPutAll: 'the characters in the string'`

- **If** you want to denote a character, **then** prefix the character with $, so that Smalltalk will not interpret the character as a variable name.

- **If** you want to write a character to a stream, **then** instantiate the following pattern:

  `stream nextPut: the character`

23 HOW TO WORK WITH CHARACTERS AND STRINGS

470 In this section, you learn how to extract vegetable information from a file that also contains dairy information. As you progress, you learn more about how to work with strings and characters.

471 Imagine that your data file has not only information about calories, but also code characters, with V indicating a Vegetable instance and D indicating a Dairy instance.

Further imagine that serving-size information is included, along with optional notes containing one or more words:

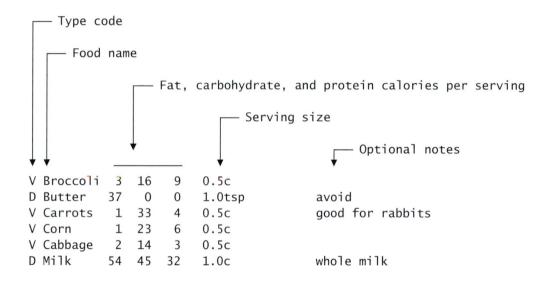

```
      Type code

        Food name

                    Fat, carbohydrate, and protein calories per serving

                        Serving size

                            Optional notes

V Broccoli  3   16   9   0.5c
D Butter   37   0    0   1.0tsp      avoid
V Carrots   1   33   4   0.5c        good for rabbits
V Corn      1   23   6   0.5c
V Cabbage   2   14   3   0.5c
D Milk     54   45   32  1.0c        whole milk
```

472 Because the number of wordlike strings varies, you should arrange to read such a file line by line. Fortunately, you can use nextLine, instead of nextWord, to read lines.

473 You can check to see whether there are any more characters in a stream by sending the stream the atEnd message, which answers true or false.

Because whitespace characters are characters, a stream with only whitespace characters answers true to atEnd.

474 Using nextLine and atEnd, you can arrange to read all the lines in a file. Note that the following definition of eatOnlyVegetables uses both methods, but does nothing with the lines other than to display them in the transcript:

```
eatOnlyVegetables: aFile
 |inputStream string|
 inputStream := File pathName: aFile.
 [inputStream atEnd]
  whileFalse:
   [Transcript show: (string := inputStream nextLine) printString; cr].
 inputStream close
```

Workspace

```
Food eatOnlyVegetables: 'c:\test\foods.dta'
```

Transcript

```
'V Broccoli  3  16   9   0.5c               '
'D Butter   37   0   0   1.0tsp         avoid'
'V Carrots   1  33   4   0.5c           good for rabbits'
'V Corn      1  23   6   0.5c'
'V Cabbage   2  14   3   0.5c'
'D Milk     54  45  32   1.0c           whole milk'
''
''
```

The first string happens to contain extra spaces after the last meaningful character. Also, there are two blank strings containing no characters.

475 Once you have a string, you can determine whether that string has no characters using the isEmpty or notEmpty predicates:

```
string isEmpty   ◄— Answers true if there are no characters.
string notEmpty  ◄— Answers true if there are characters.
```

476 Using notEmpty, you readily can weed out empty strings:

Food method definition   • class

```
eatOnlyVegetables: aFile
  |inputStream string |
  inputStream := File pathName: aFile.
  [inputStream atEnd]
   whileFalse:
    [(string := inputStream nextLine) notEmpty
      ifTrue: [Transcript show: string printString; cr]].
  inputStream close
```

Workspace

```
Food eatOnlyVegetables: 'c:\test\foods.dta'
```

Transcript

```
'V Broccoli  3  16   9   0.5c               '
'D Butter   37   0   0   1.0tsp         avoid'
'V Carrots   1  33   4   0.5c           good for rabbits'
'V Corn      1  23   6   0.5c'
'V Cabbage   2  14   3   0.5c'
'D Milk     54  45  32   1.0c           whole milk'
```

477   You cannot shorten or lengthen a string, but you can concatenate two strings to produce a new, longer string.

478   When you wish to extract a particular character from a string, you use the `at:` method, with the argument indicating the character that you wish to extract. A 1 argument indicates that you want the first character, because all string indexing is one based, as it is with arrays:

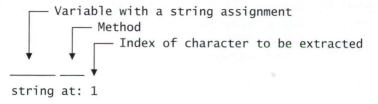

```
string at: 1
```

479   As you learned in Segment 462, you denote a particular character by prefixing that character with a $ prefix, thus distinguishing the character from, say, a variable name. For example, you denote the character *V* by writing $V.

If you want to see whether you have extracted a particular character, you compare what you have extracted with that character. Then, if you wish, you can build an `ifTrue:` expression on that comparison, as in the following example, which prints only those strings for which the first character is *V*:

```
Food method definition       • class
eatOnlyVegetables: aFile
   |inputStream string |
   inputStream := File pathName: aFile.
   [inputStream atEnd]
     whileFalse:
       [(string := inputStream nextLine) notEmpty
        ifTrue: [(string at: 1) = $V
                   ifTrue: [Transcript show: string printString; cr]]].
   inputStream close
       Workspace
Food eatOnlyVegetables: 'c:\test\foods.dta'
       Transcript
'V Broccoli  3  16   9    0.5c              '
'V Carrots   1  33   4    0.5c        good for rabbits'
'V Corn      1  23   6    0.5c'
'V Cabbage   2  14   3    0.5c'
```

480   Now, you know how to extract strings from a file and how to test particular characters. Next, you need to learn how to read information from the appropriate strings.

The simplest way to read information from a string is to covert it into a stream. Then, you can extract information from it using **nextWord**—the same method that you used before to extract information from a file stream.

In the following fragment, for example, the value of the variable, **stream**, is a stream that you produce by sending **asStream** to a string. With **stream**'s value established, you can use messages similar to those used in Segment 456 to extract the information needed to create a Food instance and to add that instance to a collection assigned to `collection`:

```
stream := string asStream.
stream nextWord.
collection add:
  (Food new name: stream nextWord;
    fCalories: stream nextWord asInteger;
    cCalories: stream nextWord asInteger;
    pCalories: stream nextWord asInteger.
```

The fragment skips over the type code and ignores everything in the string after the protein-calories number.

481 Thus, the following version of `eatOnlyVegetables` extracts name and calorie information for the vegetables found in the `foods.dta` file. Then, `eatOnlyVegetables` creates Food instances for those vegetables, and adds those Food instances to an ordered collection. That ordered collection is the answer produced by `eatOnlyVegetables`:

```
Food method definition        • class
eatOnlyVegetables: aFile
  |inputStream collection string stream |
  inputStream := File pathName: aFile.
  collection := OrderedCollection new.
  [inputStream atEnd]
    whileFalse:
      [(string := inputStream nextLine) notEmpty
       ifTrue:
         [(string at: 1) = $V
             ifTrue: [stream := string asStream.
                      stream nextWord.
                      collection add:
                        (Food new name: stream nextWord;
                          fCalories: stream nextWord asInteger;
                          cCalories: stream nextWord asInteger;
                          pCalories: stream nextWord asInteger)]]].
  inputStream close.
  ^ collection
```
```
      Workspace
(Food eatOnlyVegetables: 'c:\test\foods.dta')
  do: [ :element | Transcript show: element name printString; cr].
      Transcript
'Broccoli'
'Carrots'
'Corn'
'Cabbage'
```

130

Occasionally, you need to specify various special characters. You can specify the space character, straightforwardly, as $. Alternatively, you can specify the space character, and several others, by accessing the `CharacterConstants` dictionary with various strings:

String	Character value
'Space'	space
'Tab'	tab
'Cr'	carriage return
'Lf'	line feed
'Ff'	form feed
'Bs'	backspace

For example, if you need the tab character, you can fetch it from the `CharacterConstants` dictionary via the following expression:

```
CharacterConstants at: 'Tab'
```

Modify the definition shown in Segment 481 such that no food information is ignored. Instead, vegetable information is to create instances of the `Vegetable` class; `dairy` information is to create instances of the `Dairy` class.

Modify the definition shown in Segment 481 such that, if there is no one-character food-type indicator, the food is presumed to be a vegetable, but a warning message is displayed in the transcript.

- You cannot add characters to a string or delete characters from a string.

- If you want a read an entire line from a file stream, **then** instantiate the following pattern:

  `stream` nextLine

- If you want to determine a stream is empty, **then** instantiate the following pattern:

  `stream` atEnd

- If you want to determine whether a string is empty, then instantiate one of the following patterns:

  `string` isEmpty
  `string` notEmpty

- If you want to extract a character from a string, **then** instantiate the following pattern:

  `string` at: `index`

- **If** you want to read information from a string as though it were a stream, **then** instantiate the following pattern to produce a stream, **and then** read from the stream using, for example, `nextWord`.

```
string asStream
```

486 Because you are expected to use the features of a graphical user interface to display information on a screen, most Smalltalk implementations do not offer any methods for displaying formatted text on the transcript or for writing formatted text to a file.

Fortunately, Smalltalk provides all the tools that you need to write your own formatting methods easily. Read this section only if you need to use those tools.

487 Generally, doing formatted display and formatted writing means writing information into **fields** of prescribed width.

Suppose, for example, that you want to define a method, `formatWithWidth:`, for strings, such that `formatWithWidth:` produces a string whose length is equal to a prescribed field width. Your method is to add **padding** spaces on the left. In the following example, `formatWithWidth:` produces a string of length 10; the string is concatenated with vertical bars so as to make the presence of the spaces clear:

```
      Workspace
Transcript show: '|' , ('Broccoli' formatWithWidth: 10) , '|'
      Transcript
|  Broccoli|
```

488 You can determine the width of a string using the `size` method:

```
      Workspace
Transcript show: 'Broccoli' size printString
      Transcript
8
```

489 You can create a string of a given width by using the `new:` method. For example, the following expression creates a `String` instance of length 3:

```
String new: 3
```

Next, you can fill a string with spaces using the `atAllPut:` method.

```
      Workspace
(String new: 3) atAllPut: $
```

↑
└── Space

490 Evidently, to produce a string of a prescribed length from a given string, you determine how many padding characters you need, you create a new string filled with that number of padding characters, and you concatenate the new string with the given string. All these steps are expressed in the following definition of the `formatWithWidth:` method:

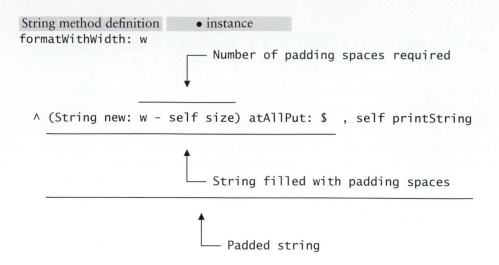

String method definition   • instance

```
formatWithWidth: w
```

— Number of padding spaces required

```
∧ (String new: w - self size) atAllPut: $   , self printString
```

— String filled with padding spaces

— Padded string

491   Of course, the version of formatWithWidth: defined in Segment 490 crashes in the event the prescribed width is less than the length of the given string. Accordingly, you should test the length of the given string, and, if it is too big, produce a string of the prescribed length filled with * characters. Filling the field with * characters is the standard way of informing human readers that you made an attempt to squeeze a too-large item into a too-narrow space:

String method definition   • instance

```
formatWithWidth: w
  self size <= w
    ifTrue: [∧ ((String new: w - self size) atAllPut: $ )   , self]
    ifFalse: [∧ (String new: w) atAllPut: $*]
```

492   Once you have defined formatWithWidth: for strings, you can define formatWithWidth: for numbers. All you need to do is to convert the number to a string, using asString, and then to activate the formatWithWidth: method:

Number method definition   • instance

```
formatWithWidth: w
  ∧ self asString formatWithWidth: w
```

493   Defining a formatting method for Float instances is a little more involved, because you usually want to specify not only the field width, but also the number of digits to follow the decimal point. Accordingly, you might want to define a method with an argument, formatWithWidth:andFraction:, with the andFraction: argument controlling the number of post–decimal-point digits.

494 To implement the `formatWithWidth:andFraction:` method, you need the `truncated` method. Whenever it is sent to a `Float` instance, the `truncated` method answers with an `Integer` instance equal to the truncated `Float` instance:

> Workspace
> ```
> Transcript show: 3.14159 truncated printString
> ```
> Transcript
> ```
> 3
> ```

Using `truncated` and `abs`, the method that produces the absolute value of a number, you can produce the fraction portion of a floating-point number:

```
Transcript show: (3.14159 truncated - 3.14159) abs printString; cr;
          show: (-3.14159 truncated - -3.14159) abs printString; cr
```
> Transcript
> ```
> 0.14159
> 0.14159
> ```

495 Now, you can assemble part of a string with the correct characteristics by first converting the truncated `Float` instance to a string:

```
self truncated printString , '.'
```

Then, to add the post–decimal-point digits, you repeatedly multiply the fractional part by 10 to push the required fractional digits to the left of the decimal point:

```
fraction := (self - self truncated) abs.
f timesRepeat: [fraction := 10 * fraction.
              ↑].
```
↑
└─ argument of andFraction:

Then, truncating the result, taking the absolute value, and converting to a string produces a digit ready for concatenation:

```
fraction := (self - self truncated) abs.
f timesRepeat: [fraction := 10 * fraction.
              string := string , fraction truncated printString.
              ↑].
```

496 All that remains is to package what you have learned so far and to ensure that the resulting string is not too wide:

```
formatWithWidth: w andFraction: f
  | string fraction |
  fraction := (self - self truncated) abs.
  string := self truncated printString , '.'.
  f timesRepeat: [fraction := 10 * fraction.
                  string := string , fraction truncated printString.
                  fraction := fraction - fraction truncated].
  string size <= w
    ifTrue: [^ ((String new: w - string size) atAllPut: $ ) , string]
    ifFalse: [^ (String new: w) atAllPut: $*]
```

Workspace

```
Transcript show: '|'
                  , (547.08988 formatWithWidth: 8 andFraction: 2)
                  , '|'
                  , (-547.08988 formatWithWidth: 8 andFraction: 2)
                  , '|'
                  , (5470898.8 formatWithWidth: 8 andFraction: 2)
                  , '|'
```

Transcript

```
|  547.08| -547.08|********|
```

497   Using what you have learned in this section, you can amend the program shown in Segment 460 by redefining `printFoodLine:` to produce aligned output:

Food method definition   • instance

```
printFoodLine: aStream
  aStream nextPutAll:
    (name formatWithWidth: 10)      , ' ' ,
    (fCalories formatWithWidth: 5) , ' ' ,
    (cCalories formatWithWidth: 5) , ' ' ,
    (pCalories formatWithWidth: 5);
    cr
```

Workspace

```
Food outputFoods:
      ((Food collectFrom: 'c:\test\vtbls.dta')
         asSortedCollection: [:x :y | x fCalories <= y fCalories])
      to: 'c:\test\foods.tab'
```

The result, in the file `\test\foods.tab`, is as follows:

```
  Broccoli      3      16      9
   Cabbage      2      14      3
   Carrots      1      33      4
      Corn      1      23      6
```

498   Amend the definition of `formatWithWidth:` for strings such that a positive argument
PRACTICE   places the padding on the left and a negative argument places the padding on the right.

- **If** you want to control display spacing, **then** you must implement methods that format strings, integers, and floating-point numbers according to your desires.

- **If** you want to determine the length of a string, **then** send the `size` message.

- **If** you want to create a new string of a specified length, **then** use the `new:` method.

- **If** you want to fill a string with a specified character, **then** send the `atAllPut:` method.

- **If** you want to convert a `Float` instance into an `Integer` instance representing the truncated float, **then** send `truncated`.

25 HOW TO USE SORTED COLLECTIONS IN SIMULATIONS

500 In Section 17, you learned about a mathematical formula that determines how fast rabbits multiply, and you examined an `Integer` method that embodies that formula.

Sometimes, however, individual behavior may be so complex so as to defy easy mathematical analysis. In such situations, you may choose to **model** the characteristics of the **individuals** that constitute a **system** so that you can **simulate** the **events** that determine system behavior. In this section, you learn how to model rabbit behavior to simulate growth in a rabbit population.

501 The state of an individual female rabbit is determined by the month of her next delivery of a baby rabbit, expressed as an integer. To model an individual, you define the `Rabbit` class so as to include an instance variable that records the next month that the rabbit will deliver a new baby rabbit:

Rabbit class definition
```
Object subclass: #Rabbit
  instanceVariableNames: 'deliveryMonth'
  classVariableNames: ''
  poolDictionaries: ''
```

When you simulate the growth of a population of rabbits, there will be just one rabbit instance at first, born at month 0.

502 The behavior of rabbits is determined by the characteristics you learned about in Segment 324:

- Female rabbits mature 1 month after birth.
- Once they mature, female rabbits have one female child each month.
- At the beginning of the first month, there is one immature female rabbit.
- Rabbits live forever.
- There are always enough males on hand to mate with all the mature females.

Evidently, the delivery month of a rabbit born at month 0 is month 2, because it takes 1 month to mature and then 1 more month to produce a new baby.

503 To model rabbit behavior, you need to define setter and getter methods for the delivery month: the `deliveryMonth:` method sets the month of delivery for a rabbit; and the `deliveryMonth` method gets the month of delivery:

Rabbit method definition   • instance
```
deliveryMonth: anInteger
  deliveryMonth := anInteger
```
Rabbit method definition   • instance
```
deliveryMonth
  ^ deliveryMonth
```

504 As suggested in Segment 324, the growth of the rabbit population is proportional to the number of females because there are always enough males on hand to mate with all the mature females. Hence, the simulation ignores male-rabbit production.

505 Using the deliveryMonth and deliveryMonth: methods, you can define bear, a method that answers with a daughter rabbit after setting the daughter rabbit's first delivery month and the mother rabbit's next delivery month:

Rabbit method definition   • instance

```
bear
   | daughter |
   daughter := Rabbit new.
   daughter deliveryMonth: (self deliveryMonth) + 2.
   self deliveryMonth: (self deliveryMonth) + 1.
   ^ daughter
```

506 Next, you are ready to define a class, RabbitApplication, to help you keep track of the simulated rabbit population.

There will be just one RabbitApplication instance, and, from the definition of the RabbitApplication class, you see that the one RabbitApplication instance contains just one instance variable: rabbits. The rabbits instance variable determines the state of the RabbitApplication instance.

RabbitApplication class definition

```
Object subclass: #RabbitApplication
   instanceVariableNames: 'rabbits'
   classVariableNames: ''
   poolDictionaries: ''
```

Two RabbitApplication instance methods are to be defined. One, the initialize method, initializes rabbit simulations; the other, the tickTo: method, executes rabbit simulations for a specified number of steps.

507 When you create a RabbitApplication instance, you need to initialize that instance such that the value of the rabbits variable is a SortedCollection instance that is sorted according to the delivery months of the rabbits. The rabbit with the earliest delivery month will always be at the front:

RabbitApplication method definition   • instance

```
initialize
   rabbits := SortedCollection
               sortBlock:
               [:x :y | x deliveryMonth < y deliveryMonth].
   rabbits add: (Rabbit new deliveryMonth: 2)
```

Note that initialize inserts exactly one Rabbit instance, born at month 0, into the sorted collection assigned to the rabbits instance variable.

140

508 The `rabbits` sorted collection is an example of an **event queue** because the elements correspond to events that are arranged by the times that those events will occur. Specifically, each element corresponds to forthcoming baby-rabbit–delivery events.

509 Event queues allow you to simulate a sequence of events by way of the following recipe:

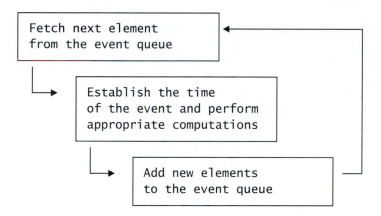

510 To capture the event-queue simulation recipe, you define `step`, a `RabbitApplication` instance method.

Because the `Rabbit` instance that has the earliest delivery month is always at the front of the `rabbits` collection, `step` can obtain that `Rabbit` instance by sending the `removeFirst` message, which both removes the `Rabbit` instance from the collection and makes the `Rabbit` instance available for assignment to the `mother` instance variable:

RabbitApplication method definition   • instance
```
step
  | mother daughter |
  mother := rabbits removeFirst.
  ...
```

511 Now, it is an easy matter to create a new daughter rabbit from the mother rabbit using `bear`, which was defined in Segment 505:

RabbitApplication method definition   • instance
```
step
  | mother daughter |
  mother := rabbits removeFirst.
  daughter := mother bear.
  ...
```

512 The final task in `step` is to reinsert the mother back into the event queue and to insert the daughter into the event queue:

```
step
    | mother daughter |
    mother := rabbits removeFirst.
    daughter := mother bear.
    rabbits add: mother.
    rabbits add: daughter
```

513   The step method removes the mother from the event queue, and then reinserts that mother
       after she bears a daughter, because bear changes her next delivery month. The reinsertion
       ensures that the mother is in the proper place in the event queue after the change.

514   In this and the next several segments, you learn what happens to the individual rabbits
       in the event queue as step messages are sent. To keep track of the individual rabbits,
       you label them with letters and next delivery months. Just after the RabbitApplication
       instance is created, there is just one rabbit, A, which will deliver at the end of the second
       month:

       Initial event queue

515   Before you send the first step message, rabbit A is scheduled to deliver at the end of the
       second month; after the first step message is processed, rabbit A is scheduled to deliver at
       the end of the third month, and a new rabbit, B, is scheduled to deliver at the end of the
       forth month. Hence, the event queue is as follows:

       Event queue after one step

       | A:3 | B:4 |

516   As you send subsequent step messages. the event queue evolves as follows:

       Event queue after two steps

       | A:4 | B:4 | C:5 |

       Event queue after three steps

       | B:4 | A:5 | C:5 | D:6 |

       Event queue after four steps

       | B:5 | A:5 | C:5 | E:6 | D:6 |

Event queue after five steps

A:5	C:5	B:6	E:6	D:6	F:7

Event queue after six steps

C:5	A:6	B:6	E:6	D:6	G:7	F:7

517   Of course, to simulate the events that occur up to a specified month, you need a method that sends `step` messages until the next scheduled delivery month is later than the current month. Accordingly, you define the `tickTo:` message:

RabbitApplication method definition   • instance
```
tickTo: limit
  [rabbits first deliveryMonth <= limit]
    whileTrue: [self step].
```

518   Once you have defined `tickTo:`, you can create an instance of the `RabbitApplication` class, initialize that instance, and simulate all the steps that occur before, say, the twelfth month:

Workspace
```
RabbitApplication new initialize tickTo: 12
```

519   At this point, you have all the simulation machinery defined, but you need to add machinery to report simulation results.

There are, of course, many approaches. The approach described in the next several segments produces an ordered collection in which each element is an integer that indicates the number of rabbits after a number of months equal to the integer's position in the collection.

520   To enable reporting, you first modify the `RabbitApplication` class and the `initialize` method to include and initialize two additional instance variables.

The `month` variable is to keep track of the current month in the simulation; the `history` variable is to keep track of the number of rabbits after each month has passed, starting with month 0. Key changes are marked by change bars, ▮.

RabbitApplication class definition
```
Object subclass: #RabbitApplication
  instanceVariableNames: 'rabbits month history'        ▮
  classVariableNames: ''
  poolDictionaries: ''
```

```
initialize
  month := 0.
  history := OrderedCollection new.
  rabbits := SortedCollection
            sortBlock:
            [:x :y | x deliveryMonth < y deliveryMonth].
  rabbits add: (Rabbit new deliveryMonth: 2)
```

521 Next, you need to implement a method, updateMonth, which increments the month whenever the value of the month instance variable is different from the delivery month associated with the first element on the event queue. Also, updateMonth adds a count of the rabbits to the history ordered collection whenever the month changes:

RabbitApplication method definition   ● instance

```
updateMonth
  [month < rabbits first deliveryMonth]
    whileTrue: [history addLast: rabbits size.
                month := month + 1]
```

522 Finally, tickTo: must send the updateMonth message to check the month variable just before each step message is sent; and also, tickTo: must report the value of the history variable, using printOrderedCollectionValues, when all work is done:

RabbitApplication method definition   ● instance

```
tickTo: limit
  [month <= limit]
    whileTrue: [self updateMonth. self step].
  history printOrderedCollectionValues
```

OrderedCollection method definition   ● instance

```
printOrderedCollectionValues
  self do: [:element | Transcript show: element printString; space].
  Transcript cr
```

523 Now, with all additions in place, you can test the result:

Workspace
```
RabbitApplication new initialize tickTo: 12
```
Transcript
```
1 1 2 3 5 8 13 21 34 55 89 144 233
```

524 The rabbits simulation illustrates typical application construction: Smalltalk applications typically are built around an **application instance**, which is the sole instance of an **application class**. The application instance typically has two roles:

- The application instance holds onto the application's key values via instance variables.

- The application instance is the receiver of one or more messages that establish initial variable values and launch the application.

The rabbit-simulation application developed in this section is centered on an instance of the RabbitApplication class, which contains rabbits, month, and history instance variables. The initialize and tickTo: messages initialize variable values and launch the application. The argument supplied with the tickTo: message specifies how much time is to be simulated.

525
SIDE TRIP Application instance responsibilities are a subset of the view-manager instance responsibilities described in Section 32. In addition to the responsibilities described here for application instances, view-manager instances must deal with the chores associated with graphical user interfaces.

526
PRACTICE As given in Segment 523, the implementations of the initialize and bear methods duplicate knowledge about gestation time and the time required for a rabbit to reach maturity. Create class variables, getters, and setters for the Rabbit class such that gestation and maturity numbers reside in just one place.

527
PRACTICE Smalltalk Express does not come equipped with a **random-number generator**, but you can implement a simple random-number generator with the following, which is adapted from *Smalltalk-80: The Language*, by Adele Goldberg and David Robson (Addison-Wesley, 1989); it, in turn, is based on Lehmer's linear congruential method, described in *The Art of Computer Programming: Fundamental Algorithms, Volume 1*, by Donald Knuth (Addison-Wesley, 1968).

The random numbers vary uniformly from 0.0, exclusively, to 1.0 exclusively. The new: method takes an integer argument that provides a starting point for the generation of random numbers, so that you are not stuck with the same sequence of random numbers each time that you create an instance of the Random class. The bitAnd: method peforms bit-by-bit logic on integers:

```
Random class definition
Object subclass: #Random
  instanceVariableNames: 'seed'
  classVariableNames: ''
  poolDictionaries: ''
Random method definition       • class
new: arg ^ super new initialize: arg.
Random method definition       • instance
initialize: x  seed := x.
Random method definition       • instance
next
  | handle |
  [seed := 13849 + (27181 * seed) bitAnd: 65535.
   handle := seed / 65536.0.
   handle = 0]
    whileTrue: [].
  ^ handle.
```

Now, using an instance of the Random class assigned to Generator, a global variable, you define a method, deliveryInterval that produces random numbers distributed between 0.75 and 1.25.

528
PRACTICE Assume that the time between the deliveries of a female rabbit varies uniformly from 0.75 months to 1.25 months. Revise the program shown in Segment 523 such that the rabbits have a random delivery interval.

529
HIGHLIGHTS

- **If** you want to simulate a sequence of events, **then** create an event queue by sending a `sortBlock:` message to `SortedCollection`, initializing that event queue, and looping through the following recipe:

  - Fetch next element from the event queue.

  - Establish the time of the event and perform computations appropriate to the event.

  - Add new elements to the event queue.

- Smalltalk applications typically are built around an instance of an **application class**. That instance provides application-controlling instance variables and serves as an application-launching receiver.

26 HOW TO WORK WITH DATES AND TIMES

530 In this section, you learn about Smalltalk's rich assortment of methods for dealing with the Time and Date classes. Then, you see how to redo the rabbit simulation using date objects instead of integer objects.

531 To obtain an object representing the current time, you send a now message to the Time class:

```
Time now
```

To obtain an object representing a specific time, you send a fromSeconds: message in which the argument is the number of seconds past midnight for which you want the time:

```
Time fromSeconds: 40271
```

532 Once you have a Time instance, you can send that instance hour, minute, second messages.

```
    Workspace
TimeHandle := Time fromSeconds: 40271.
Transcript show: TimeHandle printString; cr;
          show: TimeHandle hours printString; cr;
          show: TimeHandle minutes printString; cr;
          show: TimeHandle seconds printString
    Transcript
11:11:11
11
11
11
```

533 You can add or subtract Time instances using the addTime: and subtractTime: methods:

```
    Workspace
Time1 := Time fromSeconds: 40271.
Time2 := Time fromSeconds: 3600.
Transcript show: Time1 printString; cr;
          show: Time2 printString; cr;
          show: (Time1 addTime: Time2) printString; cr;
          show: (Time1 subtractTime: Time2) printString; cr;
          show: (Time2 subtractTime: Time1) printString; cr
    Transcript
11:11:11
01:00:00
12:11:11
10:11:11
13:48:49
```

534   You can compare Time instances:

```
Time1 := Time fromSeconds: 40271.
Time2 := Time fromSeconds: 3600.
Transcript show: (Time1 = Time1) printString; cr;
          show: (Time1 = Time2) printString; cr;
          show: (Time2 < Time1) printString; cr;
          show: (Time1 < Time2) printString
```
```
true
false
true
false
```

535   To obtain an object representing the current date, you send a today message to the Date class:

```
Date today
```

To obtain an object representing a specific day in a specific month of a specific year, you send a newDay:monthNumber:year: message:

```
Date newDay: 1 monthNumber: 1 year: 2000
```

536   Once you have a Date instance, you can send that instance day and year messages. The day message answers with the number of days since January 1, 1901:

```
DateHandle := Date newDay: 36 year: 2000.
Transcript show: DateHandle printString; cr;
          show: DateHandle year printString; cr;
          show: DateHandle day printString; cr
```
```
Feb  5, 2000
2000
36194
```

537   You can also extract the day of the week and the month name:

```
DateHandle := Date newDay: 36 year: 2000.
Transcript show: DateHandle printString; cr;
          show: DateHandle dayName printString; cr;
          show: DateHandle monthName printString
```
```
Feb  5, 2000
Saturday
February
```

538   You can add or subtract a specified number of days to a **Date** instance, and you can determine the number of days between two **Date** instances:

```
      Workspace
Date1 := Date newDay: 1 year: 2000.
Date2 := Date1 addDays: 30.
DateHandle3 := Date1 subtractDays: 30.
Transcript show: Date1 printString; cr;
          show: Date2 printString; cr;
          show: DateHandle3 printString; cr;
          show: (Date2 subtractDate: DateHandle3) printString
      Transcript
Jan  1, 2000
Jan 31, 2000
Dec  2, 1999
60
```

539   You can compare **Date** instances, just as you can compare **time** instances:

```
      Workspace
Date1 := Date newDay: 1 year: 2000.
Date2 := DateHandle addDays: 30.
Transcript show: (Date1 = Date1) printString; cr;
          show: (Date1 = Date2) printString; cr;
          show: (Date1 < Date2) printString; cr;
          show: (Date2 < Date1) printString
      Transcript
true
false
true
false
```

540   Instances that can be said to be less than, equal to, or greater than one another are said to be **magnitudes**. Thus, times and dates are magnitudes, and, like the **Number** class, the **Time** and **Date** classes are direct subclasses of the **Magnitude** class.

On the other hand, many arithmetic operations make no sense when used with dates and times. For example, neither can you multiply a **Date** instance times an integer, nor can you raise a **Time** instance to a power:

```
      Workspace
Date today * 3            ◀—— Message not understood
      Workspace
Time now raisedTo: 8      ◀—— Message not understood
```

541   Once you understand dates, you can revise the rabbit-simulation program, shown in Segment 523, to use **Date** instances, rather than **Integer** instances. Each revision is marked by a change bar, ▮, except the changes in variable names from month orientation to date

orientation. Note that the principal changes are the replacement of 0 by Date today and the replacement of + 1 and + 2 by addDays: 30 and addDays: 60.

Rabbit class definition
```
Object subclass: #Rabbit
  instanceVariableNames: 'deliveryDate'
  classVariableNames: ''
  poolDictionaries: ''
```
Rabbit method definition   • instance
```
deliveryDate: aDate deliveryDate := aDate
```
Rabbit method definition   • instance
```
deliveryDate ^ deliveryDate
```
RabbitApplication class definition
```
Object subclass: #RabbitApplication
  instanceVariableNames: 'rabbits date history'
  classVariableNames: ''
  poolDictionaries: ''
```
RabbitApplication method definition   • instance
```
initialize
  date := Date today.
  history := OrderedCollection new.
  rabbits := SortedCollection
            sortBlock: [:x :y | x deliveryDate < y deliveryDate].
  rabbits add: (Rabbit new deliveryDate: (Date today addDays: 60))
```
RabbitApplication method definition   • instance
```
step
  | mother daughter currentDate |
  mother := rabbits removeFirst.
  daughter := Rabbit new.
  currentDate := mother deliveryDate.
  mother deliveryDate: (currentDate addDays: 30).
  daughter deliveryDate: (currentDate addDays: 60).
  rabbits add: mother.
  rabbits add: daughter.
```
RabbitApplication method definition   • instance
```
tickTo: limit
  [date <= limit]
    whileTrue: [self updateDate. self step].
  history printOrderedCollectionValues
```
RabbitApplication method definition   • instance
```
updateDate
  [date < rabbits first deliveryDate]
    whileTrue: [history addLast: rabbits size.
              date := date addDays: 30]
```
OrderedCollection method definition   • instance
```
printOrderedCollectionValues
  self do: [:element | Transcript show: element printString; space].
  Transcript cr
```

```
RabbitApplication new initialize tickTo: (Date today addDays: 12 * 30)
```
```
1 1 2 3 5 8 13 21 34 55 89 144 233
```

542
PRACTICE

Write `stopwatch:` a class method for the `Time` class that prints `Time is up` in the transcript when the number of seconds indicated by the argument have elapsed. You may find it helpful to use `totalSeconds`, a class method that answers the number of seconds past midnight when sent to the `Time` class, and `fromSeconds:`, described in Segment 531.

543
PRACTICE

Write a class method for the `Time` class that prints the time in the transcript every 5 seconds.

544
HIGHLIGHTS

- If you want to create a new `Time` instance, **then** instantiate one of the following patterns:

```
Time now
Time fromSeconds: seconds past midnight
```

- If you want to extract hours, minutes, or seconds from a `Time` instance, **then** instantiate one of the following patterns:

```
Time instance hours
Time instance minutes
Time instance seconds
```

- If you want to add or subtract `Time` instances, then instantiate one of the following patterns:

```
Time instance addTime: another Time instance
Time instance subtractTime: another Time instance
```

- If you want to compare `Time` instances, then instantiate one of the following patterns:

```
Time instance = another Time instance
Time instance < another Time instance
```

- If you want to create a new `Date` instance, **then** instantiate one of the following patterns:

```
Date today
Date newDay: day in year (an integer)
      year: year (an integer)
```

- If you want to extract integer information from a `Date` instance, **then** instantiate one of the following patterns:

  ```
  Date instance day
  Date instance year
  ```

- If you want to extract information from a `Date` instance, **then** instantiate one of the following patterns:

  ```
  Date instance dayName
  Date instance monthName
  ```

- If you want to add or subtract a specified number of days from a `Date` instance, then instantiate one of the following patterns:

  ```
  Date instance addDays: Integer instance
  Date instance subtractDays: Integer instance
  ```

- If you want to compare `Date` instances, then instantiate one of the following patterns:

  ```
  Date instance = another Date instance
  Date instance < another Date instance
  ```

27 HOW TO DEFINE BINARY METHODS

545   In this segment, you learn how to define binary methods and you learn how to define your own numberlike classes.

In particular, you learn how to define a `Weight` class, so that you represent weight quantities explicitly, using `Weight` instances, rather than implicitly, using instances of one of the number classes. The `Weight` class has some numberlike properties, such as answering to magnitude-comparison, addition, and subtraction methods, buts lack others, such as answering to exponentiation methods. Thus, the `Weight` class is reminiscent of the built-in `Time` and `Date` classes, which you learned about in Section 26.

546   You define binary methods in the same way you define unary and keyword methods. Binary methods are distinguished only in that they have names corresponding to arithmetic operations and comparisons, such as + and <=.

547   Because you can define your own binary methods, you can create new numberlike object classes. For example, you can create a `Weight` class for representing weights. Once you have defined such a class, you do not need to use ordinary `Number` instances for weights; instead, you can use `Weight` instances, and can perform calculations using those instances as receivers, such as the following, in which `gm` is an abbreviation for **grams**:

```
3gm + 2gm        ← Answers 5gm
3gm < 2gm        ← Answers false
```

548   First, you need to define the `Weight` class as a subclass of the `Magnitude` class so that methods, such as `max:` and `min:`, are inherited from the `Magnitude` class.

The `Weight` class has but one instance variable, `magnitude`:

> Weight class definition
```
Magnitude subclass: #Weight
  instanceVariableNames: 'magnitude'
  classVariableNames: ''
  poolDictionaries: ''
```

549   The getter for the `magnitude` instance variable is the `magnitude` method:

> Weight method definition   • instance
```
magnitude
  ^ magnitude
```

There is no corresponding setter because you cannot change the value of a `Weight` instance, just as you cannot change the value of, for example, an `Integer` instance.

550   To construct new instances, you depart from normal practice by sending a `gm` message to an instance of the `Number` class, instead of sending a `new` message to the `Weight` class.

The number, which may be an `Integer`, `Float`, or `Fraction` instance, then sends a `new` message to the `Weight` class, which produces and initializes an instance:

```
gm
   ^ Weight new initialize: self
```
```
initialize: aNumber
   magnitude := aNumber
```

Using `gm`, you create new instances with expressions that look like denominate numbers. For example, 3gm is actually an expression that creates a new instance of the `Weight` class with 3 as the value of the `magnitude` instance variable.

551   There is no danger that Smalltalk will think that 3gm is an variable named 3gm, rather than a `gm` message sent to 3, even though there is no space between the 3 and the g, because variable names are not allowed to begin with integers.

552   So that you can display `Weight` instances that have the same look as those you type, you define a `printOn:` instance method for the `Weight` class, thereby overriding the definition of the `printOn:` instance method provided for the `Object` class.

```
printOn: aStream
   aStream nextPutAll: magnitude asString , 'gm'
```

Redefining the `printOn:` method changes the result produced by `printString` because the `printString` method uses `printOn:` to do the work of producing a string.

553   The proper approach is to define `printOn:`, rather than `printString`, for the `Weight` class, because the `printOn:` method not only helps `printString` to produce strings, but also helps other methods. Defining `printString` would fail to bring the behavior of those other methods into a state that is consistent with the behavior exhibited by the newly defined `printString`.

554   Next, you define an addition method that adds `Weight` instances. That new method works by first adding the magnitudes and then creating a new instance with the sum as that new instance's magnitude:

```
+ aWeight
   ^ (self magnitude + aWeight magnitude) gm
```

555   Finally, you define a method for comparison:

```
< aWeight
   ^ (self magnitude < aWeight magnitude)
```

556   Now you are ready to bring together all the fragments for testing:

```
Weight class definition
Magnitude subclass: #Weight
  instanceVariableNames: 'magnitude'
  classVariableNames: ''
  poolDictionaries: ''
```

```
Weight method definition        • instance
magnitude
  ^ magnitude
```

```
Number method definition        • instance
gm
  ^ Weight new initialize: self
```

```
Weight method definition        • instance
initialize: aNumber
  magnitude := aNumber
```

```
Weight method definition        • instance
printOn: aStream
  aStream nextPutAll: magnitude asString , 'gm'
```

```
Weight method definition        • instance
+ aWeight
  ^ (self magnitude + aWeight magnitude) gm
```

```
Weight method definition        • instance
< aWeight
  ^ (self magnitude < aWeight magnitude)
```

```
        Workspace
Transcript show: 3gm printString; cr;
          show: (3gm + 2gm) printString; cr;
          show: (3gm < 2gm) printString; cr
```

```
        Transcript
3gm
5gm
false
```

557   Implement -, *, and / methods for weights such that your methods can handle the following
PRACTICE   examples:

```
3gm - 2gm        ←— Answers 1gm
3gm * 2          ←— Answers 6gm
3gm / 2          ←— Answers (3/2)gm
```

558   Explain why it would be more difficult to implement a method to handle 2 * 3gm than to
PRACTICE   implement a method to handle 3gm * 2.

559   Add >, <=, and >= methods to the weight class. Define all three methods in terms of the <
PRACTICE   method.

560   In Smalltalk Express, Transcript is a global variable bound to an instance of a class.
PRACTICE   Implement <<, a binary method that prints its argument in the text window provided as

the receiver. Using <<, you can write display expressions that resemble those used in C++, such as the following:

```
    Workspace
Transcript << 2 << ' + ' << 2 << ' = ' << (2 + 2)
    Transcript
2 + 2 = 4
```

- **If** you want to define a binary method for a particular class, **then** define that binary method by instantiating the following instance-method pattern:

  name anArgument
  . . .

- **If** you want to define a new numberlike class, **then** define the class to be a subclass of the `Magnitude` class, **and then** implement an instance-creation method with a name that mimics the ordinary word or abbreviation used to denote the units involved, **and then** implement the appropriate binary methods.

28 HOW TO USE DEBUGGING TOOLS

562   When a program crashes, you need access to information. You might want to know which method Smalltalk was evaluating when the crash occurred, or the class in which that method is defined, or the sequence of messages that led up to the evaluation of that method, or the values of various parameters and variables in that method; or you might want to start over and step slowly through program evaluation. Smalltalk's debugging system readily delivers all such information to you, making that debugging system one of the special strengths of the language.

563   You use the definition of + provided in Segment 554 to add together two weights, as in the expression 3gm + 2gm.

To illustrate Smalltalk's debugging capabilities, suppose that you intentionally omit the second gm message:

3gm + 2

You attempt to evaluate the expression by selecting it and clicking **right→Show It**; you see a **walkback window**:

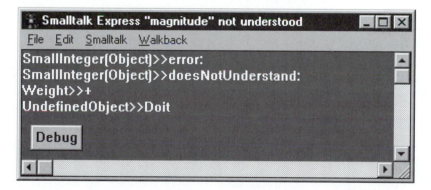

564   At first, the information in the walkback window may seem intimidating because several lines describe messages sent by Smalltalk in the course of handling the error. Do not despair. Instead, zero in on the line containing +. That line tells you that the receiver–message combinations that lead to the error report include a + message sent to a Weight instance:

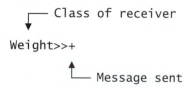

565   Similarly, the line containing doesNotUnderstand: tells you that the receiver–message combinations leading to the error report includes a doesNotUnderstand: message sent to a SmallInteger instance.

157

The line also tells you, via the name inside the parentheses, that no doesNotUnderstand: method is defined in the SmallInteger class, but the SmallInteger instance inherits a doesNoteUnderstand defined in the Object class:

┌─ Class from which doesNotUnderstand:
│ method is inherited
▼

SmallInteger(Object)>>doesNotUnderstand:

566 From the entire list of receiver–message pairs that you see in the walkback window, you see that an error occurs during the evaluation of the + method defined for the Weight class, and that the error causes doesNotUnderstand: to be sent to a SmallInteger instance.

Then, during the evaluation of the doesNotUnderstand: method defined for Object instances, error: is sent to a SmallInteger instance, and that causes the walkback window to appear.

All this activity occurs after the Doit message is sent to the expression, 3gm + 2, in response to **right**→**Show It**. The expression never produces an answer; hence, the expression is represented in the walkback window as an instance of UndefinedObject:

SmallInteger(Object)>>error:
SmallInteger(Object)>>doesNotUnderstand:
Weight>>+
UndefinedObject>>Doit

567 Occasionally, the information in the walkback window is sufficient for you to determine what has gone wrong. Usually, however, you need more help, so you to click **Debug** in the walkback window; that action closes the walkback window and opens a **debugger window**:

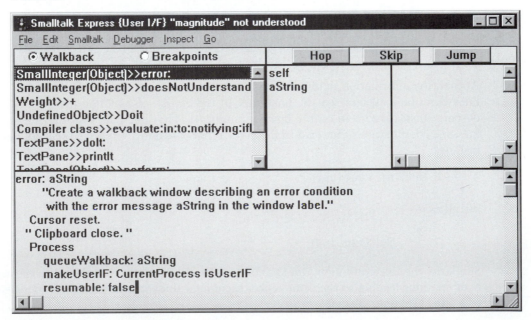

568 The pane in the upper-left corner of the debugging window contains a display of walkback information similar to the information seen previously in the walkback window. The debugging-window version of that information includes lines for Smalltalk messages sent before reaching the list that begins with the doIt message and ends with the error: message.

569 The lower pane in the debugging window contains the definition of the method referenced in the selected line of the walkback pane. When the debugging window opens, as shown in Segment 567, the first line is selected, so the definition shown is the definition of the error: method.

570 When you select the line containing +, you see the definition of the + method for the Weight class. You also see aWeight magnitude highlighted because the error occurred as Smalltalk attempted to send magnitude to the value of the aWeight parameter:

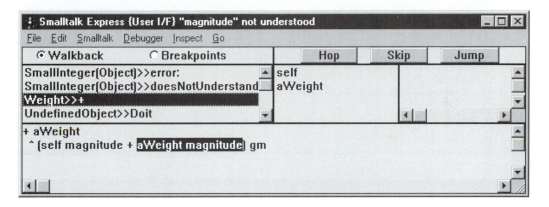

571 If you still need help to determine what has gone wrong, you use the upper-middle and upper-right panes, which together constitute an **inspector** for the receiver, parameters, and local variables of the method shown in the lower window.

Inspectors allow you to examine values. For example, if you select aWeight in the upper-middle pane, you see 2 in the upper-right pane.

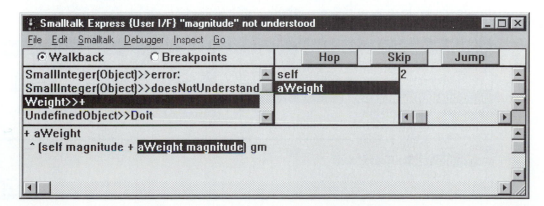

572 Now, suspending disbelief, suppose that you are still stumped. You might decide that you need a detailed understanding of what is going on. Fortunately, you can get that detailed understanding by using Smalltalk's **stepper** to examine the course of events leading up to the error.

573 In anticipation of using the stepper, you evaluate an `Object halt` expression in the workspace in addition to `3gm + 2`:

```
Object halt.
3gm + 2
```

The expression `Object halt` causes Smalltalk to enter the walkback window, at which point you can click the debug button to enter the debugger. Then, if you click the **hop** button, you see the following:

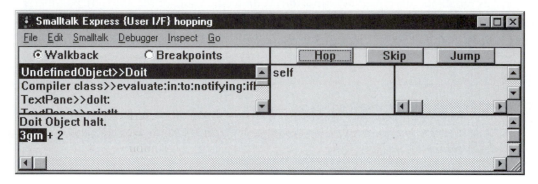

574 Now, you can use Smalltalk Express's hop, **skip**, and **jump** buttons to move the evaluation along. The hop button causes the least evaluation; the skip button causes a little more:

- When you press hop, the debugger continues to the next receiver–message combination.

- When you press skip, the debugger continues to the next receiver–message combination shown in the lower window. The debugger skips receiver–message combinations that occur inside called methods.

575 For example, if you press hop, you see that the next receiver–message combination occurs during the evaluation of the `gm` method:

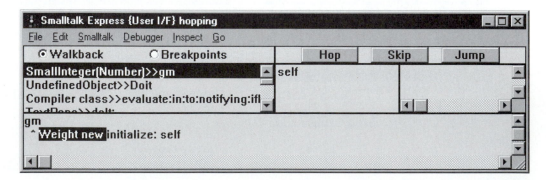

On the other hand, if you press skip instead, you see the next receiver–message combination that appears in the lower window:

576 You can also set a **breakpoint** for a receiver–message combination, and arrange for evaluation to proceed up to that breakpoint:

• When you press jump, the debugger continues to the next receiver–message combination for which a breakpoint has been set.

577 To see how a breakpoint is set, you repeat the actions prescribed in Segment 573 up to the point where you enter the debugger. Next, you click **Debugger→Add Breakpoint**. Then, in the prompt window, you type `Weight>>+`, the combination for which you want a breakpoint. Then, you click **OK**.

578 Now, with a breakpoint set, you first reactivate the walkback pane in the debugger window by pressing the walkback button; then you press the jump button. Smalltalk takes you to the point where + is sent to a `Weight` instance. From there, you can move forward using the hop and skip buttons:

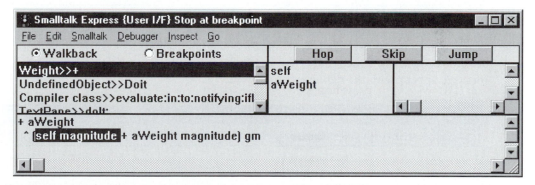

579 In addition to the walkback and debugging windows, and the class-hierarchy browser, various other windows help you to navigate through your definitions and to look at various values.

Suppose, for example, that you use the class-hierarchy browser to examine the definition of the + method for the weight class. Then, with the + method selected, you can click

Methods→Senders to produce a **method browser** that displays a list of all methods that send + messages:

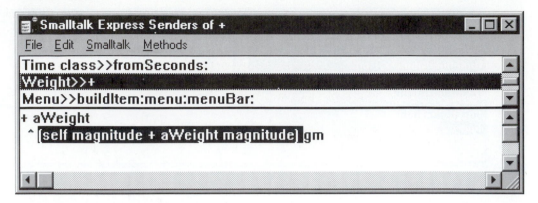

Alternatively, you can click **Methods**→**Implementers** to produce a **method browser** that displays a list of all methods that implement + methods:

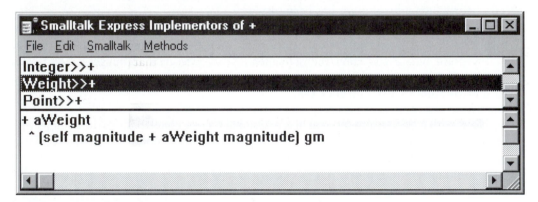

580 Also, with a method selected, you can click **Methods**→**messages** to produce a **message-selector browser** in which all the message selectors that appear in the definition of the + message appear with the definition:

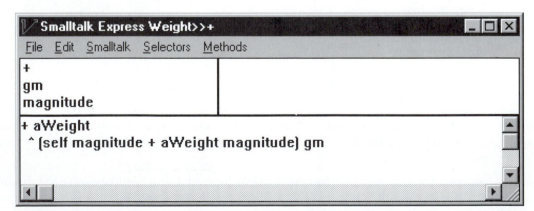

581　In a message-selector browser, you click **Selectors→Senders** to produce a list of all methods that send messages using the selected selector:

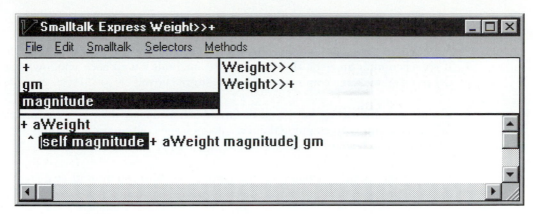

Similarly, in a message-selector window, you click **Selectors→Implementers** to produce a list of all methods that implement methods for the selected selector.

582　Finally, you can call up an **inspector window** to examine the contents of a global variable, such as `ColorConstants`. You need only to type `ColorConstants` in a workspace, to select it, and then to click **right→Smalltalk→Inspect It**. At that point, an inspector displays the keys in the `ColorConstants` dictionary:

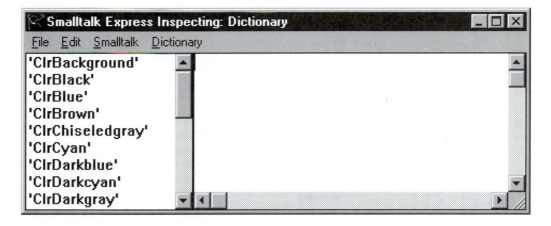

When you select a key in the left pane, the value associated with that key is shown in the right pane.

583　Type the expression 3 + 2gm in a workspace, select it, and click **right→Show It**. Then,
PRACTICE　work your way through the walkback window to the debugger as though you were tracking down a bug.

584　As described in Segment 583, evaluate 3 + 2gm in a workspace. After the walkback
PRACTICE　window appears, set a breakpoint for the + method defined for the `Weight` class. Then, use the jump button to determine whether that breakpoint is encountered.

Define the `rabbits` method as described in Segment 328. Then, determine all the senders and implementers of `rabbits`, `previousMonth`, and `penultimateMonth`.

Determine all the keys that appear in the `CharacterConstants` dictionary.

- If you encounter an error, **then** you can use Smalltalk's walkback window to see the receiver–message combinations leading to the error.

- If you press the debug button in the walkback window, **then** you can use the debugger window to examine the receiver–message combinations leading to the error and to determine values for receivers, parameters, and local variables.

- If you want to step through an evaluation, **then** instantiate and evaluate the following pattern in a workspace:

```
Object halt.
expression to be stepped through
```

    and then press the hop, skip, and jump buttons. The hop button steps the least; the skip button steps a little more; and the jump button steps to the next breakpoint.

- If you want to set a breakpoint, **then** click **Debugger→Add Breakpoint** while you are in the debugger.

- If you want to determine the senders or implementers of a method with a given name, **then** select that method name using the class-hierarchy browser, **and then** click **Methods→Senders** or **Methods→Implementers**.

29 HOW TO PROGRAM DEFENSIVELY

588　When you practice **defensive programming,** you embellish your programs with expressions that help you to zero in on where problems occur and why they occur. In this section, you learn about `implementedBySubclass` and `error:`, both of which are methods that help you to practice defensive programming.

589　Suppose that you use a < message with instances of a class that is not a subclass of the `Magnitude` class, and you have not yet implemented < for that class:

NotMagnitudeSubclass class definition
```
Object subclass: #NotMagnitudeSubclass
  instanceVariableNames: ''
  classVariableNames: ''
  poolDictionaries: ''
    Workspace
NotMagnitudeSubclass new < NotMagnitudeSubclass new
```

You would see a screen such as the following, which indicates that the message could not be understood:

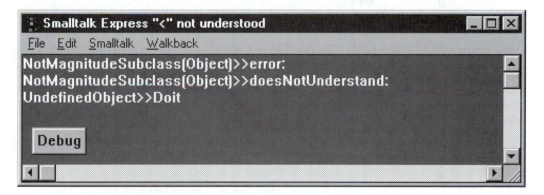

590　On the other hand, suppose that you use a < message with instances of a class that is a subclass of the `Magnitude` class, and you have not yet implemented < for that class:

MagnitudeSubclass class definition
```
Magnitude subclass: #MagnitudeSubclass
  instanceVariableNames: ''
  classVariableNames: ''
  poolDictionaries: ''
    Workspace
MagnitudeSubclass new < MagnitudeSubclass new
```

You would see a screen such as the following:

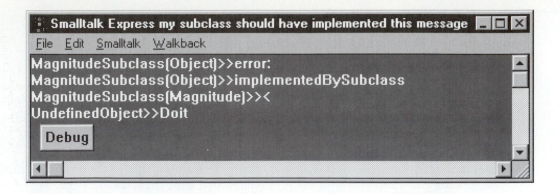

Evidently, there is something special about the Magnitude class, such that you are informed that you are expected to equip all subclasses of Magnitude with a definition for <.

591 The < method actually is defined as follows for the Magnitude class:

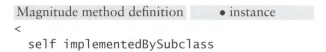

```
<
    self implementedBySubclass
```

Evidently, if you send a < message to a Magnitude instance, and the < method is not overridden by a lower-level class, then the < method defined for the Magnitude class sends a implementedBySubclass to self, which produces the appropriate error display.

Thus, the definition of < for the Magnitude class reminds you that every subclass of Magnitude is to be equipped with a < method. You see the corresponding error display if you attempt to use < without defining it.

592 Of course, when you define < for the Weight class, defined in Segment 556, the definition in the Magnitude class is overridden for all Weight instances, and there is no reason for an error display to appear:

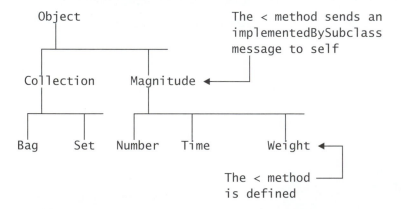

593 You can view the implementedBySubclass method as a tool for alerting users when they send messages with methods that should have been defined, but have not been.

594　Next, suppose that you attempt to evaluate the following expression, which includes an instance of the weight class created by the instance-creation method, gm:

```
3gm + 2
```

Because 2 is not a Weight instance, you will see an error display:

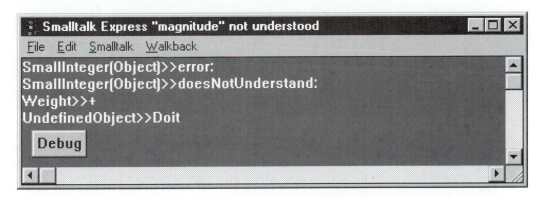

You would, of course, prefer a more specific indication of what is wrong, such as the following:

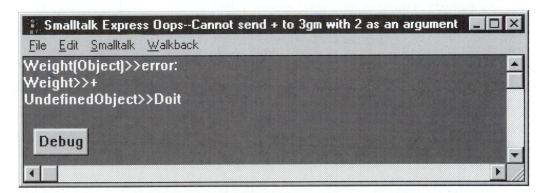

595　To detect and report such errors, you first must define a class predicate, isWeight. Most magnitudes are not weight instances, so you define isWeight for the Magnitude class to answer false:

Magnitude method definition　　　● instance
```
isWeight ∧ false
```

On the other hand, Weight instances are Weight instances, so you define isWeight for the Weight class to answer true:

Weight method definition　　　● instance
```
isWeight ∧ true
```

Thus, as you can see from the following diagram, one `isWeight` method overrides the other exactly for instances of the `Weight` class, but not for instances of other classes:

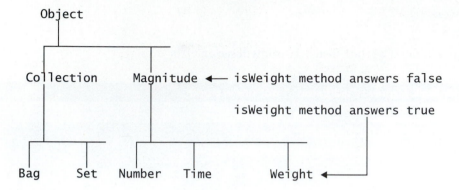

596   Next, you make use of `isWeight` in a new definition of the + method, defined previously in Segment 556. If the argument is a `Weight` instance, then activity proceeds as before. If the argument is not a `Weight` instance, then the `error:` message is sent, with an argument that is used in the error display:

Weight method definition	• instance

```
+ aWeight
  aWeight isWeight
    ifTrue: [^ (self magnitude + aWeight magnitude) gm]
    ifFalse: [self error: 'Oops--Cannot send + to '
                        , self printString
                        , ' with '
                        , aWeight printString
                        , ' as an argument']
```

597   Implement `shouldNotImplement:`, a method defined for the `Object` class. When sent to
PRACTICE   an instance of any class, `shouldNotImplement:` is to use the `error:` message to send an error message that opens an error window with the following title:

The `the class` should not implement `the argument`

Then, using `shouldNotImplement`, define < for the Food class, such that any attempt to use < on a food or on an instance of any of, say, the `Vegetable` subclasses of the `Food` class, prints the following:

The Vegetable class should not implement <

598
HIGHLIGHTS

   • **If** you want to indicate that a definition of a method is expected in a subclass, **then** instantiate the following instance–method pattern:

`method`
    `self implementedBySubclass`

- **If** you want to alert yourself when you unexpectedly arrive at a particular place in a method, **then** instantiate the following pattern:

```
...
self error: a string that explains the problem
...
```

30 HOW TO EXCHANGE SOFTWARE

599   Once you have defined various classes and methods, you may want to share them with another programmer. This section explains how.

600   When you work with many programming languages, you write a program using an editor, producing a text file. If you want to share that program with another programmer, you simply provide that programmer with a copy of the text file.

When you work with Smalltalk, you do everything in a development environment; hence, there is, ordinarily, no file to copy. You must invoke the **file-out mechanism** to convey your programs to others.

When you **file out**, you tell Smalltalk that you want to write the definitions of certain classes or methods into a file in a form that allows those class or method definitions to be absorbed back into another programmer's development environment. Absorption is done when you **file in**.

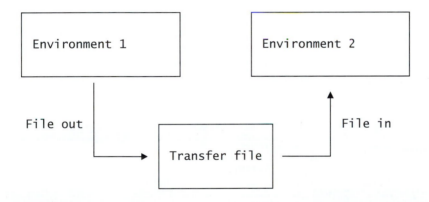

601   For example, suppose you have produced a `Weight` class, and all of that class's allied methods, as defined in Segment 556. Together, the `Weight` class and the allied methods constitute a small application.

If you decide to share the application for use by another programmer, you must execute the file-out ritual prescribed by the development environment. For the Smalltalk Express development environment, for example, you proceed as follows:

- First, activate the class-hierarchy browser, as explained in Segment 85.

- Click **Magnitude**, and then click **Weight**. You see the following:

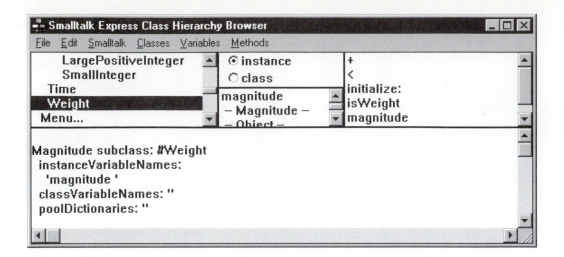

- Next, click **right** in the class column. A menu will emerge.

- Click **File out....** A text-input box will emerge.

- Provide a file name, such as \test\weight.cls, and click **Ok**.

After you have followed this ritual, Smalltalk will have written the definition of the Weight class and all the methods associated with the weight class into the file that you specified.

602 Of course, to file out the definitions of all the methods associated with weights, you must also file out the gm method of the Number class and the isWeight method of the Magnitude class. To file out those methods, you amend the procedure of Segment 601 slightly. Instead of selecting a class and clicking **right** to start the filing out process, you select the gm or isWeight method, of the appropriate class, as displayed in the following example:

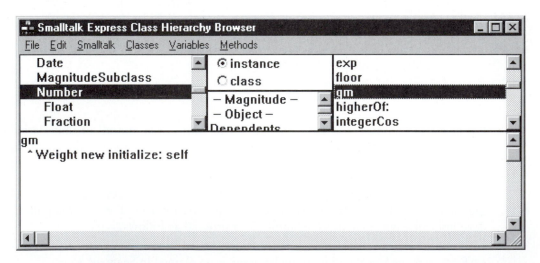

Then, you click **right//File out...** in the method column, and provide a file name, such as \test\gm.mth or \test\isweight.mth.

603   Note that you cannot file out global variables and their values. Whenever you want to exchange software or to preserve a body of work for posterity, you must be sure that you include initialization methods that recreate the global variables and global-variable values.

604   Now suppose that you want to read definitions from a filed-out file. You have two choices. One choice is to use the Smalltalk environment's point-and-click tools:

- Click **File→Open...**, select a file, and click **Ok**. You then see the file's contents in a workspace.

- Select the entire contents of the file.

- Click **Smalltalk→File It In**.

605   Alternatively, you can file in filed-out files by evaluating file-in expressions in a workspace.

You first produce an instance of the `FileStream` class by sending a `pathName:` message to the `File` class with a path-name argument. Then, you send a `fileIn` message to that file stream, as in the following examples:

```
     Workspace
(File pathName: 'c:\test\weight.cls') fileIn.
(File pathName: 'c:\test\gm.mth') fileIn.
(File pathName: 'c:\test\isweight.mth') fileIn
```

606   You must file in a class's definition before you file in method definitions that refer to that class. Thus, you must file in `weight.cls` before you file in `gm.mth`, because `gm.mth` contains the definition of a method that sends the `new` message to the `Weight` class.

607   When you file out definitions, they are written in a special **chunk format**. As you learn in the remainder of this section, the chunk format is human readable, and, in principal, you can write programs in the chunk format using an ordinary text editor. Such programming is strongly discouraged, however. When you write programs using an ordinary text editor, all the point-and-click tools and the visual guidance provided by the development environment are *hors de combat*.

608   Consider, for example, the definition of the `Weight` class shown previously in Segment 556. The definition in filed-out form, in the `weight.cls` file, is as follows:

```
Magnitude subclass: #Weight
        instanceVariableNames: 'magnitude '
        classVariableNames: ''
        poolDictionaries: '' !
```

Thus, the principal difference between what you see in the class-hierarchy browser and what you see in the filed-out `weight.cls` file is the terminating exclamation point.

609   The definitions of class methods and instance methods in the `weight.cls` file begin with a prefix line, marked on both ends by exclamation points. The prefix line records the class to which the method belongs.

Each individual method is terminated by an exclamation point. The complete set of methods is terminated by a space and yet another exclamation point.

610   Because there are no class methods for the `Weight` class, you see the following:

```
!Weight class methods ! !
```

On the other hand, you see several instance methods:

```
!Weight methods !
+ aWeight
  ^ (self magnitude + aWeight magnitude) gm!
...
printOn: aStream
  aStream nextPutAll: magnitude asString , 'gm'! !
```

611   Bringing everything together, the contents of the `weight.cls` file describing the `Weight` class and all the associated methods has the following contents:

```
Magnitude subclass: #Weight
  instanceVariableNames:
    'magnitude '
  classVariableNames: ''
  poolDictionaries: ''     !
!Weight class methods ! !
!Weight methods !
+ aWeight
  ^ (self magnitude + aWeight magnitude) gm!
< aWeight
  ^ (self magnitude < aWeight magnitude)!
initialize: aNumber
  magnitude := aNumber!
magnitude
  ^ magnitude!
printOn: aStream
  aStream nextPutAll: magnitude asString , 'gm'! !
```

612   The `gm.mth` and `isweight.mth` files are simpler because they contain no class definition. The contents of the `gm.mth` file follow:

```
!Number methods !
gm
  ^ Weight new initialize: self! !
```

And the contents of the `isweight.mth` file follow:

```
!Magnitude methods !
isWeight
  ^ false! !
```

613
PRACTICE

Define the Food class, with setters and getters, as shown in Segment 455. Next, file out the Food class to a file. Then, read the file using your favorite text editor, and replace the fCalories, cCalories, and pCalories variables with f, c, and p. Finally, exit from Smalltalk without saving the image, start Smalltalk again, file in the altered file, and examine the Food class using the class-hierarchy browser.

614
HIGHLIGHTS

- If you want to prepare an application for use by another programmer, **then** file out the application using the development environment's file-out point-and-click ritual.

- You can file out a class and all its methods or just a single method.

- If you want to make use of an application that has been filed out, **then** file in the application using the development environment's file-in point-and-click ritual.

- If you want a program to file in an application, **then** instantiate the following pattern:

```
(File pathName: 'file name') fileIn
```

- You can write programs using an ordinary editor by exploiting the chunk format, but such programming practice is strongly discouraged.

31 HOW TO CREATE POINTS AND RECTANGLES

615   In Section 26, you learned that Smalltalk offers not only traditional classes, such as those that deal with various sorts of numbers, but also more sophisticated classes, such as the `Time` and `Date` classes. In this segment, you learn about two other sophisticated classes, `Point` and `Rectangle`, both of which are put to heavy use in Section 32, which describes how to get started with graphical output.

616   A display on your screen consists of points of light laid out in a two-dimensional array. Each point is called a **pixel**—an abbreviation derived from the words **picture element**.

A typical screen has on the order of a million pixels. Black-and-white screens need just 1 bit of memory per pixel to remember whether that pixel is bright or dark. By devoting 1 byte to each pixel, color screens can display any of $2^8 = 256$ colors.

617   Each pixel lies at a place that can be referred to by an instance of the `Point` class. Such `Point` instances contain the coordinates of the point, expressed in terms of two nonnegative integer instance variables, x and y.

You can create a new point, with coordinates 5 and 3, by sending the x:y: class method to the `Point` class:

```
Point x: 5 y: 3   ⟵ The point with x=5 and y=3
```

Note that x and y are measured with respect to the left side and top of a window, rather than to the left side and bottom. The *x* coordinate of the point shown in the following, for example, is 5, and the *y* coordinate is 3:

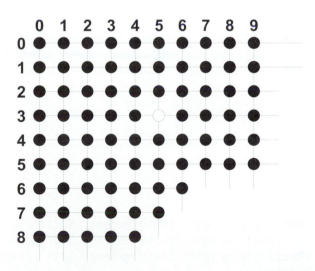

618   You can also create a new point by sending the @ method, with an argument, to a number. Thus, the point with coordinates 5 and 3 can be expressed as 5 @ 3:

5 @ 3 ◄─── The point with x=5 and y=3

You can also write the same point as 5@3 if you prefer a space-free look.

619   To extract coordinate values from a `Point` instance, you send an x or y message to the point:

> Workspace

```
Transcript show: (5 @ 3) x printString; cr;
          show: (5 @ 3) y printString; cr
```

> Transcript

```
5
3
```

620   Smalltalk offers a `Rectangle` class as well as a `Point` class. One way to create a `Rectangle` instance is to send the `origin:corner:` method to the `Rectangle` class. The following, for example, creates a rectangle with an upper-left corner specified by the point 16@10 and with a lower-right corner specified by 21@13.

```
Rectangle origin: 16 @ 10 corner: 21 @ 13
```

621   You also can create `Rectangle` instances using messages that specify rectangle origin and size independently. Such messages allow you to shift from one coordinate system to another simply by adding an offset to the origin. For example, the `origin:extent:` message's first argument specifies the location of a rectangle relative to the current coordinate system, and the second argument specifies the size of the rectangle in width and height. Accordingly, the following creates a rectangle that is identical to the one created by the example in Segment 620.

```
Rectangle origin: 16 @ 10 extent: 5 @ 3
```

622   You also can create `Rectangle` instances with separately specified origins and sizes using the `rightBottom:` message with a point receiver, rather than the `Rectangle` class. The following creates a rectangle that is identical to the one created by the example in Segment 620.

```
16 @ 10 rightBottom: 21 @ 13
```

623   To extract information from a `Rectangle` instance, you send an `origin`, `corner`, or `extent` message to the rectangle:

> Workspace

```
Transcript
   show: (Rectangle origin: 16@10 extent: 5@3) origin printString; cr;
   show: (Rectangle origin: 16@10 extent: 5@3) corner printString; cr;
   show: (Rectangle origin: 16@10 extent: 5@3) extent printString; cr
```

> Transcript

```
16 @ 10
21 @ 13
5 @ 3
```

624   The Rectangle class also has width and height methods, which answer with number instances representing the width and height of the rectangle, and a center method, which answers with a point instance representing the center of the rectangle. The center coordinates are rounded to the nearest integer:

       Workspace
```
Transcript
  show: (Rectangle origin: 16@10 extent: 5@3) height printString; cr;
  show: (Rectangle origin: 16@10 extent: 5@3) width printString; cr;
  show: (Rectangle origin: 16@10 extent: 5@3) center printString; cr
```
       Transcript
```
3
5
18 @ 11
```

625   Now that you know about points, you can understand the difference between **identity** and **equality**.

Two variables with point assignments satisfy the == predicate, and are said to have identical values, if they both refer to the same point. In the following illustration, the second test answers false, because the @ method produces a distinct point each time that it is sent, and distinct points with the same x and y values are still distinct points.

       Point method definition   • instance
```
testForIdentity: aPoint
  Transcript show: (self == self) printString; cr;
            show: (self == aPoint) printString; cr.
```
       Workspace
```
3 @ 4 testForIdentity: 3 @ 4
```
       Transcript
```
true
false
```

On the other hand, two variables with point assignments satisfy the = predicate, and are said to have equal values, if they both refer to points that have the same x and y values. Thus, both of the tests answer true in the following illustration:

       Point method definition   • instance
```
testForEquality: aPoint
  Transcript show: (self = self) printString; cr;
            show: (self = aPoint) printString; cr.
```
       Workspace
```
3 @ 4 testForEquality: 3 @ 4
```
       Transcript
```
true
true
```

626   The == and = predicates behave differently for points because of the way = is defined for the Point class. Otherwise, the = predicate would be inherited from the Object class, in which the = predicate is defined to provide the same answers as the == predicate.

Thus, if you want the = predicate to answer **true** if two instances have the same instance-variable values, you must provide a definition that overrides the definition provided in the `Object` class. In that definition, you must decide whether having the same instance-variable values means having identical values or having equal values.

627 When used with numbers, the = predicate answers **true** if two numbers are numerically equal, even if they are not the same instance:

Number method definition • instance
```
testTwoNumbers: aNumber
  Transcript show: (self = self) printString; cr;
            show: (self = aNumber) printString; cr;
            show: (self == self) printString; cr;
            show: (self == aNumber) printString; cr.
```
Workspace
```
3 testTwoNumbers: 3.0
```
Transcript
```
true
true
true
false
```

628 Write `area`, a method that answers with the area of a rectangle.
PRACTICE

629 Define Box, a class with three instance variables: `width`, `height`, and `depth`. Write getters
PRACTICE and setters for all the instance variables.

630 Write `side`, `base`, and `end` for the Box class that you defined to solve the problem posed
PRACTICE in Segment 629. The `side` method is to answer a `Rectangle` instance with dimensions equal to the width and height of the box; `base` is to answer a rectangle with dimensions equal to the width and depth; and `end` is to answer a rectangle with dimensions equal to the depth and height.

631
HIGHLIGHTS

- To assist you in displaying information graphically, Smalltalk offers the `Point` and `Rectangle` classes.

- If you want to create a point, **then** instantiate one of the following patterns:

  Point x: `x coordinate value` y: `y coordinate value`

  `x coordinate value` @ `y coordinate value`

- If you want to extract information from a point, **then** send an x or y message to the point.

- If you want to create a rectangle, **then** instantiate one of the following patterns:

```
Rectangle origin: upper-left point
         corner: lower-right point

Rectangle origin: upper-left point
         extent: point representing width and height

upper-left point
  rightBottom: lower-right point
```

- **If** you want to extract information from a rectangle, **then** send an `origin`, corner, extent, height, width, or center message to the rectangle.

32 HOW TO DRAW LINES AND DISPLAY TEXT IN WINDOWS

632 In this section, you learn how to create windows, and how to draw lines of the sort that you need to produce a drawing of a meter, which eventually becomes part of a food-calories display.

633 Programs that have graphical user interfaces seem much more powerful than programs that provide services via character-only interfaces. Accordingly, to please users, you need to learn how to build graphical user interfaces.

Much of the work required to build a **graphical user interface**, or GUI, is invested in creating rectangular **windows**, with attached menus, buttons, choice boxes, text fields, text editors, and drawing spaces. Each such attached graphical element is called a **widget**.

634 To see how Smalltalk supports GUI development, you learn how to draw a meter that is part of a calorie-dictionary application:

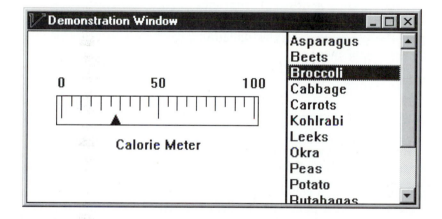

635 Once you learn how to draw a single line, you easily can draw a meter, such as the one shown in Segment 634. Paradoxically, you need to learn a lot to draw a single line, because to draw a single line, you need to learn how instances of various GUI-oriented classes interact.

In particular, you need to learn about the SubPane class, the TopPane class, and the ViewManager class.

636 All GUI applications include instances of the SubPane, the TopPane, and the ViewManager class. Of these, you need to add instance variables and methods to those supplied with the SubPane and ViewManager classes. Accordingly, you create the MeterGraphPane and the CalorieViewManager classes, which fit together with various superclasses as follows:

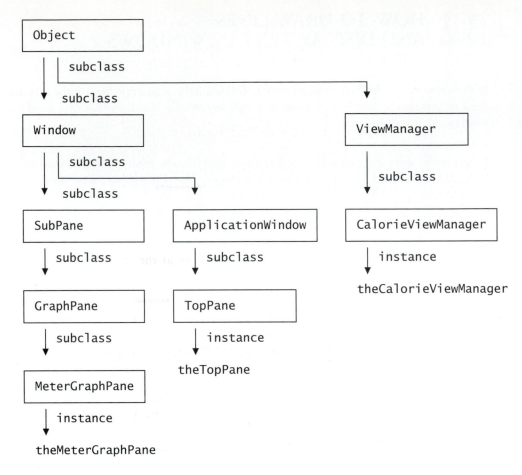

637   By defining your own subclasses of Smalltalk supplied classes, you easily can share particular classes, along with all the methods defined for those classes, as described in Section 30.

On the other hand, if you were to develop multiple applications by working directly with the classes supplied by Smalltalk, then you would have difficulty separating those applications from one another or even keeping track of which methods belong to which application.

638   As shown in Segment 636, you are to work with an instance of the MeterGraphPane class, an instance of the TopPane class, and an instance of the CalorieViewManager class. These instances are referred to as a **graph pane** or **meter pane**, a **top pane**, and a **view manager**. Similarly, when referring to an instance of any SubPane class, that instance is referred to as a **subpane**.

639   Conceptually, subpanes have two important roles.

- Subpanes appear as visual elements.

- Subpanes receive messages whenever an event occurs, such as the event that indicates that a mouse operation requires graphical information to be redrawn.

640   Like subpanes, top panes appear as visual elements and receive messages.

Visually, a top pane surrounds one or more subpanes. The top pane typically supplies a title, a minimize button, a maximize button, and a close button.

641   Both subpanes and top panes are **views**. In Smalltalk Express, views are managed by a **view manager**.

A view manager serves as a command center, enabling information to flow from one subpane to another:

- Instance methods defined for the view manager respond to requests for action forwarded from top pane and subpane views in response to events.

- Instance methods defined for the view manager send messages to subpanes asking for action.

642   A view manager also has an important responsibility at the time that an application is started:

- The **open** message, when sent to the view manager, causes the top-pane instance, and all the subpanes connected to the top pane, to appear on your screen.

643   Finally, the view manager typically contains instance variables that tie together an entire application.

644   Because an application's view manager has so many responsibilities, you can think of it as the hub that ties the entire application together. Accordingly, `ViewManager` subclasses typically have names that include the word *application*, and some programmers would prefer to use `CalorieApplication`, rather than `CalorieViewManager`, to name a subclass of the `ViewManager` class. Using `CalorieViewManager` has the virtue of identifying the class clearly as a subclass of the `ViewManager` class.

645   View-manager instance responsibilities are a superset of application instance responsi-
SIDE TRIP bilities described in Segment 524. In addition to the responsibilities described there for application instances, view managers must deal with all the chores associated with GUIs.

646   You easily can define `MeterGraphPane` and `CalorieViewManager`—the required classes—because variables are not yet needed in those classes:

CalorieViewManager class definition
```
ViewManager subclass: #CalorieViewManager
  instanceVariableNames: ''
  classVariableNames: ''
  poolDictionaries: ''
```

MeterGraphPane class definition
```
GraphPane subclass: #MeterGraphPane
  instanceVariableNames: ''
  classVariableNames: ''
  poolDictionaries: ''
```

647 Once class definitions are in place, you can write **createViews**, a method that is sent to a view manager whenever **open**, a Smalltalk-supplied method, is sent to that same view manager. Later on, in Section 37, you learn that you can use Smalltalk Express's built-in GUI builder to define **createViews**. Before you can understand what the GUI builder does for you, however, you need to understand exactly how **createViews** works.

648 According to the following definition, the **createViews** method starts the GUI machinery in motion by creating a top pane and a graph pane, and assigning those instances to local variables, **theTopPane** and **theMeterPane**. The value of another local variable, **theCalorieViewManager**, is the **CalorieViewManager** instance itself, which is also, of course, the value of **self**. The local variable is established because its name helps to make the relations among the instances clearer as **createViews** grows more complex.

CalorieViewManager method definition   ● instance

```
createViews
  | theCalorieViewManager theTopPane theMeterPane |
  theCalorieViewManager := self.
  theTopPane := TopPane new.
  theMeterPane := MeterGraphPane new.
  ...
```

649 Next, several messages establish connections between the panes and the view manager:

CalorieViewManager method definition   ● instance

```
createViews
  | theCalorieViewManager theTopPane theMeterPane |
  theCalorieViewManager := self.
  theTopPane := TopPane new.
  theMeterPane := MeterGraphPane new.

  "Set up the top pane"
  theCalorieViewManager addView: theTopPane.
  theTopPane owner: theCalorieViewManager.
  ...
  "Set up the meter pane"
  theTopPane addSubpane: theMeterPane.
  theMeterPane owner: theCalorieViewManager.
  ...
```

The **addView:** message establishes that the view manager manages the top pane. This connection enables the view manager to display the panes on your screen and to close the application when you press the close button.

The **owner:** messages establish that the view manager is to receive information forwarded from the top pane and from the graph pane whenever the top pane or the graph pane receive notifications of events, such as mouse operations that require graphical information to be redrawn.

The **addSubpane:** message establishes that the graph pane is contained visually within the top pane.

186

650 With the `addView:`, and `owner:`, and `addSubpane:` messages in place in `createViews`, you can send `open` to an instance of the `CalorieViewManager` class:

> Workspace

```
CalorieViewManager new open
```

The `open` method sends the `createViews` method to the view manager, producing a display.

651 Having succeeded in displaying the top pane and the empty graph pane, you proceed to add a few messages that alter their appearance. One provides a label for the top pane. Another deletes the menu bar from the top pane. Two more establish the size and positioning of the top pane and the graph pane. And yet another suppresses the scroll bars that otherwise appear in the graph pane: Each change are marked by a change bar:

> CalorieViewManager method definition • instance

```
createViews
  | theCalorieViewManager theTopPane theMeterPane |
  theCalorieViewManager := self.
  theTopPane := TopPane new.
  theMeterPane := MeterGraphPane new.
  "Set up the top pane"
  theCalorieViewManager addView: theTopPane.
  theTopPane owner: theCalorieViewManager.
  theTopPane labelWithoutPrefix: 'Demonstration Window'.
  theTopPane noSmalltalkMenuBar.
  theTopPane framingRatio: (1/4 @ (3/8) rightBottom: 3/4 @ (5/8)).
  "Set up the meter pane"
  theTopPane addSubpane: theMeterPane.
  theMeterPane owner: theCalorieViewManager.
  theMeterPane noScrollBars.
  theMeterPane framingRatio: (0 @ 0 rightBottom: 1 @ 1).
  ...
```

652 The argument of the `framingRatio:` message sent to the top pane is a rectangle instance. The upper-left corner of the rectangle is a point with fractional x and y values. Those fractions determine where the upper-left corner of the top pane lies relative to the left edge and top of your screen. The lower-right corner of the rectangle is a point with fractional x and y values that determine where the lower-right corner of the top pane lies relative to the left edge and top of your screen.

Similarly, the argument of the `framingRatio:` message sent to the graph pane is a rectangle instance that establishes where the graph pain lies relative to the top pane. The `0 @ 0` and `1 @ 1` points indicate that the graph pane is to fill the top pane.

653 Note that you often see ratios surrounded by parentheses in `framingRatio:` expressions. The parentheses are mandatory, because, without them, Smalltalk would misunderstand your meaning. For example, if you strip the parentheses from 3/4 @ (5/8), you have 3/4 @ 5/8, which Smalltalk interprets as (3/4 @ 5) / 8, which is (3/32) @ (5/8).

654   When no `framingRatio:` message is sent to a subpane, Smalltalk assumes that the subpane is to fill the top pane. Accordingly, you never need to send a `framingRatio:` message with a (0 @ 0 rightBottom: 1 @ 1) argument.

655   With the appearance-establishing messages in place, you now see the following when you send an `open` message to an instance of the `CalorieViewManager` class:

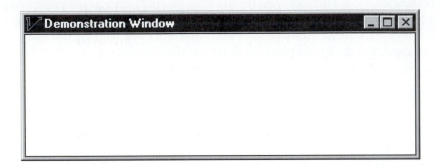

656   Now, finally, you need to add just one more, crucial message: the message that tells the graph pane what to do when it is time to draw information on the graph pane. In particular, you need to add a message that tells the graph pane to send a message to the view manager that causes information in the graph pane to be displayed. For example, you might choose to tell the graph pane to send the `callDrawMeter:` message (at first `callDrawMeter` will do the drawing itself; later, in Segment 667, `callDrawMeter` is defined to call upon another method, `drawMeter`, that does the drawing).

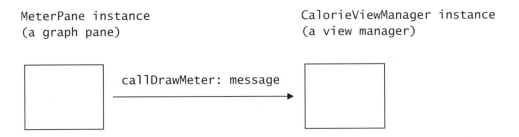

657   You add a `when:perform:` message to the `createViews` method to tell the graph pane when to send the `callDrawMeter:` message.

The `when:perform:` message has two arguments: the first, `#display`, identifies a Smalltalk **event** triggered, ultimately, by the operating system; the second, `#callDrawMeter:`, names the message to be sent to the view manager:

```
createViews
    | theCalorieViewManager theTopPane theMeterPane |
    theCalorieViewManager := self.
    theTopPane := TopPane new.
    theMeterPane := MeterGraphPane new.
    "Set up the top pane"
    theCalorieViewManager addView: theTopPane.
    theTopPane owner: theCalorieViewManager.
    theTopPane labelWithoutPrefix: 'Demonstration Window'.
    theTopPane noSmalltalkMenuBar.
    theTopPane framingRatio: (1/4 @ (3/8) rightBottom: 3/4 @ (5/8)).
    "Set up the meter pane"
    theTopPane addSubpane: theMeterPane.
    theMeterPane owner: theCalorieViewManager.
    theMeterPane noScrollBars.
    theMeterPane framingRatio: (0 @ 0 rightBottom: 1 @ 1).
    theMeterPane when: #display perform: #callDrawMeter:.
```

658   The method called in response to an **event** is called a **callback method**. Thus, events lead to callbacks.

659   Now, you define the `callDrawMeter:` callback method for the `calorieViewManager` class.

Note that each callback method sent to a view manager via the `when:perform:` mechanism travels with an argument, and the value of that argument is the subpane from which the message is sent:

CalorieViewManager method definition   • instance

```
callDrawMeter: thePane
    ...
```

660   Now, to make a drawing, you need a tool with which to draw. You obtain that tool by sending the `pen` message to the graph pane:

CalorieViewManager method definition   • instance

```
callDrawMeter: thePane
    | thePen |
    thePen := thePane pen.
    ...
```

661   Now, if you want to draw a simple horizontal line, at position (0, 50), with length equal to 100, you use the pen as the receiver of the `lineFrom:to:` message:

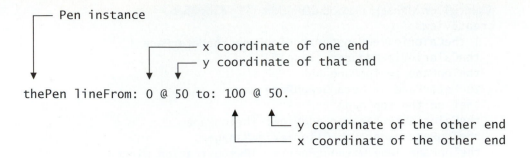

```
thePen lineFrom: 0 @ 50 to: 100 @ 50.
```

662 Inserting the `lineFrom:to:` message into the `callDrawMeter:` method, you have the following:

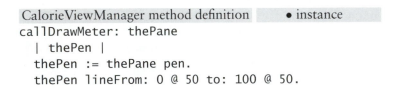

CalorieViewManager method definition   • instance
```
callDrawMeter: thePane
  | thePen |
  thePen := thePane pen.
  thePen lineFrom: 0 @ 50 to: 100 @ 50.
```

663 With `createViews` and `callDrawMeter:` now defined, you can, at last, draw a line on your display by sending the `open` message to an instance of the view manager:

    Workspace
```
CalorieViewManager new open
```

The result is as follows:

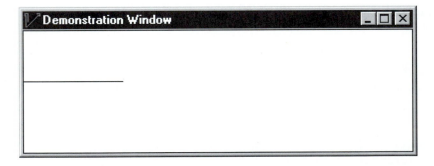

664 The `createViews` definition contains an unnecessary substitute for `self` and no cascades so that the identity of the receivers is clear. An experienced Smalltalk programmer might write `createViews` as follows, employing `self`, exploiting the values of assignment expressions, and using cascades liberally:

```
createViews
  | theTopPane theMeterPane |
  self addView: (theTopPane := TopPane new).
  theMeterPane := MeterGraphPane new.
  "Set up the top pane"
  theTopPane owner: self;
    labelWithoutPrefix: 'Demonstration Window';
    noSmalltalkMenuBar;
    framingRatio: (1/4 @ (3/8) rightBottom: 3/4 @ (5/8)).
  "Set up the meter pane"
  theTopPane addSubpane: theMeterPane.
  theMeterPane owner: self;
    noScrollBars;
    framingRatio: (0 @ 0 rightBottom: 1 @ 1);
    when: #display perform: #callDrawMeter:.
```

665   At this point, you could add more drawing messages to the `callDrawMeter:` method, building toward a display such as the one shown in Segment 634.

Such drawing messages belong in a method defined for the `MeterGraphPane` class, however, because the behavior of `MeterGraphPane` instances should be captured by instance methods of the `MeterGraphPane` class, rather than by instance methods of a view manager class.

666   If you incorporate meter-drawing messages into a method defined for the `MeterGraphPane` class, you simplify the exportation of your meter to another application. Using the file-out mechanism described in Section 30, you need to file out only the `MeterGraphPane` class, rather than the `MeterGraphPane` class and the drawing method, which you would have to redefine for the application's view-manager class.

667   You can move meter-drawing messages from the `callDrawMeter:` method to a method defined for the `MeterGraphPane` class by redefining the `callDrawMeter:` method to call a drawing method defined for the `MeterGraphPane` class:

CalorieViewManager method definition   ● instance

```
callDrawMeter: thePane
  thePane drawMeter.
```

Then, drawing previously done in `callDrawMeter:`, a view-manager method, must be done in `drawMeter`, a meter method:

MeterGraphPane method definition   ● instance

```
drawMeter
  | thePen |
  thePen := self pen.
  thePen lineFrom: 0 @ 50 to: 100 @ 50.
```

668   Now, whenever you enlarge or shrink the window, or bring it to the front of your display, Smalltalk transmits the following messages:

- The `display` message to the graph pane

- The `callDrawMeter:` message from the graph pane to the view manager

- The `drawMeter` message from the view manager back to the view pane

Thus, the view manager acts as a command center, receiving requests for attention, and issuing requests for action.

669 Now, it is time for you to learn how to take advantage of the information provided by various methods inherited by `Window` instances, so that you can produce more sophisticated drawings.

For example, you can obtain the width and height values of a `MeterGraphPane` instance by sending the `width` and `height` messages.

With the width and height variable values in hand, you can arrange for the horizontal line to fill out the window and stay centered, even as you move, or change the size of, the window. And while you are at it, you can add a short, pointerlike vertical line, 10 pixels long, emerging from the middle of the horizontal line:

```
MeterGraphPane method definition        • instance
drawMeter
  | thePen meterWidth xLft yBot |
  meterWidth := self width * 3 // 4.
  xLft := self width - meterWidth // 2.
  yBot := self height // 2.
  thePen := self pen.
  thePen lineFrom: xLft @ yBot to: (xLft + meterWidth) @ yBot.
  thePen lineFrom: (xLft + (meterWidth // 2)) @ yBot
              to: (xLft + (meterWidth // 2)) @ (yBot - 10).
```

670 Note that `lineFrom:to:` and other drawing commands expect integer arguments. Accordingly, in Segment 669, all the divisions are done with the `//` message, rather than with the `/` message.

671 You can use the pen to display text as well as lines. The display work is done by `displayText:at:` or `centerText:at:` messages. In the following, one argument of `centerText:at:` is a string to be printed, and the other specifies a position just under the primitive meter.

The exact distance under the primitive meter is twice the height of the font. To determine that height, you send a `font` message to extract the current font instance associated with the pen, and then you send a `height` message to determine the font instance's height:

```
drawMeter
  | thePen meterWidth xLft yBot |
  meterWidth := self width * 3 // 4.
  xLft := self width - meterWidth // 2.
  yBot := self height // 2.
  thePen := self pen.
  thePen lineFrom: xLft @ yBot to: (xLft + meterWidth) @ yBot.
  thePen lineFrom: (xLft + (meterWidth // 2)) @ yBot
              to: (xLft + (meterWidth // 2)) @ (yBot - 10).
  thePen centerText: 'Untitled'
                at: ((self width) // 2)
                   @ ((self height // 2)
                     + (2 * thePen font height)).
```

Using the definition of `drawMeter` provided in this segment, you produce the following display:

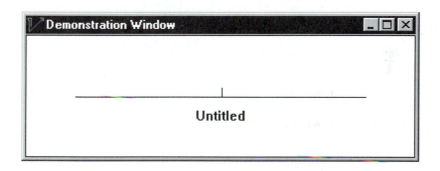

672   So far, your meter display presents wired-in data: the title is *Untitled* and the pointer is in the middle. The next step toward a real meter is to define `MeterGraphPane` with instance variables for the minimum and maximum values expected, for a value, and for a title. The following includes those instance variables, as well as listing `ColorConstants` in the pool-dictionary specification, for use later, in Segment 680.

MeterGraphPane class definition
```
GraphPane subclass: #MeterGraphPane
  instanceVariableNames: 'min max value title'
  classVariableNames: ''
  poolDictionaries: 'ColorConstants'
```

673   With those instance variables in place, you can incorporate their values into the meter, taking care to draw the pointer and to display the title only if the necessary values have been set. Note that `drawMeter` now includes an **erase** message, which ensures that previously drawn lines and text are erased before new lines and text are drawn.

```
drawMeter
  | thePen meterWidth xLft yBot pointer |
  self erase.
  meterWidth := self width * 3 // 4.
  xLft := self width - meterWidth // 2.
  yBot := self height // 2.
  thePen := self pen.
  thePen lineFrom: xLft @ yBot to: (xLft + meterWidth) @ yBot.
  min notNil & max notNil & value notNil
    ifTrue:
      [pointer :=
        (value - min) * meterWidth // (max - min).
      thePen lineFrom: (xLft + pointer) @ yBot
                  to: (xLft + pointer) @ (yBot - 10)].
  title notNil
    ifTrue:
      [thePen centerText: title
                    at: ((self width) // 2)
                        @ ((self height // 2)
                            + (2 * thePen font height))].
```

674   At this point, you know how to draw lines and to display text. In Section 33, you learn how to change the appearance of lines and text. In Section 35, you learn, in general, how to connect together various elements of a GUI. In particular, you learn how to connect the meter display to a selected food by supplying values for `min`, `max`, `value` and `title`.

675   Modify the `drawMeter` method such that it prints `Drawing...` in the transcript each time
PRACTICE   that it is called. Watch the transcript as you hide, reveal, enlarge, and shrink the window.

676   Define `ChartGraphPane`, a subclass of `GraphPane`. Instances are to have two variables:
PRACTICE   `values` and `title`. Also define `drawChart`, modeled on `drawMeter`, such that `drawChart` draws a chart using the values assigned to the `values` and the `title` variables. For example, given that the value of the `values` variable is the array `#(1 1 2 3 5 8)` and the value of the `title` variable is `Rabbit Population`, `drawChart` is to produce the following:

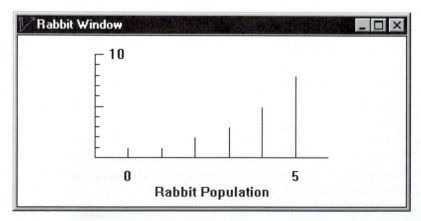

- If you want to display a window containing a drawing, **then** create subclasses of the `ViewManager`, `TopPane`, and `GraphPane` classes.

  then define a `createViews` method for the view-manager class, such as the following:

  ```
  createViews
      | theCalorieViewManager theTopPane theMeterPane |
      theCalorieViewManager := self.
      theTopPane := TopPane new.
      theMeterPane := MeterGraphPane new.
      "Set up the top pane"
      theCalorieViewManager addView: theTopPane.
      theTopPane owner: theCalorieViewManager.
      theTopPane labelWithoutPrefix: a title string .
      theTopPane noSmalltalkMenuBar.
      theTopPane framingRatio: a rectangle .
      "Set up the meter pane"
      theTopPane addSubpane: theMeterPane.
      theMeterPane owner: theCalorieViewManager.
      theMeterPane noScrollBars.
      theMeterPane framingRatio: a rectangle .
      theMeterPane when: #display perform: # a view-manager method .
  ```

  then define the method for the view manager named by the `when:perform:` message:

  ```
  the view-manager method named by when:perform:  thePane
      thePane a graph pane method .
  ```

  and then define a drawing method for the graph pane:

  ```
  the graph pane method
      ...
  ```

- If you want to draw lines or display text, **then** extract a pen from the graph pane by sending a pen message:

  ```
  the graph pane method
    | thePen |
    thePen := self pen.
    ...
  ```

- If you want to draw a line, **then** send the `lineFrom:to:` message to the pen:

  ```
  the pen lineFrom: start point to: end point
  ```

- If you want to display text, then send the `displayText:at:` or the `centerText:at:` message to the pen:

  `the pen` `displayText:` `a string` `at:` `a point`
  `the pen` `centerText:` `a string` `at:` `a point`

33 HOW TO USE THE GRAPHICS CONTEXT TO ALTER APPEARANCE

678 In Section 32, you learned how to draw lines. In this section, you learn how to change the appearance of lines and text. In Section 35, you learn how to connect together various elements of a GUI.

679 A pen is also called a **graphics context**, because a pen acts as a conduit that determines exactly how graphical commands affect an instance of the `GraphPane` class.

```
                    Graphics context, a pen
Graphical           ─────────────────────────
commands        ───────────────────────────────────▶   The graph pane
                    ─────────────────────────
```

680 You can set state information in the graphics context, as well as get state information. For example, if you want to draw a heavy red line, rather than an ordinary black one, you easily can modify the example of Segment 671 by adding messages that change line width and change color.

To get line width, you send the `lineWidth` message; to set line width, you send the `setLineWidth:` message with an integer argument.

To get line and text color, you send the `foreColor` message; to set line and text color, you send the `foreColor:` message with a color name—such as `ClrRed`, `ClrWhite`, or `ClrBlue`—used as an index into the `ColorConstants` pool dictionary established in Segment 672:

MeterGraphPane method definition	• instance

```
drawMeter
  | thePen meterWidth xLft yBot |
  meterWidth := self width * 3 // 4.
  xLft := self width - meterWidth // 2.
  yBot := self height // 2.
  thePen := self pen.
  thePen setLineWidth: 5.
  thePen foreColor: ClrRed.
  thePen lineFrom: xLft @ yBot to: (xLft + meterWidth) @ yBot.
  thePen lineFrom: (xLft + (meterWidth // 2)) @ yBot
              to: (xLft + (meterWidth // 2)) @ (yBot - 10).
  thePen centerText: 'Untitled'
            at: ((self width) // 2)
                @ ((self height // 2)
                  + (2 * thePen font height)).
```

681 Whenever you make a change to the value of a graphics context variable, you should first obtain the current value, and you should restore that value later.

Suppose, for example, that you want to change the color of the lines, but not to change the text. You use the `foreColor` method to obtain the current color associated with the graphics context. Then, you use `foreColor:` to change to another color temporarily. Finally, you use `foreColor:` again to restore the graphics context to the original state:

MeterGraphPane method definition   • instance

```
drawMeter
  | thePen meterWidth xLft yBot oldColor oldWidth |
  meterWidth := self width * 3 // 4.
  xLft := self width - meterWidth // 2.
  yBot := self height // 2.
  thePen := self pen.
  "Remember old values"
  oldColor := thePen foreColor.
  oldWidth := thePen width.
  "Set new values"
  thePen setLineWidth: 5.
  thePen foreColor: ClrRed.
  thePen lineFrom: xLft @ yBot to: (xLft + meterWidth) @ yBot.
  thePen lineFrom: (xLft + (meterWidth // 2)) @ yBot
            to: (xLft + (meterWidth // 2))
                @ (yBot - 10).
  "Reset to old values"
  thePen setLineWidth: oldWidth.
  thePen foreColor: oldColor.
  thePen centerText: 'Untitled'
            at: ((self width) // 2)
                @ ((self height // 2)
                    + (2 * thePen font height)).
```

682   You can change the font by sending a `font:` message to the graphics context, along with a suitable argument. In the following definition, for example, the suitable argument is a constructed font that you produce by sending the `faceName:` message to a font instance with an `'Algerian'` argument, and then sending the result the `bold:` message with a `true` argument:

MeterGraphPane method definition   • instance

```
drawMeter
  | thePen meterWidth xLft yBot oldFont |
  meterWidth := self width * 3 // 4.
  xLft := self width - meterWidth // 2.
  yBot := self height // 2.
  thePen := self pen.
  thePen lineFrom: xLft @ yBot to: (xLft + meterWidth) @ yBot.
  thePen lineFrom: (xLft + (meterWidth // 2)) @ yBot
            to: (xLft + (meterWidth // 2))
                @ (yBot - 10).
```

```
"Remember old values"
oldFont := thePen font.
"Set new values"
thePen font: (Font new faceName: 'Algerian'; bold: true).
thePen centerText: 'Untitled'
              at: ((self width) // 2)
                  @ ((self height // 2)
                      + (2 * thePen font height)).
"Reset to old values"
thePen font: oldFont.
```

The result is text printed in bold Algerian:

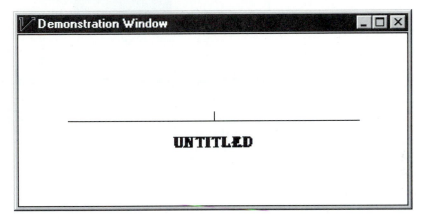

683 All Smalltalk environments provide many drawing messages. Two of the most useful are the `polygon:` and the `polygonFilled:` messages. Both are sent to graphics contexts; both take an array of points, which collectively defines a polygon. In the following, `polygon:` draws an open rectangle and `polygonFilled:` draws a filled rectangle.

MeterGraphPane method definition   • instance
```
drawMeter
  | thePen rectangleWidth rectangleHeight array1 array2 |
  rectangleWidth := self width * 1 // 4.
  rectangleHeight := self height * 1 // 3.
  array1 := Array with: rectangleWidth @ rectangleHeight
                  with: (rectangleWidth * 2) @ rectangleHeight
                  with: (rectangleWidth * 2) @ (rectangleHeight * 2)
                  with: rectangleWidth @ (rectangleHeight * 2).
  array2 := Array with: (rectangleWidth * 2) @ rectangleHeight
                  with: (rectangleWidth * 3) @ rectangleHeight
                  with: (rectangleWidth * 3) @ (rectangleHeight * 2)
                  with: (rectangleWidth * 2) @ (rectangleHeight * 2).
  thePen := self pen.
  thePen setFillColor: ClrBlack.
  thePen polygon: array1.
  thePen polygonFilled: array2.
```

The **setFillColor:** message is essential—it changes the fill color from white to black:

684 The **drawMeter** revision shown in Segment 683 produces the following result:

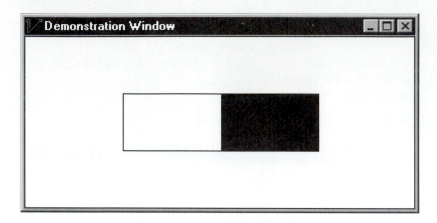

685 If you want to exert fine control over text placement, you need to know about the
SIDE TRIP **descender** and the **stringWidthOf:** messages.

When you display strings, the characters are placed on a **baseline**. Portions of all characters
appear above the baseline. Characters such as g have **descenders** that appear below the
baseline.

The distance by which a font extends above the baseline is that font's **height**, whereas the
distance by which the font's characters extends below the baseline is the font's **descent**.
The **height** and **descender** methods answer the maxima for the height and descent when
sent to a font instance:

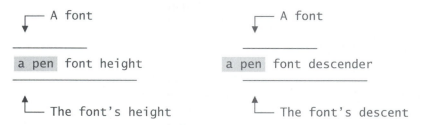

The **stringWidthOf:** method, when sent to a graphics context, answers the width that
a specified string would occupy if the string were displayed in the font associated with
graphics context:

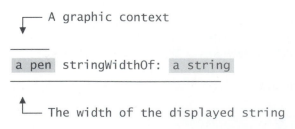

686
SIDE TRIP

The `ColorConstants` dictionary provides keys for common colors. If you need other colors, you can create your own by sending the `red:green:blue:` class method to the `GraphicsTool` class. The three arguments specify the intensity of red, green, and blue in the color, on a scale that ranges from 0 to 255. In the following example, the answer produced, 6553600, is a large integer that represents dark blue.

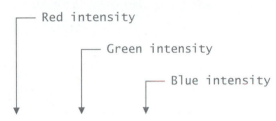

```
GraphicsTool red: 0 green: 0 blue: 100
```

687
PRACTICE

Define `ThermometerGraphPane`, a class that produces a drawing that looks like a traditional glass thermometer with a reading halfway between maximum and minimum. Pattern your definition on the `MeterGraphPane` class defined in Segment 681. Use the `circleFilled:` and the `setFillColor:` methods to draw the bulb. Use the `polygon:` and `polygonFilled:` methods to draw the rest of the thermometer.

688
PRACTICE

Define a class, `TrafficLight`, that produces a drawing that looks like a traffic light. Use the `setFillColor:`, `circleFilled:`, and `polygon:` methods.

689
HIGHLIGHTS

- Pens, also known as graphics contexts, contain information that determines how drawing is done.

- If you want to change line width, **then** instantiate the following pattern:

  `the pen` `setLineWidth:` `new width` .

- If you want to change the color with which lines are drawn and text displayed, **then** include `ColorConstants` in the pool-dictionary specification of the class, **and then** instantiate the following pattern, with a color such as `ClrRed`.

  `the pen` `foreColor:` `string-naming color` .

- If you want to change the font in which strings are displayed, **then** instantiate the following pattern:

  `the pen` `font: (Font new faceName:` `string-naming face` `)` .

- If you want to draw an open polygon, **then** instantiate the following pattern:

  `the pen` `polygon:` `an array of points` .

201

- **If** you want to draw a filled polygon, **then** include `ColorConstants` in the pool-dictionary specification of the class, **and then** instantiate the following pattern:

```
the pen setFillColor: string-naming color .
the pen polygonFilled: an array of points .
```

690   In this section, you learn how to create a list box, from which you can select a food. Then, you learn how to connect the selected food to the meter that you learned about in Section 32.

691   Your first objective is to produce a list box, such as the following:

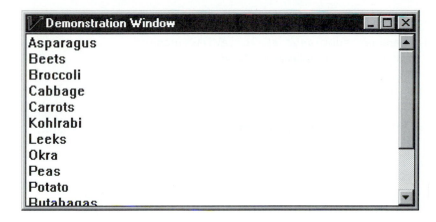

692   To create a list box, you alter the `createViews` method shown in Segment 664 in two ways: you add a `ListBox` instance, instead of a `MeterGraphPane` instance; and you arrange to respond to `select` and `getContents` events, rather than `display` events:

CalorieViewManager method definition   • instance

```
createViews
  | theTopPane theListBox |
  "Set up all panes"
  self addView: (theTopPane := TopPane new).
  theListBox := ListBox new.
  "Set up the top pane"
  theTopPane owner: self;
    labelWithoutPrefix: 'Demonstration Window';
    noSmalltalkMenuBar;
    addSubpane: theListBox;
    framingRatio: (1/4 @ (1/3) rightBottom: 3/4 @ (2/3)).
  "Set up the list box pane"
  theListBox owner: self;
    when: #getContents perform: #initializeListBox:;
    when: #select perform: #itemSelected:.
```

693   Now, having referred to `initializeListBox:` and `itemSelected:` in `when:perform:` messages, you must define those two callback methods for the `CalorieViewManager` class.

694 The `getContents` Smalltalk event occurs when a list box is created. Smalltalk responds by sending an `initializeListBox:` message to the `CalorieViewManager` instance.

To do its work, the `initializeListBox:` callback method must first obtain a list of foods. In preparation, you define the Food class as in Segment 455, you employ the file-reading program shown in Segment 456, and you define `tCalories` as in Segment 236.

695 Next, to enable the list box to be loaded with a list of food names, and to provide a handle for the selected food, you add two instance variables to the `CalorieViewManager` class:

CalorieViewManager class definition
```
ViewManager subclass: #CalorieViewManager
  instanceVariableNames: 'food foodList'
  classVariableNames: ''
  poolDictionaries: ''
```

696 Then, you define `initializeListBox:` to set the `foodList` variable:

CalorieViewManager method definition   • instance
```
initializeListBox: theListBox
  foodList := (Food collectFrom: 'c:\test\vtbls.dta').
  ...
```

697 Next, you arrange for the `initializeListBox` callback method to send a `contents:` message that provides the list box with food names obtained using a `collect:` message:

CalorieViewManager method definition   • instance
```
initializeListBox: theListBox
  foodList := (Food collectFrom: 'c:\test\vtbls.dta').
  theListBox contents: (foodList collect: [:p | p name]).
```

Thus, when the `#getContents` event occurs, in the course of creating the list box, the `initializeListBox:` message is sent; it, in turn, reads food information from a file, and uses that food information to set the contents of the list box.

698 The `select` event calls on the `itemSelected:` callback method when you click the mouse on a displayed item. For the moment, the `itemSelected:` callback method merely displays in the transcript the name of the selected food. To identify the selected food, `itemSelected:` uses the `selection` message to obtain the index of the selected name in the displayed list; then `itemSelected:` uses the `at:` message to obtain the corresponding Food instance from the Food-instance collection:

CalorieViewManager method definition   • instance
```
itemSelected: theListBox
  food := foodList at: theListBox selection.
  Transcript show: food name; cr.
```

204

In Smalltalk Express, the `ListBox` class happens to be a direct subclass of the `ControlPane` class, which, in turn, is a direct subclass of the `SubPane` class, which is a superclass of all widgets. The `ControlPane` class is a superclass of all widgets that are implemented by the operating system; other `SubPane` classes implement widgets in Smalltalk itself.

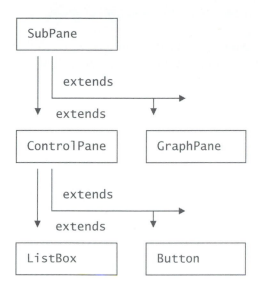

Alter the definition of `itemSelected` shown in Segment 698 such that not only the name of the selected food, but also the total number of calories in a serving is displayed in the transcript.

An instance of `MultipleSelectListBox` responds to the `selection` message with the index of the first item selected; it responds to the `selections` message with an ordered collection of the indexes selected. Alter the definition of `createViews` shown in Segment 692 such that `createViews` creates a `MultipleSelectionListBox` instance. Then, alter the definition of `itemSelected` such that the answers produced by both the `selection` and the `selections` messages are displayed whenever an item is selected.

- **If** you want to include a list box in an application, **then** insert a list-box variable, assign to it a `ListBox` instance, and instantiate the following pattern in the `createViews` definition:

```
the list box owner: the view manager .
the list box when: #getContents
             perform: initialization method
the list box when: #select
             perform: action method .
```

- If you want to define a list-box initialization method, **then** instantiate the following pattern for a view-manager method:

```
initialization key word theListBox
   theListBox contents: an ordered collection of strings .
```

- If you want to define a list-box action method, **then** instantiate the following pattern for a view-manager method, noting that the `selection` method answers an integer index:

```
selector theListBox
   ··· (theListBox selection) ···
```

HOW TO CONNECT TOGETHER DISPLAY ELEMENTS

703 In Section 32, you learned how to create a meterlike display. In Section 34, you learned how to work with list boxes. In this section, you learn how to connect the two together.

704 Your objective is to produce a list box, such as the following, from which you can select a food via a mouse click, and have the calorie content of the food displayed on a meter:

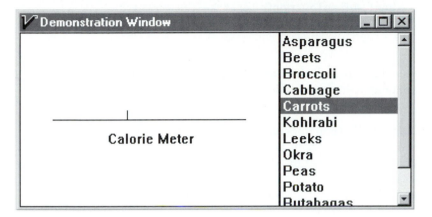

705 The first step toward connected display elements is to rewrite `createViews` such that both a `MeterGraphPane` and a `ListBox` are included. Now, both require `framingRatio:` messages, because both occupy only a fraction of the top pane to which they are connected by `addSubpane:` messages. Similarly, both require `when:perform:` messages so that they can send appropriate callback messages to the view manager in response to the `getContents` events that occur when the meter pane and the list box are created.

Also, you soon need to be able to refer to the meter by name; accordingly, you send the graph pane the `paneName:` message, with a string argument, `'CalorieMeter'`.

CalorieViewManager method definition   • instance

```
createViews
  | theTopPane theListBox theMeterPane |
  "Set up all panes"
  self addView: (theTopPane := TopPane new).
  theListBox := ListBox new.
  theMeterPane := MeterGraphPane new.
  "Set up the top pane"
  theTopPane owner: self;
    labelWithoutPrefix: 'Demonstration Window';
    noSmalltalkMenuBar;
    addSubpane: theListBox;
    addSubpane: theMeterPane;
    framingRatio: (1/4 @ (1/3) rightBottom: 3/4 @ (2/3)).
```

```
    "Set up the list-box pane"
    theListBox owner: self;
      when: #getContents perform: #initializeListBox:;
      when: #select perform: #itemSelected:;
      framingRatio: (2/3 @ 0 rightBottom: 1 @ 1).
    "Set up the meter pane"
    theMeterPane owner: self;
      paneName: 'CalorieMeter';
      noScrollBars;
      when: #getContents perform: #initializeMeter:;
      when: #display perform: #callDrawMeter:;
      framingRatio: (0 @ 0 rightBottom: 2/3 @ 1).
```

706 To set the `min` and `max` variables of the meter, you first expand the definition of the `MeterGraphPane` to include setters:

MeterGraphPane method definition • instance
```
setMin: aNumber min := aNumber
```
MeterGraphPane method definition • instance
```
setMax: aNumber max := aNumber
```
MeterGraphPane method definition • instance
```
setValue: aNumber value := aNumber
```
MeterGraphPane method definition • instance
```
setTitle: aString title := aString
```

707 Next, you add the `setMin:`, `setMax:` and `setTitle:` setters to the `initializeMeter:` callback method. You also send the `event:` message, with an argument, `#display`. The `event:` message tells the meter pane to act as though the event, `#display`, has occurred:

CalorieViewManager method definition • instance
```
initializeMeter: theMeter
  theMeter setMin: 0;
          setMax: 100;
          setTitle: 'Calorie Meter';
          event: #display.
```

From the definition of `createViews` in Segment 705, you know that the response to the `event:` message, with a `#display` argument, is to send the `callDrawMeter:` message to the view manager, thus drawing the meter.

708 The `initializeMeter:` callback method is sent when the list box is initialized because, as shown in Segment 705, the view manager's `createViews` method contains a `when:perform:` message, and that `when:perform:` message connects the `getContents` event with the `initializeMeter:` callback method.

709   At this point, if you send open to a CalorieViewManager instance, you see the following display:

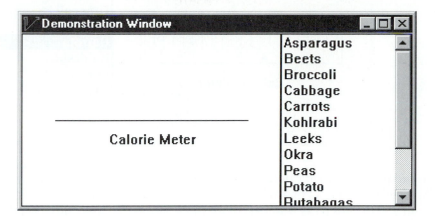

The meter displays a title, but does not yet display a value, because the value variable of the MeterGraphPane instance has yet to be set.

710   Now, you need to connect to the meter changing food names and changing food-calorie values. One way to connect them is to redefine the itemSelected: callback method, defined previously in Segment 698, such that itemSelected: sends messages to the meter, identified by the name identified by the definition shown in Segment 705.

```
CalorieViewManager method definition        • instance
itemSelected: theListBox
  food := foodList at: theListBox selection.
  (self paneNamed: 'CalorieMeter')
    setValue: food tCalories;
    event: #display.
```

The first message sent to the meter sets the value variable. The second message tells the meter to act as though the #display event has occurred, as explained in Segment 707.

711   When you send open to a CalorieViewManager instance now, you first see the same display shown in Segment 709. Then, however, when you click on a food name, you see the same display shown in Segment 704.

712   Using the more elaborate meter shown in Appendix A, produces the following, more elaborate display, in which the minimum and maximum values are displayed, as well as a value:

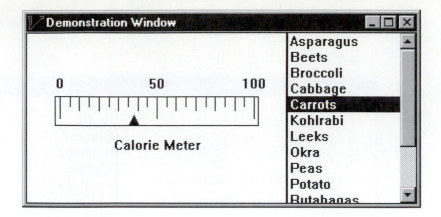

713   At this point, the food-calorie display is spread out over many segments in several sections. Accordingly, versions of all class and method definitions are brought together, so you can study the various parts with less trouble, in Appendix A. Note, however, that Appendix A contains the extra methods required to implement a menu bar, all of which are explained in Section 36.

714   The open method that you use to actuate the view manager sends default preInitWindow
side trip and initWindow methods that do nothing. By overriding those do-nothing methods, you can arrange for various initializations that do not fit conveniently in other places.

The preInitWindow message is sent to the view manager by the open method before graphical elements are created. You can define the preInitWindow method to load data into an application.

The initWindow message is sent to the view manager by the open method after graphical elements are created, but before they appear on your screen. You can define the initWindow method to set variables in graphical elements.

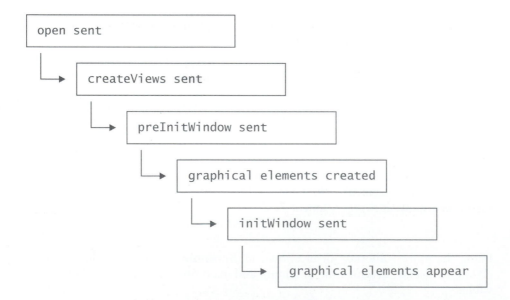

You are unlikely to need either the `preInitWindow` method or the `initWindow` method because you can take care of most initialization work using initialization methods launched by `getContents` events via the `when:perform:` mechanism.

715
PRACTICE Alter the calorie-dictionary application such that the food list is on the left, rather than on the right.

716
PRACTICE Alter the calorie-dictionary application such that, each time that a food item is selected, the number of fat grams in one serving of the food is shown, rather than the total number of calories. Adjust the meter's title and range appropriately.

717
PRACTICE Alter the calorie-dictionary application such that, each time that a food item is selected, the number of calories in one serving of the food is added to the total of all items so far selected, and that total is shown on the meter. The meter's title should be `Total Calories`, and the values shown on the meter should range from 0 to 2000, as in the following illustration:

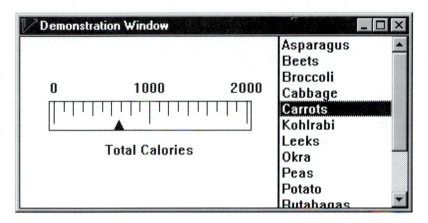

718
HIGHLIGHTS

- If you want a subpane to fill only part of a top pane, **then** instantiate the following pattern in the definition of `createViews`:

  `the subpane` `framingRatio:` `a rectangle`

  The rectangle's upper-left and lower-right corners are fractions that determine where the subpane begins and ends relative to the top pane.

- If you want a view-manager method to send a message to a particular view, **then** name the view by instantiating the following pattern in the `createViews` method:

  `the pane` `paneName:` `a string`

- If you want a view manager method to send a message to a named view, **then** instantiate the following pattern:

  `(self paneNamed:` `pane name, a string` `)` `message selector`

- A `preInitWindow` message is sent to the view manager by the `open` method before graphical elements are created.

- An `initWindow` message is sent to the view manager by the `open` method after graphical elements are created, but before they are displayed.

36 HOW TO DISPLAY MENUS AND FILE DIALOG WINDOWS

719 In this section, you learn to incorporate menus and menu bars in an application. You also learn to use a file-dialog window so that you no longer have to wire a file name into your application. Such features enable your application to present a polished look and feel.

720 **Menu bars** exhibit labels, each of which, when clicked, exhibits a **menu**. Each menu, in turn, exhibits **menu items**, some of which may, themselves, be menus.

As the following shows, the emerging application has a menu bar with one menu, `Options`. When clicked, the `Options` menu presents two menu items: `Food Type` and `Mode`. The purpose of the `Food Type` menu item is to open a file-dialog window that enables you to load new information into the application; the purpose of the `Mode` menu item is to determine whether the meter shows total calories or only fat calories.

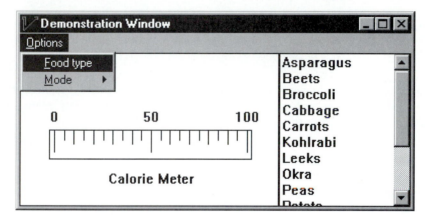

721 You create menus and menu bars as illustrated in the following examples:

```
MenuWindow new      ←── Creates a new menu bar.
Menu new            ←── Creates a new menu.
```

722 You create `MenuWindow` and `Menu` instances inside the **createViews** method, in which the value of **self** is the view manager. Each menu has a title and an owner; you establish both by sending messages. The owner is the view manager assigned to the **self** variable:

```
Menu new
  title: 'Options';
  owner: self;
  ...
```

723 For your program to be fully compliant with operating-system guidelines, you must designate a character in each menu title as the **mnemonic**. When you designate such a character, you can select the menu by pressing the corresponding key while holding the `Alt` key down.

To designate a character as the mnemonic, you precede that character with the tilde character, as in the following, in which the O in Options is the mnemonic:

```
Menu new
   title: '~Options';
   owner: self;
   ...
```

724 You add menu items to a menu using the appendItem:selector: message. The first argument is the string that appears in the menu; the second argument is a literal symbol that identifies the callback message to be sent to the view manager, the owner, whenever the item is selected from the menu:

```
Menu new
   title: '~Options';
   owner: self;
   appendItem: '~Food Type' selector: #resetListBox;
   ...
```

725 You can divide menu items into groups by adding a line, called a **separator**, between them. To add a separator, you use the appendSeparator method. For example, the following adds a separator after the Options item:

```
Menu new
   title: '~Options';
   owner: self;
   appendItem: '~Food Type' selector: #resetListBox;
   appendSeparator;
   ...
```

726 Menu items can be menus. For example, the following uses the appendSubMenu: method to establish that the Options menu has a submenu, the Mode menu:

```
Menu new
   title: '~Options';
   owner: self;
   appendItem: '~Food Type' selector: #resetListBox;
   appendSubMenu: (Menu new
                    title: '~Mode';
                    owner: self;
                    ...)
```

727 The Mode menu, in turn, has menu items. By using nil in place of an ordinary selector, you defer the need to define a method; if the item is selected, no message is sent:

```
Menu new
  title: '~Options';
  owner: self;
  appendItem: '~Food Type' selector: #resetListBox;
  appendSubMenu: (Menu new
                    title: '~Mode';
                    owner: self;
                    appendItem: '~Fat Calories' selector: nil;
                    appendItem: '~Total Calories' selector: nil)
```

728 Once you have created a menu, such as the `Options` menu, you must connect that menu to a menu window using the `addMenu:` message. Then, you also must connect the menu window to the top pane of an application. Both connections occur in the `createViews` method of a view manager.

The following definition illustrates the connections by way of additions to the `createViews` method shown in Segment 705. The definition also includes a name for the list box, which you need later in Segment 737.

CalorieViewManager method definition • instance

```
createViews
  | theTopPane theListBox theMeterPane theMenuWindow |
  "Set up all panes"
  self addView: (theTopPane := TopPane new).
  theListBox := ListBox new.
  theMeterPane := MeterGraphPane new.
  "Set up the top pane"
  theTopPane owner: self;
    labelWithoutPrefix: 'Demonstration Window';
    noSmalltalkMenuBar;
    addSubpane: theListBox;
    addSubpane: theMeterPane;
    menuWindow: (theMenuWindow := MenuWindow new);
    framingRatio: (1/4 @ (1/3) rightBottom: 3/4 @ (2/3)).
  "Set up the menu window"
  theMenuWindow addMenu:
    (Menu new
       title: '~Options';
       owner: self;
       appendItem: '~Food Type' selector: #resetListBox;
       appendSubMenu:
         (Menu new
            title: '~Mode';
            owner: self;
            appendItem: '~Fat Calories' selector: nil;
            appendItem: '~Total Calories' selector: nil)).
  "Definition continued on next page"
```

215

```
"Definition continued from previous page"
"Set up the list-box pane"
theListBox owner: self;
  paneName: 'ListBox';
  when: #getContents perform: #initializeListBox:;
  when: #select perform: #itemSelected:;
  framingRatio: (2/3 @ 0 rightBottom: 1 @ 1).
"Set up the meter pane"
theMeterPane owner: self;
  paneName: 'CalorieMeter';
  noScrollBars;
  when: #getContents perform: #initializeMeter:;
  when: #display perform: #callDrawMeter:;
  framingRatio: (0 @ 0 rightBottom: 2/3 @ 1).
```

729 At this point, the revised application has a menu bar, a menu, and two menu items, but clicking on those display elements has no effect.

To put function behind your menu bar, menu, and menu items, you define the callback methods identified in appendItem:selector: messages. For example, you define the resetListBox method to create an instance of the FileDialog class, which ultimately enables a new value to be assigned to the foodList variable of the view manager.

730 Creating an instance of the FileDialog class, assigned to the theFileDialog variable, is straightforward:

```
theFileDialog := FileDialog new.
```

731 To arrange for a file-dialog window to display only those files that have a particular extension, you restrict display using the fileSpec: method, with a wildcard character, *, as in the following example:

```
theFileDialog fileSpec: '*.dta'.
```

732 When you are ready to display the file-dialog window, you use the open method:

```
theFileDialog open.
```

The open method defined for FileDialog instances does not produce an answer until you act by clicking the Open or Cancel button in the file-dialog window.

733 To obtain the selected file name, once you click the Open button in the file-dialog window, you use the file method, as in the following example, which assigns the file name to the file variable:

```
file := theFileDialog file.
```

734 If you click the Cancel button, rather than the Open button, the file method answers nil.

735 Now, you can assemble what you have just learned into the `resetListBox` callback method defined for the `CalorieViewManager` class. Note that callback methods sent in response to menu selections do not have arguments:

CalorieViewManager method definition   • instance

```
resetListBox
  | theFileDialog file |
  (theFileDialog := FileDialog new)
    fileSpec: '*.dta';
    open.
  file := theFileDialog file.
  ...
```

736 Next, you add the apparatus required to determine that a file has been selected, to extract information from the file, and to assign a value to the `foodList` variable:

CalorieViewManager method definition   • instance

```
resetListBox
  | theFileDialog file |
  (theFileDialog := FileDialog new)
    fileSpec: '*.dta';
    open.
  (file := theFileDialog file) notNil
    ifTrue:
      [foodList := (Food collectFrom: file).
       ...].
```

737 To respond properly to a request to look at a new file, the `resetListBox` callback method must communicate with the list box and with the meter pane. The `resetListBox` callback method communicates with the list box and with the meter pane using names, as explained in Section 35. The contents of the list box is changed, and the value in the meter is set to `nil`:

CalorieViewManager method definition   • instance

```
resetListBox
  | theFileDialog file |
  (theFileDialog := FileDialog new)
    fileSpec: '*.dta';
    open.
  (file := theFileDialog file) notNil
    ifTrue:
      [foodList :=  (Food collectFrom: file).
       (self paneNamed: 'ListBox')
         contents: (foodList collect: [:p | p name]).
       (self paneNamed: 'CalorieMeter')
         setValue: nil; event: #display].
```

738 The calorie-dictionary application is now complete. All the methods required to implement the calorie dictionary, including the methods required to implement a menu bar, are brought together in Appendix A.

739 To package your work for application users, you perform a ritual, described in Appendix B, that separates applications from your development environment. Packaged applications have no transcripts or workspaces. You see those windows intended for users only; you do not see those intended for programmers.

740 **PRACTICE** Write methods to be activated by the `Fat Calories` and `Total Calories Mode` menu options. Your methods are to change the title of the meter and to change the value presented accordingly.

741 **PRACTICE** Alter the definition of `createViews` shown in Segment 728 such that the `Mode` submenu is elevated to the menu bar, as shown in the following illustration:

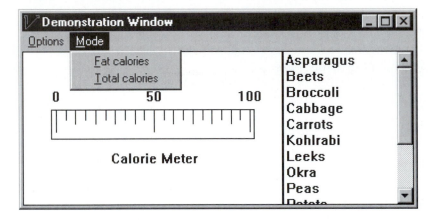

742 **HIGHLIGHTS**

- If you want to make use of a menu bar, **then** create instances of the `Menu` class by instantiating the following pattern inside the definition of the `createViews` method:

```
Menu new
    title:  menu-naming string ;
    owner: self;
    appendItem:  item-naming string
      selector: # view-manager method name ;
    appendItem:  another item-naming string
      selector: # another view-manager method name ;
    ...
```

- If you want to have a program react when a particular menu item has been selected, **then** define a `view manager` method named by a `appendItem:selector:` message.

218

- **If** you want to specify submenus, **then** use the `appendSubMenu:` method, rather than the `appendItem:selector:` method:

```
Menu new
   title: menu-naming string ;
   owner: self;
   appendSubMenu: (Menu new
                     title: menu-naming string ;
                     owner: self;
                     ...);
   appendSubMenu: (Menu new
                     title: another menu-naming string ;
                     owner: self;
                     ...);
   ...
```

- **If** you want to tie a menu to a menu window, **then** instantiate the following pattern in the definition of the **createViews** method:

```
...
   the top pane  menuWindow: (theMenuWindow := MenuWindow new).
...
   the menu window  addMenu: a menu
...
```

- **If** you want to open a file-dialog window, **then** instantiate the following pattern:

```
( file-dialog variable  := FileDialog new)
   fileSpec: file-specifying string ;
   open.
```

- `FileDialog` instances answer a file name when sent the `file` message if you have clicked the Open button; such instances answer `nil` when sent the `file` message if you have clicked the `cancel` button.

- **If** you want to extract and make use of the file name answered by a file-dialog window, **then** instantiate the following pattern:

```
( file name  := file-dialog variable  file) notNil
   ifTrue: [ appropriate action-specifying expressions ].
```

37 HOW TO DEVELOP A GUI USING A GUI BUILDER

743   Since Section 32, you have been learning about how to construct GUIs of growing complexity. In this section, you learn how to use a GUI builder to simplify your work and to increase your productivity.

744   You can develop an extremely fancy GUI using Smalltalk, but when you develop an extremely fancy GUI, the `createViews` method defined for the view manager grows complex in proportion:

- The `createViews` method requires program fragments for each graphical element. You must supply all such fragments.

- Each graphical element supports a collection of clicked events. You must specify the events that your application is to recognize, along with the names of the responding callback methods.

- Each graphical element requires a message specification of where it is to appear in the application window. You must write complex specifications if you want to include information about how the graphical element is to move and shrink or grow as the surrounding window shrinks or grows.

- Your application may require a menu bar. You must write a complex specification for that menu bar inside the `createViews` method if the menu has many elements, particularly if there are many submenus.

All these facts ensure that the definition of `createViews` for complex applications will be tedious and error prone.

The facts also ensure that changes will be difficult and time consuming.

745   From what you learned in Segment 744, you readily conclude that you need help whenever you define and maintain the `createViews` method for a complex application. You need the most help in arranging graphical elements and organizing details.

746   Fortunately, GUIs are especially good at supplying help with arranging graphical elements and organizing details. Accordingly, Smalltalk suppliers implement GUIs that help you build GUIs.

747   As an illustration, you see how to build a simple meter-testing application containing two buttons and a meter:

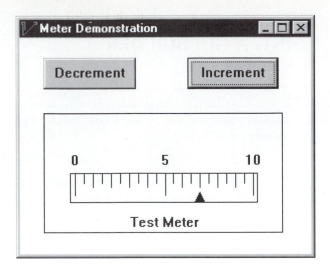

Each time that you click Decrement, the meter dial is to move down 1 unit; each time that you click Increment, the meter dial is to move up 1 unit.

748　To access Smalltalk Express's GUI builder, you click **WindowBuilder Pro→New Window** in the transcript window. Then, you see the following appear:

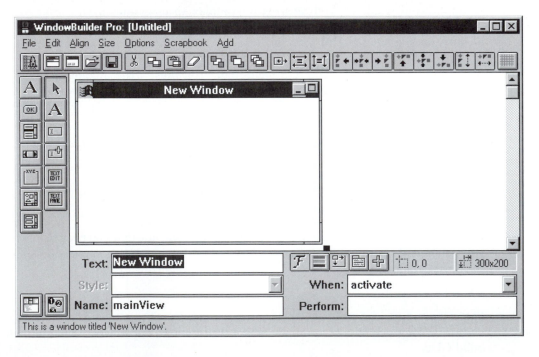

749　Building your GUI becomes a matter of using the menu bar, buttons, and text fields of the GUI builder to place graphical elements, to supply titles, and to establish connections between events and callback methods.

For example, to supply a title for your application, you replace **New Window** in the Text field with, say, **Meter Demonstration**. Your application window immediately exhibits the new title:

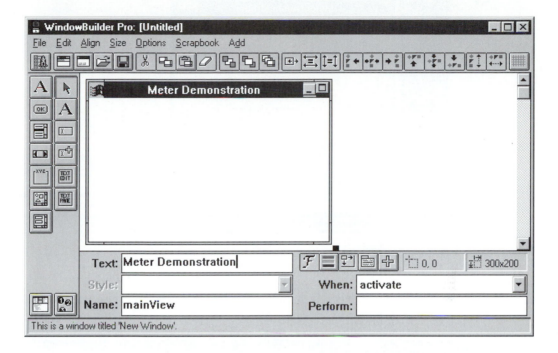

750   Next, suppose that you decide to install a Decrement button. You first click the button on the left side showing the OK-button icon, the one under the button labeled A.

Then, a new set of buttons appears in the adjacent column. You click the OK-button icon in that adjacent column, indicating that you want a labeled button.

At this point, you move the cursor inside the application window, which is now titled Meter Demonstration. A click, drag, and release produces a button.

You proceed to replace **Button** in the Text field with your preferred label, **Decrement**.

Next, you move to the When: list box and the Perform: text field. You select the clicked option from the list box, and type decrementMeter, without a colon, in the text field. By so doing, you indicate that you will supply a callback method named decrementMeter:, with a colon, for the clicked event associated with the button.

As soon as you supply the method name, an asterisk appears in front of clicked, which indicates that a callback method name has been supplied.

All this work leads to the following display:

Click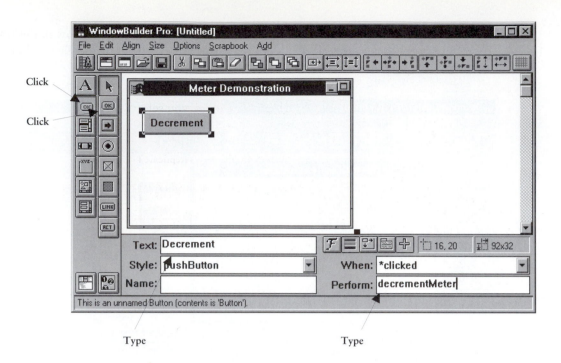

Click

Type   Type

751 Now, you install an `Increment` button following the steps that you used to install the `Decrement` button shown in Segment 750:

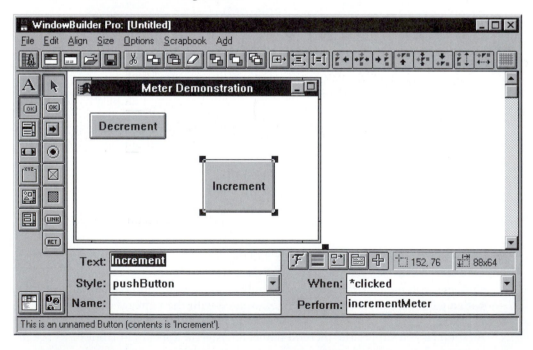

752 Alas, your buttons differ in size and show no alignment. But a few button clicks are all you need to correct the size and alignment.

To arrange for the height and width of the buttons to be the same, you first select one button, the **master**, and then, with the shift key held down, you select the second button, the **slave**. Then, clicking the replicate-height and replicate-width buttons forces the dimensions of the slave to be the same as the master.

Similarly, to align the buttons along, say, their centers, you select the master and the slave, and then click on the align-by-vertical-centers button:

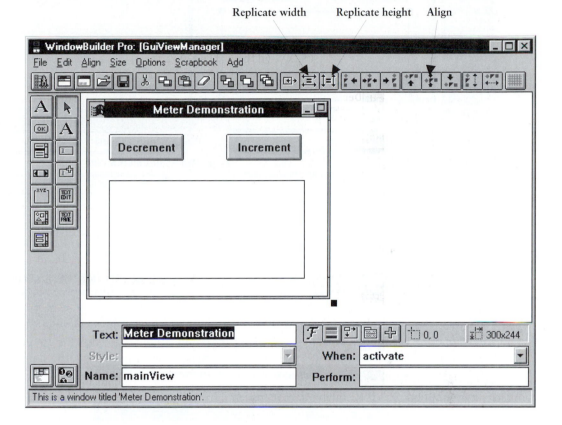

753   Now, you need to install the meter. You click **Add→Add Custom Pane**, and then select `MeterGraphPane`. A click, drag, and release produces a rectangle in which a meter is to appear when the application is launched.

Note, however, that the rectangle, being a graph pane, has scroll bars. You eliminate them by selecting `noScrollBars` in the `Style:` list box.

Next, you supply a name for the meter by typing `the meter` in the `Name:` field. You need the name later when you define the `decrementMeter:` and `incrementMeter:` methods.

Finally, you move to the `When:` list box and the `Perform:` text field to specify two callback methods. For the `display` event, you specify `callDrawMeter`. For the `getContents` event, you specify `initializeMeter`.

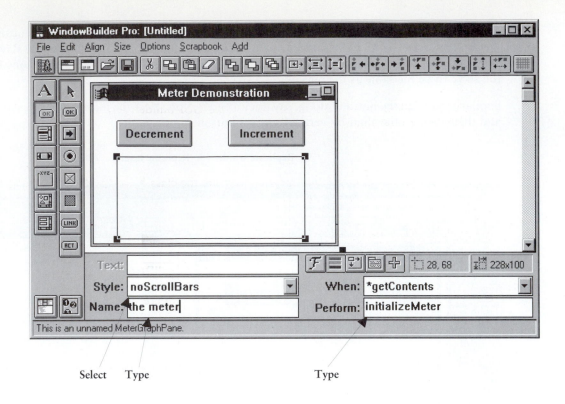

Select   Type   Type

754 At this point, all the graphical elements are complete, but all you have is a graphical
     Potemkin village. Many software vendors use such villages to sell software projects.

755 To convert your graphical Potemkin village into a real application, you must first cre-
     ate a subclass of the VewManager class for the application. You do this by clicking
     File→Save As..., at which point a dialog box emerges, in which you type the name of a
     subclass of the VewManager class, say GuiViewManager:

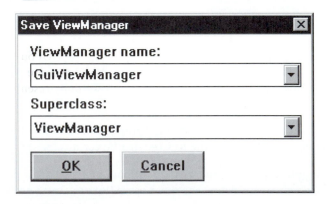

756 Now, just after you specify the name of the new subclass of the VewManager class, the
     GUI builder does a great deal of work for you:

- The GUI builder defines the `createViews` method for the new class.

- The GUI builder defines templates for all the callbacks that you need to complete the application.

For the `GuiViewManager` class, for example, the GUI builder defines templates for the `decrementMeter:`, `incrementMeter:`, `initializeMeter:`, and `callDrawMeter:` methods.

757   To see what the GUI builder has done, you activate the class-hierarchy browser, and then you move to the `GuiViewManager` class. You note that five methods are defined.

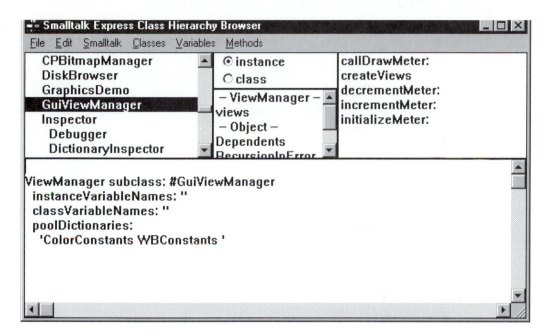

758   If you select the `createViews` method, you see that the GUI builder has defined a complex `createViews` method. The coding style differs from the one that you have seen in other definitions of `createViews`, but you readily see a family resemblance.

759   Novices should never edit the `createViews` method defined by the GUI builder. The Smalltalk Express GUI builder is able to handle certain manual changes, such as changes to strings and numbers; in general, however, manual changes may make it impossible for the GUI builder to maintain the `createViews` definition as your requirements change or grow.

760   Now, you should select one of the callback methods, such as the `decrementMeter:` method. You see a template:

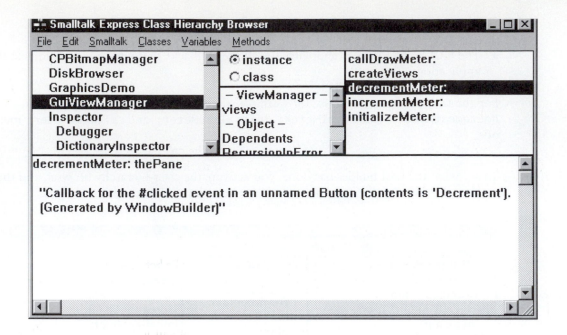

761 All that remains is to fill in the templates to provide the behavior you want. For example, in the decrementMeter: method—the callback method for the clicked event—you arrange to set the value, in the meter named 'the meter', to 1 less than the current value. Then, you activate the display event to redraw the meter with the new value.

GuiViewManager method definition   • instance
```
decrementMeter: theButton
  | meter |
  meter := self paneNamed: 'the meter'.
  meter setValue: meter getValue - 1;
        event: #display
```

You define the incrementMeter callback method analogously:

GuiViewManager method definition   • instance
```
incrementMeter: theButton
  | meter |
  meter := self paneNamed: 'the meter'.
  meter setValue: meter getValue + 1;
          event: #display
```

762 To initialize the meter, using the initializeMeter method—the callback method for the getContents event—you arrange to set various variable values and actuate the display event:

```
initializeMeter: theMeter
  theMeter setMin: 0;
           setMax: 10;
           setValue: 5;
           setTitle: 'Test Meter';
           event: #display
```

763 Finally, to respond to the `display` event, you define the `callDrawMeter` callback method. That method simply sends the `drawMeter` method to the meter:

```
callDrawMeter: theMeter
  theMeter drawMeter
```

764 If a value established by the `setValue:` method does not lie between the values established by the `setMin:` and `setMax:` methods, `drawMeter`, as defined in Appendix A, does not draw a pointer.

765 After you have defined the four callback methods, you can launch your application by pressing the rocket button:

Press

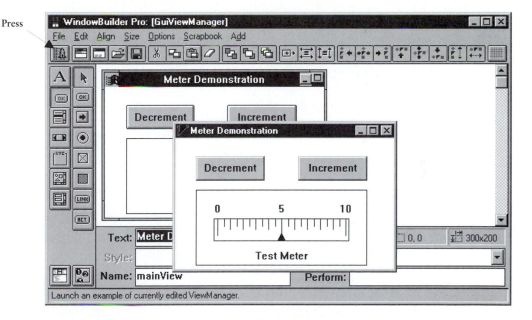

766 Note that you do little work in creating the sample application. You need to define only four callback methods—the more complex work of defining `createViews` is done for you.

In general, a GUI builder raises your productivity a great deal. Your productivity rises even more if your GUI builder provides sophisticated built-in graphical elements, such as meters and various charts, in addition to the usual buttons and list boxes.

767
SIDE TRIP

In Segment 739, you learned that you can perform a ritual, described in Appendix B, that separates applications from your development environment. The same ritual works for applications produced with the GUI builder.

768
SIDE TRIP

If you wish, you can align the graph pane precisely with respect to the buttons, but first you must create a temporary graphical element with respect to which you size and align the meter. Then, you align the left edge of the `Decrement` button with respect to the left edge of the temporary element, and the right edge of the `Increment` button to the right edge of the temporary element. Finally, you delete the temporary element. Just about anything will do as a temporary element—a button, for example.

769
SIDE TRIP

The WindowBuilder Pro™interface is available not only for Smalltalk Express, but also for Visual Age for Smalltalk™; see page 289.

770
PRACTICE

Use the Smalltalk Express GUI builder to implement a version of the `createViews` method defined in Appendix A.

771
PRACTICE

Use the Smalltalk Express GUI builder to implement an application that allows you to display growth in the population of rabbits as suggested by the following illustration:

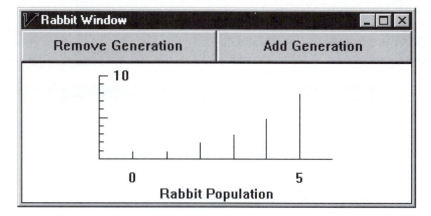

Each time that the `Remove Generation` button is pressed, the number of generations is to decrease by 1. Each time that the `Add Generation` button is pressed, the number of generations is to increase by 1. You are to use the `ChartGraphPane` class and `drawChart` method that you defined in Segment 676.

772
HIGHLIGHTS

- **If you want to create a GUI, then** do the work using a GUI builder.

- GUI builders help you to incorporate various graphical elements into your applications.

- GUI builders help you to size and align graphical elements.

- GUI builders help you to label graphical elements.

- GUI builders help you to connect events to callback methods.

38 HOW TO WORK WITH A COMMERCIAL SMALLTALK

773 When you migrate from a free Smalltalk, such as Smalltalk Express, to a commercial Smalltalk, such as VisualWorks™, you find that the core of the language changes little, but that there are important extensions that increase your productivity. Category and protocol grouping and input–output extensions are described in this section. Other extensions, described in subsequent sections, deal with the extremely important model–viewer–controller paradigm and the construction of GUIs.

774 When you start VisualWorks, you are presented with a transcript and a workspace. If you click **Browse→All Classes** in the transcript, VisualWorks opens the system browser. If you then click **Magnitude-General** in the first column, **Magnitude** in the second, **comparing** in the third, and < in the fourth, you see the following:

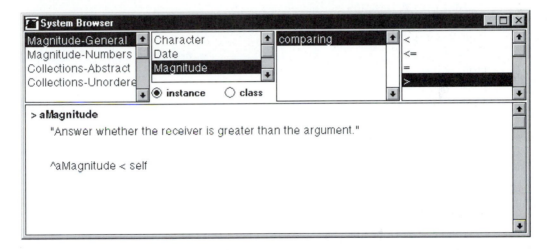

775 In the system browser, the `Magnitude` class is grouped with other classes into a **category** named `Magnitude-General`. VisualWorks uses such categories to group together classes with a common purpose. The `Magnitude` and `Date` classes, for example, are in the same category because they work together to solve problems involving date manipulation.

776 VisualWorks not only adds category grouping for classes, but also adds **protocol** grouping for methods.

VisualWorks uses protocols to group together methods that share a common purpose. In the `Magnitude` class, there is only one protocol, named `comparing`. In other classes, you find protocols with names such as `initialize-release`, `accessing`, `changing`, and `updating`.

777 **Category names** begin with an uppercase character; **protocol names** begin with a lowercase character.

778   The virtue of categories and protocols is that they provide mechanisms for organizing your work.

In particular, you are likely to place all the classes in a particular application into one new category of your own choosing.

In the examples shown in the rest of this book, for example, the Experiment category and the experimenting category are widely used.

779   Suppose that you added category and protocol information to the definitions presented in Segment 556. If you use a compact rendering of what you would see in the system browser—a rendering that includes category and protocol information—you have the following:

Experiment	Weight		

```
Magnitude subclass: #Weight
  instanceVariableNames: 'magnitude'
  classVariableNames: ''
  poolDictionaries: ''
  category: 'Experiment'
```

Experiment	Weight	• instance	accessing

```
magnitude
  ^ magnitude
```

Magnitude-Numbers	Number	• instance	conversion

```
gm
  ^ Weight new initialize: self
```

Experiment	Weight	• instance	initialize-release

```
initialize: aNumber
  magnitude := aNumber
```

Experiment	Weight	• instance	displaying

```
printString
  ^ magnitude printString , 'gm'
```

Experiment	Weight	• instance	arithmetic

```
+ aWeight
  ^ (self magnitude + aWeight magnitude) gm
```

Experiment	Weight	• instance	comparing

```
< aWeight
  ^ (self magnitude < aWeight magnitude)
```

780   In Segment 779, note that the definition of the Weight class, like all class definitions, carries an additional argument, marked by category:, which specifies the category to which the class belongs.

781   Categories and protocols simplify the filing-out operations initially explained in Section 30. In that section, you learned that you can file out the definition of particular class, along with all the methods defined for that class, or, alternatively, you can file out just one method. Now, with categories and protocols, you have additional flexibility: you can file out by category, thus filing out all the associated classes and methods, and you can file out by protocol, thus filing out all the associated methods.

232

782   Of course, the chunk-file format for VisualWorks differs slightly from that of Smalltalk Express, because it must carry information about categories and protocols.

For example, if you file out the definitions shown in Segment 779, the specification of the `Weight` class has an extra `category:` argument, and the specification of each method includes a protocol designation:

```
Magnitude subclass: #Weight
        instanceVariableNames: 'magnitude '
        classVariableNames: ''
        poolDictionaries: ''
        category: 'Experiment'!
!Weight methodsFor: 'accessing'!
magnitude
  ^ magnitude! !
!Weight methodsFor: 'initializing'!
initialize: aNumber
  magnitude := aNumber! !
!Weight methodsFor: 'displaying'!
printString
  ^ magnitude printString , 'gm'! !
!Weight methodsFor: 'arithmetic'!
+ aWeight
  ^ (self magnitude + aWeight magnitude) gm! !
!Weight methodsFor: 'comparing'!
< aWeight
  ^ (self magnitude < aWeight magnitude)! !
```

783   The next major distinction between VisualWorks and Smalltalk Express lies in the handling of input and output from files. In Section 22, you learned to create input streams, using Smalltalk Express, as demonstrated by the following example:

```
inputStream := File pathName: 'c:\test\input.dta'.
```

In VisualWorks you create an input stream as follows:

```
inputStream := 'c:\test\input.dta' asFilename readStream.
```

Similarly, you create an output stream as follows:

```
outputStream := 'c:\test\output.dta' asFilename writeStream.
```

784   Alas, input–output distinctions often wreck your ability to translate a program written in one implementation of a programming language into another implementation. In particular, many details of the input–output framework differ between VisualWorks and Smalltalk Express.

785

HIGHLIGHTS

- VisualWorks, in contrast to Smalltalk Express, groups classes into categories and methods into protocols. Categories and protocols are formed around common purposes.

- Because VisualWorks has categories and protocols, the chunk-file format of VisualWorks differs from that of Smalltalk Express.

- Many details of input–output programming differ between VisualWorks and Smalltalk Express.

HOW TO WORK WITH THE MODEL–VIEWER–CONTROLLER PARADIGM

786   The most distinctive difference between VisualWorks and Smalltalk Express is that VisualWorks uses a different, more complex approach to separating user-interface classes and instances from those classes and instances that are not part of the user interface. VisualWorks's approach is called the model–viewer–controller paradigm. In this section, you learn how model instances communicate with dependent-part instances and with controller instances.

In this section's illustrations, you see various objects manually assigned to global variables. Such manual assignment to global variables is for illustration only; ordinarily, a GUI builder attaches models, viewers, and controllers to one another using instance variables, as described in Section 41.

787   In VisualWorks, instances of the `Model` class and the `DependentPart` class work together. The work begins when the model instance sends itself a **change message**:

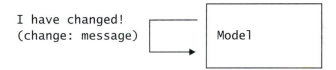

The sole purpose of a change message is to activate a method in the model that sends **update messages** to dependent parts, telling those dependent parts that a change in the model may require an update in the dependent parts:

Then, the dependent part examines the model to see what exactly has changed, and responds accordingly:

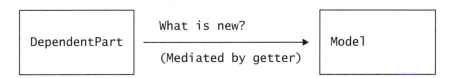

788   Typically, the dependent part is an instance of the `View` class: a graphic-managing subclass of the `DependentPart` class. Such dependent parts are **viewers** of the **model**.

789   A model instance can have many viewers. Thus, the information in one model can be displayed by multiple, up-to-date graphical elements, via update and getter messages:

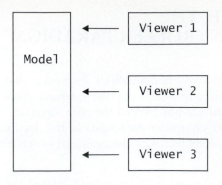

790 A **controller** is in charge of dealing with input devices—typically, the keyboard and mouse. When a controller notes that a keystroke or mouse click is of interest, that controller sends a message to the corresponding model:

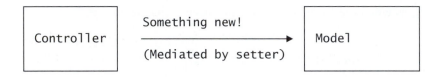

791 Thus, in the **model–viewer–controller paradigm**, the following sequence of messages represents what typically occurs after, for example, a mouse click is noted by a controller:

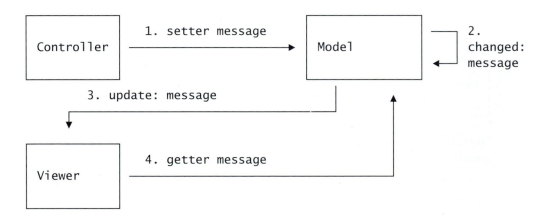

792 Typically, for every viewer, there is an associated controller that handles keyboard and mouse activity during the time that the corresponding viewer is the one associated with the **active window**.

793 To see the model–viewer–controller paradigm at work on a deeper level, you start by creating subclasses of the Model, View, and Controller classes. Note that instances of the ModelSubclass class have two instance variables, x and y, in the following definition:

```
      Experiment        ModelSubclass
Model subclass: #ModelSubclass
  instanceVariableNames: 'x y'
  classVariableNames: ''
  poolDictionaries: ''
  category: 'Experiment'
      Experiment        ViewSubclass
View subclass: #ViewSubclass
  instanceVariableNames: ''
  classVariableNames: ''
  poolDictionaries: ''
  category: 'Experiment'
      Experiment        ControllerSubclass
Controller subclass: #ControllerSubclass
  instanceVariableNames: ''
  classVariableNames: ''
  poolDictionaries: ''
  category: 'Experiment'
```

You need these classes so that you can define certain illustrative methods without either cluttering up the system-supplied classes or obliterating existing methods on which other subclasses depend.

794   Next, suppose that you construct model and dependent part instances:

```
M := ModelSubclass new.
V := ViewSubclass new.
```

795   With a model and a viewer in hand, and attached to global variables for the sake of experimentation, you can attach the viewer to the model using the `model:` method, which is defined for the `Model` class:

```
V model: M.
```

796   The `model:` message accomplishes two key objectives:

- The model becomes the assignment of the `model` instance variable residing in the viewer instance. This assignment allows the model to be obtained from the viewer instance via `model`, a getter defined for all dependent parts, including, of course, all dependent viewers.

- The viewer instance becomes part of a list of dependent parts attached to the model instance. The model instance uses this list to send update messages to all dependent parts, including, of course, all viewers.

797   Now, suppose that you evaluate the fragments shown in Segment 794 and Segment 795 in a workspace, and then you send a change message to the model. Specifically, you send a `changed:` message to the model with, say, `#test` as the argument:

237

```
M := ModelSubclass new.
V := ViewSubclass new.
V model: M.
M changed: #test.
```

Because the model receives a `changed:` message, the model sends an `update:` message to all dependent parts, one viewer in the example, with `#test` as the argument. Because the `View` class defines `update:` to do nothing in such circumstances, nothing seems to happen.

798   The argument sent with an `update:` message, usually a literal symbol, is called the **aspect argument**. By convention, the aspect argument usually is a literal symbol that identifies an instance variable in the model that has been reset. That is, the aspect argument identifies which **aspect** of the model has changed.

799   To see that an `update:` message is sent, you can define the `update:` message for the `ViewSubclass` class, thus overriding the do-nothing version found higher in the hierarchy:

Experiment	ViewSubclass	• instance	experimenting

```
update: aspect
 Transcript show:
   'Sample viewer receiving '
   , aspect printString
   , ' update message'; cr.
```

Workspace

```
M changed: #test.
```

Transcript

```
Sample viewer receiving #test update message
```

800   So far, you have seen that a `changed:` message causes `update:` messages to be sent. Now, you need to know that such changed messages are most often sent inside setters, as in the following setters of the x and y instance variables. Note that the aspect argument identifies the instance variable—that is, the aspect—that changes.

Experiment	ModelSubclass	• instance	experimenting

```
setX: value
  x := value.
  self changed: #x.
```

Experiment	ModelSubclass	• instance	experimenting

```
setY: value
  y := value.
  self changed: #y.
```

Workspace

```
M setX: 0.
M setY: 1.
```

Transcript

```
Sample viewer receiving #x update message
Sample viewer receiving #y update message
```

801 Next, you can redefine the update: method such that it responds only to update: messages with specified aspect arguments:

Experiment	ViewSubclass	● instance	experimenting

```
update: aspect
  aspect = #x
    ifTrue:
      [Transcript show:
        'Sample viewer responding to '
        , aspect printString
        , ' update message'; cr.].
```

Workspace			

```
M setX: 0.
M setY: 1.
```

Transcript			

```
Sample viewer responding to #x update message
```

802 Usually, the viewer, or other dependent part, reaches back into the model, via a getter—defined for the model—to present the change in the display of information, as in the following example:

Experiment	ModelSubclass	● instance	experimenting

```
getX ^ x.
```

Experiment	ViewSubclass	● instance	experimenting

```
update: aspect
  aspect = #x
    ifTrue:
      [Transcript show:
        'Sample viewer responding to #x update message'; cr.
       Transcript show:
        'Model x value, determined in viewer, is '
        , self model getX printString; cr.]
```

Workspace			

```
M setX: 0.
M setY: 1.
```

Transcript			

```
Sample viewer responding to #x update message
Model x value, determined in viewer, is 0
```

803 Next, to complete the model–view–controller illustration, you need to attach the model to a controller. You attach a controller in the same way that you attach a dependent part, using a model: message. As are dependent parts, the model is placed in a model instance variable. The controller does not become part of the list to which update: messages are sent, however:

Workspace			

```
C := ControllerSubclass new.
C model: M.
```

804 Change in a model is typically initiated by a button click or key press observed by a controller. The following illustrates such a button click or key press by employing a method that simulates a button click, rather than a real button click. Each time that a click is simulated, the x instance variable in the model is incremented by way of the setter, setX, which initiates the changed:–update: sequence that leads to display by the viewer:

Experiment	ControllerSubclass	• instance	experimenting

```
simulateClick
   Transcript show: 'Button click simulated'; cr.
   self model setX: (self model getX + 1).
```
      Workspace
```
C := ControllerSubclass new.
C model: M.
C simulateClick.
C simulateClick.
C simulateClick.
```
        Transcript
```
Button click simulated
Sample viewer responding to #x update message
Model x value, determined in viewer, is 1
Button click simulated
Sample viewer responding to #x update message
Model x value, determined in viewer, is 2
Button click simulated
Sample viewer responding to #x update message
Model x value, determined in viewer, is 3
```

In the click simulation, and the resulting action, you see activity analogous to that shown graphically in Segment 791.

805

SIDE TRIP

You learn how to write controllers that respond to real button clicks in Section 42.

806

SIDE TRIP

In addition to changed:, VisualWorks offers changed:with: and update:with:, which together allow the change and update mechanism to carry along an argument. VisualWorks also offers changed, but changed is defined simply to send a changed: message with nil as the argument.

807

HIGHLIGHTS

- VisualWorks offers the Model, DependentPart, View, and Controller classes. The View class is a subclass of the DependentPart class.

- If you want a dependent part or view to depend on a particular model, **then** instantiate one of the following patterns:

  dependent part model: model
  view model: model

- If you want a model to broadcast an update: message to all its dependents, **then** send a changed: message to the model.

240

- **If** you want a dependent part to respond to an `update:` message, **then** define `update:` for the dependent part's class.

- **If** you want to obtain the model inside a viewer method, **then** send the `model` message to self.

- **If** you want a controller to work with a particular model, **then** instantiate the following pattern:

  `controller` `model:` `model`

- **If** you want to obtain the model inside a controller method, **then** send the `model` message to self.

808   The `Model` class has many subclasses. Of these, the two that you should learn about first are the `ValueHolder` and `AspectAdapter` classes, both of which are explained in this section.

VisualWorks widgets generally interact with one another and with application instances via value holders and aspect adapters, so widgets can use just two messages, `value` and `value:`, to get and set values. Such uniformity enables widget writers to develop general-purpose widgets that do not depend on application details.

In this section's illustrations, you see various objects manually assigned to global variables. Such manual assignment to global variables is for illustration only; ordinarily, a GUI builder attaches models, viewers, and controllers to one another using instance variables, as described in Section 41.

809   In Section 39, you learned that you can define setters for various instance variables in a model such that those setters send `changed:` messages, which in turn cause model instances to send `update:` messages to dependent parts. It was up to you to decide which setters send `changed:` messages.

The `ValueHolder` class comes equipped with one instance variable, `value`, with a getter, `value`, and a setter, `value:` (inherited from the `ValueModel` class), for the `value` instance variable. The setter sends the `changed:` message with `#value` as the aspect argument:

Interface-Support	ValueHolder		

```
Object subclass: #ValueHolder
  instanceVariableNames: 'value'
  classVariableNames: ''
  poolDictionaries: ''
  category: 'Interface-Support'
```

Interface-Support	ValueHolder	• instance	accessing

```
value
  ^ value
```

Interface-Support	ValueModel	• instance	accessing

```
value: newValue
  value := newValue
  self changed: #value
```

810   Suppose, for example, that you slightly redefine the `update:` method, defined previously in Segment 802, such that it works with a value holder. You replace the `getX` getter with the `value` getter:

```
       Experiment          ViewSubclass
DependentPart subclass: #ViewSubclass
  instanceVariableNames: ''
  classVariableNames: ''
  poolDictionaries: ''
  category: 'Experiment'
       Experiment          ViewSubclass          • instance          experimenting
update: aspect
  aspect = #value
    ifTrue:
      [Transcript show:
        'Sample viewer receiving #value update message'; cr.
       Transcript show:
         'Value, determined in viewer, is '
         , self model value printString; cr.]
```

811 Now, you can create a value holder and a ViewSubclass instance, and can tie them together:

```
       Workspace
H := ValueHolder new.
V := ViewSubclass new.
V model: H.
```

Then, setting the value instance variable in the value holder causes an update: message to be sent to the view:

```
       Workspace
H value: 1.
       Transcript
Sample viewer receiving #value update message
Value, determined in viewer, is 1
```

812 Of course, you can define a controller to send the sort of messages expected by a value holder:

```
       Experiment          ControllerSubclass
Controller subclass: #ControllerSubclass
  instanceVariableNames: ''
  classVariableNames: ''
  poolDictionaries: ''
  category: 'Experiment'
       Experiment          ControllerSubclass          • instance          experimenting
simulateClick
    Transcript show: 'Button click simulated'; cr.
    self model value: (self model value + 1).
```

Then, the controller can write into the same value holder that sends updates to the viewer:

```
      Workspace
C := ControllerSubclass new.
C model: H.
C simulateClick.
      Transcript
Button click simulated
Sample viewer receiving #value update message
Value, determined in viewer, is 2
```

813 An `AspectAdapter` instance looks like a `ValueHolder` instance from the perspective of a
     viewer or controller, in that the aspect adapter handles both `value` and `value:` messages.
     An aspect adapter contains no `value` instance variable, however; instead, an aspect adapter
     forwards those messages to another model, using a getter and setter appropriate to that
     model. Thus, you have the following contrast:

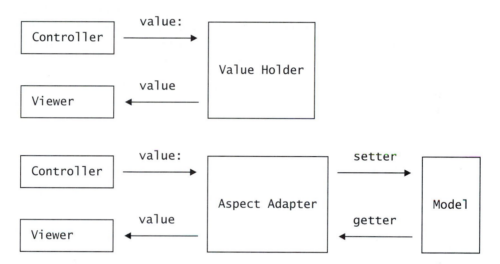

814 Thus, if you have a viewer and controller that ordinarily access a value holder via `value`
     and `value:` messages, you can substitute an aspect adapter for that value holder, without
     altering the viewer or the controller.

815 Suppose, for example, that you define the Food class, with a setter and getter for the
     `fCalories` instance variable. Note that in these definitions, Food is a subclass of `Model`,
     rather than of `Object`, and that `fCalories:` sends a `changed:` message:

```
      Experiment            Food
Model subclass: #Food
   instanceVariableNames: 'food fCalories cCalories pCalories'
   classVariableNames: ''
   poolDictionaries: ''
   category: 'Experiment'
```

```
fCalories
  ^ fCalories
```

```
fCalories: aNumber
  fCalories := aNumber.
  self changed: #fCalories
```

816 Next, you create a Food instance:

```
     Workspace
F := Food new.
```

Then, you create an aspect adapter, which you specialize with several messages. The subject: message connects the aspect adapter to the Food instance. The forAspect: message, with the #fCalories argument, stipulates that the fCalories variable, accessed by fCalories and fCalories:, is the variable of interest. The subjectSendsUpdates: message, with the true argument, stipulates that the aspect adapter is to expect the fCalories: message to generate changed: messages, which lead to the sending of update: messages, which the aspect adapter must forward to all viewers.

```
     Workspace
A := (AspectAdaptor new) subject: F;
                        subjectSendsUpdates: true;
                        forAspect: #fCalories
```

817 Now, suppose that you attach the aspect adapter to an instance of the ViewSubclass class, noting that the ViewSubclass class has an update: method defined in Segment 810.

```
     Workspace
V := ViewSubclass new.
V model: A.
```

Now, if you change the value of the fCalories variable in the food, via an fCalories: message, the view is notified by way of the attached aspect adapter, and the view obtains the current value of the fCalories instance variable through that same aspect adapter:

```
     Workspace
F fCalories: 27.
     Transcript
Sample viewer receiving #value update message
Value, determined in viewer, is 27
```

Thus, fCalories: sends changed: to the food instance, which sends update: to the aspect adapter, which sends update: to the viewer, which sends value back to the aspect adapter, which sends fCalories to the food instance.

818 Of course, the sequence of messages can be initiated by a controller that sends a value-changing message to the aspect adapter by way of the button click simulator defined in Segment 812:

```
      Workspace
C := ControllerSubclass new.
C model: A.
C simulateClick.
      Transcript
Button click simulated
Sample viewer receiving #value update message
Value, determined in viewer, is 28
```

The message sequence is longer than the one reported in Segment 817: First, the controller sends `value:` to the aspect adapter, which sends `fCalories:` to the food instance. Then, `fCalories:` sends `changed:` to the food instance, which sends `update:` to the aspect adapter, which sends `update:` to the viewer, which sends `value` back to the aspect adapter, which sends `fCalories` to the food instance.

819
SIDE TRIP

When an aspect adapter's setter has the same name as the getter, except that the setter has a colon at the end, you do not need to supply a separate setter literal, because VisualWorks can manufacture that literal by concatenating the getter literal with a colon:

```
setter , ':'
```

820
SIDE TRIP

You can, if you wish, create aspect adapters that allow the subject's instance variable and access procedures to have unrelated names

821
SIDE TRIP

So that you can specify getters and setters as literals when you are working with aspect adapters, VisualWorks implements the `perform:` and `perform:with:` methods. The `perform:` method is useful because the following have the same effect:

```
receiver getter
receiver perform: getter expressed as literal
```

The `perform:with:` method is useful because the following have the same effect:

```
receiver setter argument
receiver perform: setter expressed as literal with: argument
```

822
SIDE TRIP

When you create an aspect adapter, the getter and setter are stored in instance variables, from which they are fetched for use in `perform:` and `perform:with:` expressions.

823
HIGHLIGHTS

- Value holders have a single instance variable, `value`, which is accessed via `value` and `value:` methods.

- Value holders frequently connect controllers to viewers. Both the viewers and the controllers associated with a particular value holder access that value holder by sending a `model` message to `self`.

- If you want to create a value holder, **then** instantiate the following pattern:

  ```
  ValueHolder new
  ```

- Aspect adapters translate `value` and `value:` messages sent from viewers and controllers into model-specific getters and setters.

- **If** you want to create an aspect adapter, **then** you must specify the receiver instance (the subject), along with an indication that `update:` messages are to be forwarded, and the name for the getter and setter accessors, by instantiating one of the following patterns. Note that the names are provided as #-marked literals, with no colons:

```
(AspectAdaptor new) subject: F;
        subjectSendsUpdates: true;
                forAspect:  accessor name
(AspectAdaptor new) subject: F;
        subjectSendsUpdates: true;
                accessWith:  getter name
                assignWith:  setter name }
```

41 HOW TO USE VISUALWORKS TO BUILD APPLICATIONS

824   You have learned about the `ValueHolder` and `AspectAdapter` classes in Section 40. In this section, you learn about another subclass of the `Model` class, the `ApplicationModel` class.

825   In certain respects, the functions performed by VisualWorks's `ApplicationModel` instances parallel those performed by Smalltalk Express's `ViewManager` instances. Those functions, previously explained in Section 32, are as follows:

- An application model is the receiver of messages that start the application.

- An application model serves as a command center, enabling information to flow to and from widgets. In serving the command-center function, an application model typically contains instance variables that tie together an application.

Because an application's application model has so many responsibilities, you can think of it as the hub that ties together the entire application. Accordingly, `ApplicationModel` subclasses typically have names that include the word *application*.

826   In Section 32, you learned that, for Smalltalk Express, the `createViews` method, defined for a view manager, is used, when you start an application, to define the characteristics of the user interface.

In VisualWorks, the characteristics of the user interface are established by a `windowSpec` method defined for the application model. In contrast to the `createViews` method, which sends many messages, the `windowSpec` method sends no messages: instead, `windowSpec` answers a complex array that defines the characteristics of the user interface.

Although you learned that you can construct definitions of `createViews` by hand, you would find it impracticable to construct definitions of `windowSpec` by hand. You must construct the `windowSpec` method for an application by using VisualWorks GUI builder.

827   In most applications, the application model has instance variables with values that are value holders. The GUI builder arranges for various views and controllers to access various value holders by asking you to specify the names of the getters of the instance variables to which the value holders are assigned.

828   Suppose that, with a view toward illustrating the role of value holders, you use the VisualWorks GUI builder to construct a user interface with two **sliders** and one **input field**.

Your intent is that the sliders and the input field all show the same value. If you move a slider, the other slider and the input field are to follow the change:

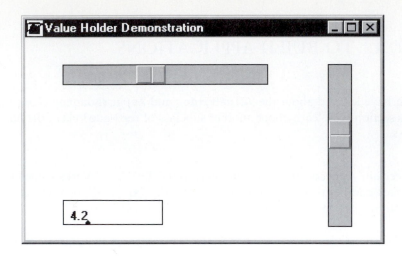

The button-clicking ritual that you use to construct the interface using the GUI builder is described in Appendix C. In the rest of this section, you learn how the interface functions, once it has been constructed.

829   Suppose that you tell the GUI builder that the subclass of the `ApplicationModel` class is to be the `ValueHolderDemonstration`.

Further suppose that you tell the GUI builder that each of the three widgets is to use a value model obtained from the application model's `commonValue` instance variable.

Then, the GUI builder will perform the following work for you:

- Define the `ValueHolderDemonstration` class with a `commonValue` instance variable.

- Define `commonValue`, the getter for the `commonValue` variable.

830   The first time a demonstration instance is sent a `commonValue` message, that `commonValue` method creates a new value holder and answers that value holder; whenever the same demonstration instance receives another `commonValue` message, that `commonValue` message answers the same value holder previously created:

Example	ValueHolderDemo···	• instance	aspects

```
commonValue
∧ commonValue isNil
    ifTrue: [commonValue := 0 asValue]
    ifFalse: [commonValue]
```

As indicated, the `commonValue` method creates a new value holder by sending the `asValue` message to a receiver, which not only creates a value holder, but also initializes that value holder. In this example, the initial value of the `value` instance variable is the integer 0.

831   The implementation of `commonValue` in Segment 830 exhibits an important Smalltalk programming idiom: if a getter sees that the value of an instance variable is `nil`, then the getter creates a suitable value. Typically, such value creation occurs only the first time that

the getter is sent; subsequently, the instance variable's value is not `nil`, so that value is answered.

832   When you open the example application, the two slider views and the input-field view, with their automatically created, associated controllers, all use the `commonValue` getter to fetch a common value holder, which each viewer and each controller subsequently installs as the value of its `model` instance variable using the `model:` message. For each viewer, the `model:` message also establishes that the view is to be informed whenever the value holder's value is changed.

833   When a value holder is created for a slider, the receiver of the `asValue` instance creation message is the number the slider produces when the slider is in the minimum position.

834   After the application is started, the value holder has many residences:

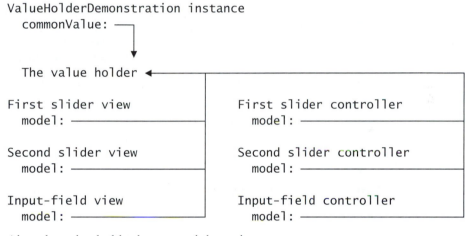

```
ValueHolderDemonstration instance
    commonValue:

    The value holder

First slider view              First slider controller
   model:                         model:

Second slider view             Second slider controller
   model:                         model:

Input-field view               Input-field controller
   model:                         model:
```

Also, the value holder has several dependents:

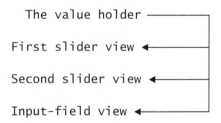

```
The value holder

First slider view

Second slider view

Input-field view
```

835   Now, if you move one of the sliders with the mouse, or type a new value in the input field, followed by a carriage return, the following occurs:

- The controller associated with the widget through which you provide new information obtains the value holder from its `model` instance variable using the `model` getter. Then, the controller writes a new value into the value holder's `value` instance variable using the `value:` setter.

- The `value:` setter causes the value holder to send the `changed:` message to itself.

- The `changed:` method sends `update:` messages to all dependent parts, which, in the example, amount to the two sliders views and the input field view.

- All three views respond to the `update:` message by extracting the new value from the value holder, held by their `model` instance variables, and then updating their displayed information.

Thus, both sliders and the input field all display the same value. If you move a slider, the other slider and the input field follow the change.

836   At this point, you know about application models, value holders, and aspect adapters. Moreover, you know that application models are models that serve as hubs around which applications are built. You also know that value holders and aspect adapters are special models that serve as conduits for information flowing to viewers.

837   The source of the information flowing to viewers may be controllers associated with viewers, or the source may be methods defined on classes specifically set up to embody **domain knowledge**. Such classes are often called **domain models** because they model the problem-solving domain. Note, however, that this use of the word *model* is different from the use of the word in connection with the model–viewer–controller paradigm—a domain model is not necessarily a subclass of the `Model` class.

838   In the example explained in this section, there is an application model, three viewers, and three controllers, but there are no domain models.

839   In applications with domain models, you typically rewrite some of the application-model getters provided by the GUI builder, such that the application-model getters produce appropriate aspect adapters, rather than value holders.

840   Application models, with various value holders and aspect adapters, allow you to separate the classes of the domain model from those associated with the GUI. The application model, the value holders, and the aspect adapters can be viewed as mediators:

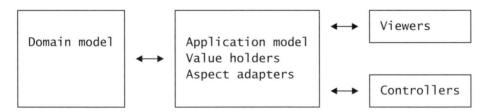

841   Separation of the domain model from the GUI is one important step toward system **modularity**. Such modularity makes systems easier to understand, build, debug, modify, and maintain. Also, you can completely change a system's GUI without changing the domain model, or you can reuse the GUI widgets in other applications.

842   Value holders and aspect adapters help to make GUI widgets reusable, because value holders and aspect adapters make it possible for widget methods to access uniformly the data that they need. Each widget that conforms to the value-holder–aspect-adapter convention

looks in the `model` slot for a value holder or aspect adapter, and accesses the information in the value holder or aspect adapter with the `value` getter and `value:` setter.

Accordingly, all you need to tell such a widget is the name of the accessor that produces a value holder or aspect adapter from the application model.

843

HIGHLIGHTS

- **If** you want to build an application, **then** use the VisualWorks GUI builder to create a subclass of the `ApplicationModel` model class to serve as the hub.

- The VisualWorks GUI builder generally installs value holders in instance variables of the application model. The value-holder installation is done by an application-model getter that creates a value holder the first time that it is called. The getter exhibits the following general pattern, in which the selector and instance variable have the same name:

```
selector
  ^ instance variable isNil
      ifTrue: [instance variable := initial value asValue]
      ifFalse: [instance variable]
```

- In typical applications, controllers send value-setting messages to value holders, which then send change messages to themselves, initiating the propagation of update messages to viewers, which look back into the value holders in the course of redrawing themselves.

- In complex applications, the application model, with value holders and aspect adapters, separates domain-model classes from viewer and controller classes. This separation is the essence of the model–viewer–controller paradigm.

42 HOW TO USE VISUALWORKS TO BUILD VIEWERS AND CONTROLLERS

844   In this section, you learn how to create your own widget using VisualWorks. You also learn how to develop an accompanying controller.

845   To illustrate VisualWorks's drawing tools, you learn how to implement the same meter-testing application that you saw implemented with Smalltalk Express in Section 37:

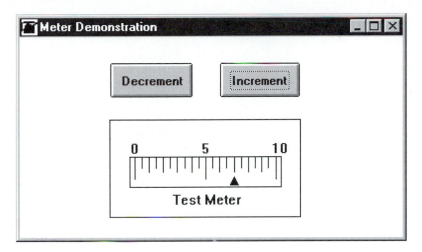

846   Following the pattern established in Section 41, the application is built around an instance of a subclass of the `ApplicationModel` class. This time, the subclass is called the `MeterDemonstration` class. That class has two instance variables, `meterValueHolder` and `meterViewHolder`:

```
    Experiment      MeterDemonstration
ApplicationModel subclass: #MeterDemonstration
  instanceVariableNames: 'meterValueHolder meterViewHolder'
  classVariableNames: ''
  poolDictionaries: ''
  category: 'Experiment'
```

847   The purpose of the `meterValueHolder` instance variable is to provide a place for the value holder that is to hold the value shown on the meter. As explained in Segment 831, the initial value of that instance variable is established by the `meterValueHolder` getter. That initial value is an initialized value holder:

```
    Experiment      MeterDemonstration      • instance        accessing
meterValueHolder
  ^ meterValueHolder isNil
      ifTrue: [meterValueHolder := 5 asValue]
      ifFalse: [meterValueHolder]
```

848   The purpose of the `meterViewHolder` instance variable is to provide a place for an instance of a subclass of the `View` class. That subclass, the `Meter` subclass, has three variables—`min`, `max` and `title`—which define the characteristics of particular meters. The values of those variables are established by setters:

Experiment	Meter

```
View subclass: #Meter
  instanceVariableNames: 'min max title'
  classVariableNames: ''
  poolDictionaries: ''
  category: 'Experiment'
```

Experiment	Meter	• instance	experimenting

```
setMin: aNumber
  min := aNumber.
```

Experiment	Meter	• instance	experimenting

```
setMax: aNumber
  max := aNumber.
```

Experiment	Meter	• instance	experimenting

```
setTitle: aString
  title := aString.
```

849   Just as the `meterValueHolder` getter creates a new value holder the first time that it is sent, the `meterViewHolder` getter creates a new meter the first time that it is sent:

Experiment	MeterDemonstration	• instance	accessing

```
meterViewHolder
  ^ meterViewHolder isNil
     ifTrue: [meterViewHolder := Meter new.
             meterViewHolder min: 0; max: 10; title: 'Test Meter'.
             meterViewHolder model: self meterValueHolder.
             meterViewHolder]
     ifFalse: [meterViewHolder]
```

Note that, the first time that it is sent, `meterViewHolder` getter also does the following:

- Initialize the instance variables of the new meter using setters.

- Set the value of the new meter's `model` instance variable to be the same as the value of the `meterValueHolder` instance variable.

850   Thus, the first time the `meterViewHolder` message is sent, the `meterViewHolder` method creates a new meter; also, the `meterViewHolder` method sends `meterValueHolder`, which creates a new value holder.

851   Next, you need to define increment and decrement methods. Both do their work on the value holder found via the `meterValueHolder` getter:

Experiment	MeterDemonstration	● instance	action

```
incrementMeter
    | valueHolder |
    valueHolder := self meterValueHolder.
    valueHolder value: valueHolder value + 1.
```

Experiment	MeterDemonstration	● instance	action

```
decrementMeter
    | valueHolder |
    valueHolder := self meterValueHolder.
    valueHolder value: valueHolder value - 1.
```

852   Now, all that remains is to connect the defined methods to a suitable GUI.

853   As explained in Appendix C, you start to create the GUI as follows:

- You click **Tools**→**New Canvas** in the transcript to create a window for building a GUI. Such a window, in VisualWorks, is called a **canvas**.

- You install two button widgets by clicking the appropriate box in the **pallet** found to the left of the canvas, and then clicking on the appropriate place in the canvas.

- You install a view-holder widget by clicking the appropriate box in the pallet, and then clicking on the appropriate place in the canvas.

- You size and align all three widgets.

854   Next, you establish properties for the three widgets by selecting the widget, and then clicking **right**→**properties**.

For the button on the right, you specify Increment as the label and incrementMeter as the action. Because the action specification is incrementMeter, the incrementMeter message is sent to the application model whenever the button is pressed. Similarly, for the button on the left, you specify Decrement as the label and decrementMeter as the action.

855   For the view holder, you specify meterViewHolder as the view. Because the view specification is meterViewHolder, VisualWorks sends the meterViewHolder message to the application model when the application is started.

Because meterViewHolder answers an instance of the Meter class, the display in the area covered by the view holder is the display specified by the Meter instance and by the drawing method defined for the Meter class.

856   Finally, you click **Install...** on the canvas tool. A window appears that invites you to specify a class. You type MeterDemonstration in the slot offered, and then click **OK**. Then, another window invites you to specify a category and to click one of several **radio buttons**. Specify Experiment as the category, and click the Application button.

857   Now, all that remains is to define the drawing method, displayOn:, that actually displays the meter using VisualWorks. The details are tedious, but overall, the drawing method is much like the one developed for Smalltalk Express, provided in Appendix A.

The key differences are explained in the next few segments. Other, less important differences are explained, and a complete display method is presented, in Appendix D.

858   You define your own `displayOn:` method to draw, because VisualWorks provides mechanisms that send `displayOn:` to a view, with a graphics-context argument, `thePen`, whenever one of the following occurs:

- The operating system notes that a change has occurred that calls for redrawing, such as uncovering or moving a window.

- The view receives an `update:` message from a model, suggesting that a value has changed that may require a change in what is displayed.

859   Recall now that the meter is a viewer of a value holder, as established by the method defined in Segment 849. Accordingly, to get at the value to be displayed, the `displayOn:` method sends the `model` message to `self`, fetching the value in the `model` instance variable. Then, as it does with all value holders, the `value` message gets the value:

```
   Experiment       MeterDemonstration       • instance       experimenting
displayOn: thePen
  | ··· modelValue ··· |
  ...
  modelValue := self model value.
  ...
```

860   At this point, you have a complete application, with all three widgets working together. Each widget, including your meter, has an automatically created, associated controller. As it stands, the meter has a default, do-nothing controller.

861   You may wish to add a flourish by defining a custom controller for the meter class, just to see how controllers work in general.

862   Suppose, for example, that you decide to attach a controller that resets the meter to the value just under the cursor when the left button is clicked in the meter window.

863   Now, suppose that you decide to name the controller class `MeterController`:

```
    Experiment        MeterController
Controller subclass: #MeterController
  instanceVariableNames: ''
  classVariableNames: ''
  poolDictionaries: ''
  category: 'Experiment'
```

864   You arrange for VisualWorks to attach an instance of this new controller class to meters by defining the `defaultControllerClass` method for the `Meter` class as follows:

Experiment	Meter	• instance	experimenting

```
defaultControllerClass
    ∧ MeterController
```

865   So far, the new controller class inherits all its behavior from the parent, do-nothing, `Controller` class. To produce new behavior, you must define a new `controlActivity` method to override the do-nothing `controlActivity` method defined for the `Controller` class. The `controlActivity` method sits in a loop in which it is sent repeatedly to the controller instance, thus executing constantly, always looking for events that it recognizes.

866   To recognize specific events, you arrange for the `controlActivity` method to send various messages to a **sensor** extracted from the corresponding controller instance using the **sensor** method. One such message, `redButtonPressed`, answers `true` if the left button is pressed at the time that the `redButtonPressed` message is sent.

867   The `redButtonPressed` message is used—instead of, say, `leftButtonPressed`—because
SIDE TRIP   early Smalltalk systems used mouse buttons that were painted with red, yellow, and blue dots to make Smalltalk easier for children to learn.

868   In the following definition, if the left button is pressed at the time the `redButtonPressed` message is sent, `controlActivity` enters a loop, which continues as long as the left button is pressed. When the button is released, `controlActivity` sends the `newModelValue` message, which determines where the mouse is, relative to the minimum and maximum values displayed on the meter, and computes the model's value accordingly:

Experiment	MeterController	• instance	experimenting

```
controlActivity
    self sensor redButtonPressed
        ifTrue: [[self sensor redButtonPressed] whileTrue: [].
            self model value: self newModelValue].
```

869   The `newModelValue` method determines the position of the cursor by sending the sensor the `lastUpPoint` message. You obtain the width of the window from the companion viewer using the `view` message. You obtain minimum and maximum values for the meter's value from the companion viewer, using `getMin` and `getMax`, two newly defined `Meter` getters. In the event that the pointer is in the window, but is not between the minimum and maximum values, the new model value is the same as the previous model value:

Experiment	Meter	• instance	experimenting

```
getMin ∧ min
```

Experiment	Meter	• instance	experimenting

```
getMax ∧ max
```

```
newModelValue
    | pointerPosition windowWidth meterWidth proportion |
    pointerPosition := self sensor lastUpPoint x.
    windowWidth := self view bounds width.
    meterWidth := windowWidth * 3 // 4.
    proportion := ((pointerPosition - (windowWidth * 1/8)) / meterWidth).
    proportion >= 0 & proportion <= 1
        ifTrue: [^ proportion * (self view getMax - self view getMin)]
        ifFalse: [^ self view model value]
```

- **If** you want to define a new widget, **then** define a subclass of the `View` class **and then** define the `displayOn:` method for that class, by instantiating the following pattern:

```
displayOn: thePen
    | ··· modelValue ··· |
    ...
    modelValue := self model value.
    ...
```

- **If** you want to deploy a widget that you have defined yourself, **then** define your application model with instance variables to hold an instance of the widget and an instance of a value holder for the widget, **and then** place a view holder in a canvas, specifying, as the view property of the view holder, an application model getter, **and then** define that application-model getter such that it produces an instance of the widget, by instantiating the following pattern, in which the selector and instance variable have the same name:

```
selector
    ^ instance variable isNil
        ifTrue: [ instance variable := widget class new.
                  instance variable model: self a value holder .
                  instance variable ]
        ifFalse: [ instance variable ]
```

- Whenever a viewer is created, a companion controller is created as well.

- **If** you want to alter the controller used as a viewer companion, **then** define `defaultControllerClass` by instantiating the following pattern:

```
defaultControllerClass
    ^ name of controller class
```

- **If** you want to define a controller, **then** define a subclass of the `Controller` class and implement the `controlActivity` method for that subclass.

APPENDIX A:
THE CALORIE APPLICATION

871   This appendix brings together all the elements of the calorie-display application developed in Smalltalk Express and shown in Segment 712.

872   The names in the application occasionally depart from the no-abbreviations convention of Smalltalk, because, as explained in Segment 197, names must fit into programs that fit into the dimensions of the page.

THE FOODS

```
Food class definition
Object subclass: #Food
  instanceVariableNames: 'name fCalories cCalories pCalories'
  classVariableNames: ''
  poolDictionaries: ''
```

```
Food method definition          • instance
name
  ^ name.
```

```
Food method definition          • instance
name: aString
  name := aString.
```

```
Food method definition          • instance
fCalories
  ^ fCalories
```

```
Food method definition          • instance
fCalories: aNumber
  fCalories := aNumber
```

```
Food method definition          • instance
cCalories
  ^ cCalories
```

```
Food method definition          • instance
cCalories: aNumber
  cCalories := aNumber
```

```
Food method definition          • instance
pCalories
  ^ pCalories
```

```
Food method definition          • instance
pCalories: aNumber
  pCalories := aNumber
```

```
Food method definition          • instance
tCalories
 ^fCalories + cCalories + pCalories
```

Food method definition   ● class
```
collectFrom: aFile
  |inputStream collection food|
  inputStream := File pathName: aFile.
  collection := OrderedCollection new.
  [(food := inputStream nextWord) notNil]
    whileTrue: [collection add:
                  ((Food new) name: food;
                    fCalories: inputStream nextWord asInteger;
                    cCalories: inputStream nextWord asInteger;
                    pCalories: inputStream nextWord asInteger)].
  inputStream close.
  ^ collection
```

874   **THE METER GRAPH PANE**

MeterGraphPane class definition
```
GraphPane subclass: #MeterGraphPane
  instanceVariableNames: 'min max value title'
  classVariableNames: ''
  poolDictionaries: 'ColorConstants'
```
MeterGraphPane method definition   ● instance
```
setMin: aNumber
  min := aNumber
```
MeterGraphPane method definition   ● instance
```
setMax: aNumber
  max := aNumber
```
MeterGraphPane method definition   ● instance
```
setValue: aNumber
  value := aNumber
```
MeterGraphPane method definition   ● instance
```
getValue
  ^ value
```
MeterGraphPane method definition   ● instance
```
setTitle: aString
  title := aString
```
MeterGraphPane method definition   ● instance
```
drawMeter
  | thePen meterWidth meterHeight xLft yBot xPointer yPointer
    ptrHeight ptrHalfWidth oldBackColor dialArray
    range step tics tickPlace tickHeight|
  self erase.
  thePen := self pen.
  meterHeight := 30.  meterWidth := self width * 3 // 4.
  ptrHeight := 10.  ptrHalfWidth := 5.
  xLft := self width - meterWidth // 2.  yBot := self height * 3 // 8.
```

```
"Draw frame for meter"
thePen drawRectangle: ((xLft - ptrHalfWidth) @ yBot)
                extent: (meterWidth + (ptrHalfWidth * 2))
                          @ meterHeight).
"Draw tick marks.  Adaped from code provided by Richard Lyon.
 Works well for all min and max values"
range := max - min.
range = 0
  ifTrue:
    [self error: 'Cannot put tics in an interval of width zero'].
range < 0
  ifTrue: [step := -1.  range := range negated]
  ifFalse: [step := 1].
[range <= 15] whileTrue: [range := range*10. step := step/10].
[range > 150] whileTrue: [range := range/10. step := step*10].
range <= 30
  ifTrue: [tics := #(1 5 10)]
  ifFalse:
    [(range <= 60)
        ifTrue: [tics := #(2 10 20)]
        ifFalse: [tics := #(5 10 50)] ].
step := step * (tics at: 1).
(((min // (step negated)) negated) to: (max // step))
  do: [:k | (k \\ ((tics at: 3) / (tics at: 1)) = 0)
                ifTrue: [tickHeight := meterHeight * 3 // 4]
                ifFalse:
                  [(k \\ ((tics at: 2) / (tics at: 1)) = 0)
                      ifTrue: [tickHeight := meterHeight // 2]
                      ifFalse: [tickHeight := meterHeight * 3 // 8]].
             tickPlace := xLft
                         + (k * meterWidth * step // max)
                         - (min * meterWidth // range).
             thePen lineFrom: (tickPlace @ yBot)
                         to: (tickPlace @ (yBot + tickHeight))].
"Write title"
title notNil
  ifTrue:
    [thePen
      centerText: title
      at: ((self width) // 2)
          @ (yBot + meterHeight + (2 * thePen font height))].
"Write scale minimum, middle, and maximum"
min notNil & max notNil
  ifTrue: [thePen centerText: min printString
              at: xLft @ yBot.
           thePen centerText: (max - min // 2 + min) printString
              at: (xLft + (meterWidth // 2)) @ yBot.
           thePen centerText: max printString
              at: (xLft + meterWidth) @ yBot].
```

```
"Draw pointer, if values set"
min notNil & max notNil & value notNil
          & (value >= min) & (value <= max)
  ifTrue:
    [xPointer := (value - min) * meterWidth // (max - min) + xLft.
     yPointer := yBot + meterHeight - 1.
     oldBackColor := thePen backColor.
     thePen backColor: ClrBlack.
     dialArray := Array with: ((xPointer + ptrHalfWidth) @ yPointer)
                        with: (xPointer @ (yPointer - ptrHeight))
                        with: ((xPointer - ptrHalfWidth) @ yPointer).
     thePen polygonFilled: dialArray.
     thePen backColor: oldBackColor]
```

875   THE VIEW MANAGER

The marked line is needed only when you wish to separate the application from the development environment, as explained in Segment 879.

CalorieViewManager class definition
```
ViewManager subclass: #CalorieViewManager
  instanceVariableNames: 'food foodList'
  classVariableNames: ''
  poolDictionaries: ''
```

CalorieViewManager method definition   • instance
```
initializeMeter: theMeter
  theMeter setMin: 0; setMax: 100;
          setTitle: 'Calorie Meter';
          event: #display.
```

CalorieViewManager method definition   • instance
```
initializeListBox: theListBox
  foodList :=
   (Food collectFrom: 'c:\test\vtbls.dta').
  theListBox contents: (foodList collect: [:p | p name]).
```

CalorieViewManager method definition   • instance
```
itemSelected: theListBox
  food := foodList at: theListBox selection.
  (self paneNamed: 'CalorieMeter')
    setValue: food tCalories;
    event: #display.
```

CalorieViewManager method definition   • instance
```
callDrawMeter: thePane
  thePane drawMeter.
```

264

```
resetListBox
  | theFileDialog file |
  (theFileDialog := FileDialog new)
    fileSpec: '*.dta';
    open.
  (file := theFileDialog file) notNil
    ifTrue: [foodList := (Food collectFrom: file).
             (self paneNamed: 'ListBox')
               contents: (foodList collect: [:p | p name]).
             (self paneNamed: 'CalorieMeter')
               setValue: nil; event: #display].
```

```
createViews
  | theTopPane theListBox theMeterPane theMenuWindow |
  "Set up all panes"
  self addView: (theTopPane := TopPane new).
  theListBox := ListBox new.
  theMeterPane := MeterGraphPane new.
  "Set up the top pane"
  theTopPane owner: self;
    labelWithoutPrefix: 'Demonstration Window';
    noSmalltalkMenuBar;
    addSubpane: theListBox;
    addSubpane: theMeterPane;
    menuWindow: (theMenuWindow := MenuWindow new);
    when: #close perform: #close:;
    framingRatio: (1/4 @ (1/3) rightBottom: 3/4 @ (2/3)).
  "Set up the menu window"
  theMenuWindow addMenu:
    (Menu new
       title: '~Options';
       owner: self;
       appendItem: '~Food type' selector: #resetListBox;
       appendSubMenu: (Menu new
                         title: '~Mode';
                         owner: self;
                         appendItem: '~Fat calories' selector: nil;
                         appendItem: '~Total calories' selector: nil)).
  "Set up the list-box pane"
  theListBox owner: self;
    paneName: 'ListBox';
    when: #getContents perform: #initializeListBox:;
    when: #select perform: #itemSelected:;
    framingRatio: (2/3 @ 0 rightBottom: 1 @ 1).
```

```
"Set up the meter pane"
theMeterPane owner: self;
  paneName: 'CalorieMeter';
  noScrollBars;
  when: #getContents perform: #initializeMeter:;
  when: #display perform: #callDrawMeter:;
  framingRatio: (0 @ 0 rightBottom: 2/3 @ 1).
```

APPENDIX B:
PACKAGING APPLICATIONS FOR USERS

876   When you finish an application, you need to separate that application from the **development environment** so that, when you start the application, you see only the application window, and do not see the transcript. Separation also eliminates various classes that are useful only during application development.

To separate an application from the development environment, producing the **delivery environment**, you perform a bit of implementation-dependent ritual. This appendix describes the procedure for Smalltalk Express applications constructed as subclasses of the `ViewManager` class.

877   Remove all uses of `halt` and `inspect` from your program. These debugging-oriented methods are available in only the development environment.

878   Redefine the `startUpApplication:` method defined for `NotificationManager` to include only an expression that starts your application. For example, for the calorie-dictionary application, you redefine `startUpApplication:` as follows:

NotificationManager method definition   ● instance

```
startUpApplication: oldWindows
  CalorieViewManager new open
```

879   Add a `when:perform:` statement to `creatViews` such that the top pane responds to a `close` event by sending a `close:` message to the view manager. For example, for the calorie-dictionary application, you add the `when:perform:` statement as follows:

CalorieViewManager method definition   ● instance

```
createViews
  | theTopPane theListBox theMeterPane theMenuWindow |
  ...
  "Set up the top pane"
  theTopPane owner: self;
    ...
    menuWindow: (theMenuWindow := MenuWindow new);
    when: #close perform: #close:;
    framingRatio: (1/4 @ (1/3) rightBottom: 3/4 @ (2/3)).
    ...
  ...
```

See Segment 875 for the complete `createViews` method.

880   Define a prescribed `close:` method for your application class such that Smalltalk Express exits properly when you close your application. For example, for the calorie-dictionary application, you define `close:` as follows:

```
close: aPane
  Smalltalk isRunTime
    ifTrue: [(MessageBox confirm: 'Are you sure you want to exit?')
              ifTrue: [self close. ^Smalltalk exit]
              ifFalse: [^self]]
    ifFalse: [^self close]
```

881   Now, click **File→Save Image...**, and save the Smalltalk Express image. All your work, along with the Smalltalk Express apparatus required to use your work, is saved in two places: the complete Smalltalk Express development environment, with your work, is saved in `vw.exe`; the delivery environment, with your work, is stored in `v.exe`.

Copy `v.exe` to a delivery directory.

Also, copy all the files with `dll` extensions to the delivery directory. Alternatively, you can read the current Smalltalk Express documentation to see which `dll` files are currently required.

882   In the delivery directory, rename the `v.exe` file in the Smalltalk Express directory to suit your application. This file is now your **application image**, ready for you to start it as you would any application using your operating system. For example, for the calorie-dictionary application, you could change `v.exe` to `Calories.exe`.

883   For further information on these steps and for information on changing the application icon and start-up display, see the `readme.txt` file in the Smalltalk Express directory.

APPENDIX C:
THE VISUALWORKS GUI BUILDER

884   This appendix explains, telegraphically, how to build the value-holder demonstration interface discussed in Section 40. In particular, you see how to create an application with two sliders and an input field, as described in Section 40, and you see how to connect all three widgets to a single, shared value holder—the one found in the `currentValue` instance variable of a `ValueHolderDemonstration` instance.

885   When you load VisualWorks, you are presented with a transcript and a workspace. To build a GUI, you click **Tools→New Canvas** in the transcript, whereupon the following appears:

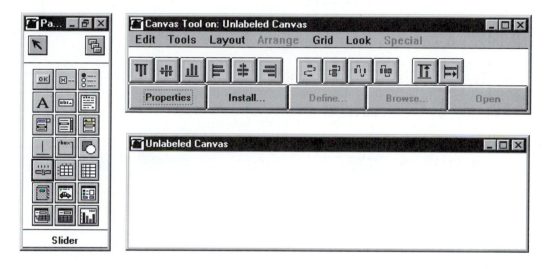

886   To create and install each widget, you click the appropriate box in the pallet found to the left of the canvas, and then click on the appropriate place in the canvas:

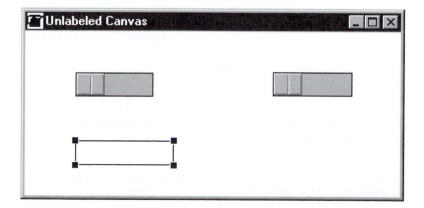

887 Next, you size the widgets using the handles. Then, you align the widgets by clicking on one, then clicking on another, then clicking the appropriate button on the **canvas tool**, found above the canvas.

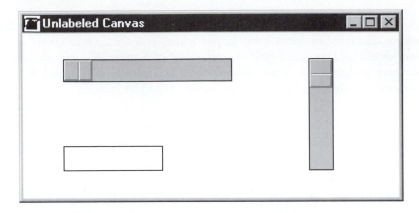

888 At this point, all the widgets are in place, and it is time to adjust their properties. For example, to change the label that appears in the title bar, you select the canvas by clicking on the canvas in an area not covered by a widget. Then, you click **right→properties**, at which point the GUI builder displays the following:

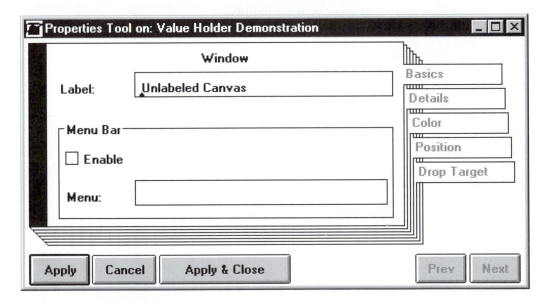

Now, you replace `Unlabeled Canvas` with `Value Holder Demonstration`. Finally, you click `Apply & Close`.

889 Next, you select one of the sliders by clicking on it. Then, you click **right→properties**, at which point the GUI builder displays the following:

Properties Tool on: Value Holder Demonstration ▬ ☐ ✕

Slider

Aspect:	
ID:	
Start:	
Stop:	
Step:	

Basics
Details
Validation
Notification
Color
Position
Drop Target

[Apply] [Cancel] [Apply & Close]   [Prev] [Next]

Now, you insert currentValue in the aspect slot, and fill in other slots to tell the GUI builder that 0 is associated with the slider's minimum value and that 10 is associated with the maximum value. The 0.1 entry tells the GUI builder that the slider is to move in steps of 0.1 as you drag the slider with the mouse.

Properties Tool on: Value Holder Demonstration ▬ ☐ ✕

Slider

Aspect:	#currentValue
ID:	
Start:	0
Stop:	10
Step:	0.1

Basics
Details
Validation
Notification
Color
Position
Drop Target

[**Apply**] [**Cancel**] [**Apply & Close**]   [Prev] [Next]

Finally, you click Apply & Close.

Whenever you click **right→properties** with a canvas or widget selected, you see that VisualWorks allows you to specify a host of properties, many of which you reach by clicking on one of the tabs projecting to the right. You can create increasingly more elaborate interfaces as you learn more about all the offered properties.

891 You establish most of the characteristics of the second slider in exactly the same way; in addition, however, you must indicate that you want the slider to move vertically. To do so, you click **Apply** after you have written `currentValue`, 0, 10, and `0.1` into the appropriate slots. Then, you click the `details` tab, and then click **vertical**. Finally, you click `Apply & Close`.

892 You establish the characteristics of the input field by selecting it and opening the properties window, as you did for the other two widgets. Then, you type `currentValue` in the aspect slot, and choose `number` and `0.00` for the `type` and `format` slots:

```
Properties Tool on: Value Holder Demonstration          _ □ ✕

                         Input Field                          ▲

    Aspect:      #currentValue                      Basics

    Menu:                                           Details

    ID:                                             Validation

    Type:        Number                     ▼       Notification

    Format:      0.00                       ▼       Color

                                                    Position
                                                         ▼

   [ Apply ] [ Cancel ] [ Apply & Close ]      [ Prev ] [ Next ]
```

Finally, you click `Apply & Close`.

893 At this point, all the widgets are properly defined, but, to complete your work, you need to tell the GUI builder to which class the application model is to belong.

Accordingly, you click **Install...** on the canvas tool. A window appears that invites you to specify a class. You type `ValueHolderDemonstration` in the slot offered, and then click **OK**. Then, another window invites you to specify a category and to click one of several **radio buttons**. Specify `Experiment` as the category, and click the `Application` button.

894 You also need to tell the GUI builder to define the `currentValue` method, used to retrieve the value holder from the application model.

Accordingly, you click **Define...** on the canvas tool. A window appears that invites you to approve the definition of a value holder associated the `currentValue` instance variable of the `ValueHolderDemonstration` class. Click **OK**.

895 At this point, the application is complete. You launch it by clicking **Open** in the canvas tool, whereupon you see the following:

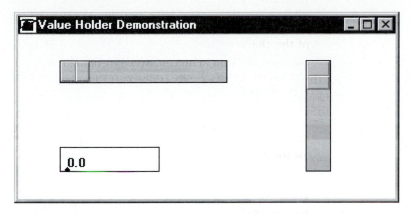

Now, you can experiment by moving the sliders with the mouse and by typing numbers into the input field, then pressing the Enter key.

APPENDIX D:
THE VISUALWORKS DRAWING METHODS

896   This appendix explains the method that draws meters for VisualWorks, and highlights the ways in which the method differs from the analogous method presented in Appendix A— the one defined for Smalltalk Express.

897   The meter-drawing method is defined for the Meter class, a subclass of the View class. The meter class has three instance variables. Three setters are defined for those variables for use in initialization:

Experiment	Meter		

```
View subclass: #Meter
  instanceVariableNames: 'min max title'
  classVariableNames: ''
  poolDictionaries: ''
  category: 'Experiment'
```

Experiment	Meter	• instance	experimenting

```
setMin: aNumber min := aNumber.
```

Experiment	Meter	• instance	experimenting

```
setMax: aNumber max := aNumber.
```

Experiment	Meter	• instance	experimenting

```
setTitle: aString title := aString.
```

898   There is no value instance variable, however. Instead, meter instances are expected to have a model, and the value to be displayed is to be fetched from that model:

```
displayOn: thePen
  | ··· modelValue ··· |
  ...
  modelValue := self model value.
  ...
```

899   The display method for View subclasses is always named displayOn: because that is the name used when VisualWorks decides that display is called for.

900   When VisualWorks sends a displayOn: message, the message includes an argument: a graphics context, which serves as the receiver of drawing messages. In contrast, in Smalltalk Express, the graphics context is extracted from the value of the self variable.

901   In VisualWorks, you erase the meter window by sending clear to the graphics context. In Smalltalk Express, you erase the meter window by sending erase to self.

902   In VisualWorks, you determine the width and height of the meter window by sending width and height to the answer produced when bounds is sent to self. In Smalltalk Express, you determine the width and height by sending width and height directly to self.

903 Drawing is done with displayRectangularBorder:at:, with displayLineFrom:to:, with displayPolygon:, and with displayString:at:.

Because there is no exact analog of centerText:at:, you must center displayed strings manually, by first converting the string to composed text, using asComposedText. The composed text then serves as the receiver of a width message.

904 Here, then, is the method:

```
   Experiment          Meter          • instance     experimenting
displayOn: thePen
   | meterWidth meterHeight xLft yBot xPointer yPointer
     ptrHeight ptrHalfWidth dialArray stringHandle modelValue
     range step tics tickPlace tickHeight|
   thePen clear.
   meterHeight := 30. ptrHeight := 10.  ptrHalfWidth := 5.
   meterWidth := self bounds width * 3 // 4.
   xLft := self bounds width - meterWidth // 2.
   yBot := self bounds height * 3 // 8.
   "Draw frame for meter"
   thePen displayRectangularBorder:
       ((0 @ 0)
         extent: (meterWidth + (ptrHalfWidth * 2)) @ meterHeight)
       at: ((xLft - ptrHalfWidth) @ yBot).


   "Draw tick marks.  Adaped from code provided by Richard Lyon.
    Works well for all min and max values"
   range := max - min.
   range = 0
     ifTrue:
       [self error: 'Cannot put tics in an interval of width zero'].
   range < 0
     ifTrue: [step := -1.  range := range negated]
     ifFalse: [step := 1].
   [range <= 15] whileTrue: [range := range*10. step := step / 10].
   [range > 150] whileTrue: [range := range/10. step := step * 10].
   range <= 30
     ifTrue: [tics := #(1 5 10)]
     ifFalse:
       [(range <= 60)
           ifTrue: [tics := #(2 10 20)]
           ifFalse: [tics := #(5 10 50)] ].
   step := step * (tics at: 1).
```

```
            (((min // (step negated)) negated) to: (max // step))
              do: [:k | (k \\ ((tics at: 3) / (tics at: 1)) = 0)
                        ifTrue: [tickHeight := meterHeight * 3 // 4]
                        ifFalse:
                          [(k \\ ((tics at: 2) / (tics at: 1)) = 0)
                              ifTrue: [tickHeight := meterHeight // 2]
                              ifFalse: [tickHeight := meterHeight * 3 // 8]].
                      tickPlace := xLft
                                  + (k * meterWidth * step // max)
                                  - (min * meterWidth // range).
                      thePen
                        displayLineFrom: (tickPlace @ yBot)
                                    to: (tickPlace @ (yBot + tickHeight))].
"Write title"
title notNil
  ifTrue:
    [thePen displayString: title
        at: ((self bounds width)
            - (title asComposedText width) // 2)
            @ (yBot + meterHeight + (thePen font height * 1.1))].
"Write scale minimum, middle, and maximum"
min notNil & max notNil
  ifTrue:
    [thePen displayString: (stringHandle := min printString)
        at: (xLft - (stringHandle asComposedText width // 2))
            @ (yBot - (thePen font height * 0.2)) asInteger.
    thePen displayString:
          (stringHandle := (max - min // 2) printString)
        at:
          (xLft + (meterWidth
                  - stringHandle asComposedText width // 2))
          @ (yBot - (thePen font height * 0.2)).
    thePen displayString: max printString
        at: (xLft + meterWidth
            - (min printString asComposedText width // 2))
            @ (yBot - (thePen font height * 0.2))].
"Continued ..."
```

```
"Draw pointer, if modelValue set"
modelValue := self model value.
min notNil & max notNil & modelValue notNil
          & (modelValue >= min) & (modelValue <= max)
  ifTrue:
    [xPointer :=
      (((modelValue - min) * meterWidth // (max - min)))
      + xLft.
    yPointer := yBot + meterHeight - 1.
    dialArray := Array
                  with: ((xPointer + ptrHalfWidth) @ yPointer)
                  with: (xPointer @ (yPointer - ptrHeight))
                  with: ((xPointer - ptrHalfWidth) @ yPointer).
    thePen displayPolygon: dialArray]
```

COLOPHON

The author created camera-ready copy for this book using TeX, Donald E. Knuth's typesetting language.

He transformed the source text into PostScript files using the products of Y&Y, of Concord, Massachusetts. Pageworks, of Cambridge, Massachusetts, produced film from the PostScript files.

The text was set primarily in 10-point Sabon Roman. The section headings were set in 14-point Sabon bold. The computer programs were set in 9-point Lucida Sans bold.

The author tested the programs in Section 37 and preceding sections with Smalltalk Express, a product of ParcPlace-Digitalk, of Sunnyvale, California. The author tested the programs in Section 38 and following sections with VisualWorks, also a product of ParcPlace-Digitalk.

INDEX

SOFTWARE

Smalltalk Express™, the principal version of Smalltalk used throughout this book, is available without charge via the Internet from ObjectShare, a division of ParcPlace-Digitalk, Incorporated. To obtain your copy of Smalltalk Express, you use your favorite network browser to connect with either of the following URLs, provided through the courtesy of ParcPlace-Digitalk, Incorporated, and ObjectShare:

```
http://www.parcplace.com/
http://www.objectshare.com/
```

The programs in this book also are available via the Internet. To obtain this software, you use the following URL, provided through the courtesy of Ascent Technology, Incorporated:

```
http://www.ascent.com/books
```

Smalltalk Express's GUI builder, WindowBuilder Pro™, is also available for Visual Age for Smalltalk™, a product of IBM, Incorporated. You can learn about WindowBuilder Pro for Visual Age for Smalltalk via the preceding Object-Share URL.

ObjectShare also markets a variety of add-on widget packages for use with Smalltalk Express, including sliders, dials, gauges, charts, graphs, and even spreadsheets.

BOOKS

BOOKS IN THIS SERIES

On To C, by Patrick Henry Winston

On To C++, by Patrick Henry Winston

On to Java, by Patrick Henry Winston and Sundar Narasimhan

The *On To* series stands on the idea that the best way to learn a new programming language is to follow an example that answers natural questions in a natural order. Then, once you understand how to express a complete program, you extend your understanding by learning about features that make your programs more efficient, flexible, and sophisticated.

Thus, you learn a new programming language in much the same way that you learned your native tongue: you learn essentials first, then you build on those essentials as situations arise that require you to know more. As you progress, you learn not only the commands and syntax, but also the idiomlike patterns that experienced programmers use instinctively.

OTHER BOOKS BY PATRICK HENRY WINSTON

Artificial Intelligence (Third Edition), by Patrick Henry Winston

Lisp (Third Edition), by Patrick Henry Winston and Berthold Klaus Paul Horn